Paint 50
LANDSCAPES

A complete guide to painting landscapes and seascapes in watercolour

Joe Francis Dowden

DAVID & CHARLES

www.davidandcharles.com

Contents

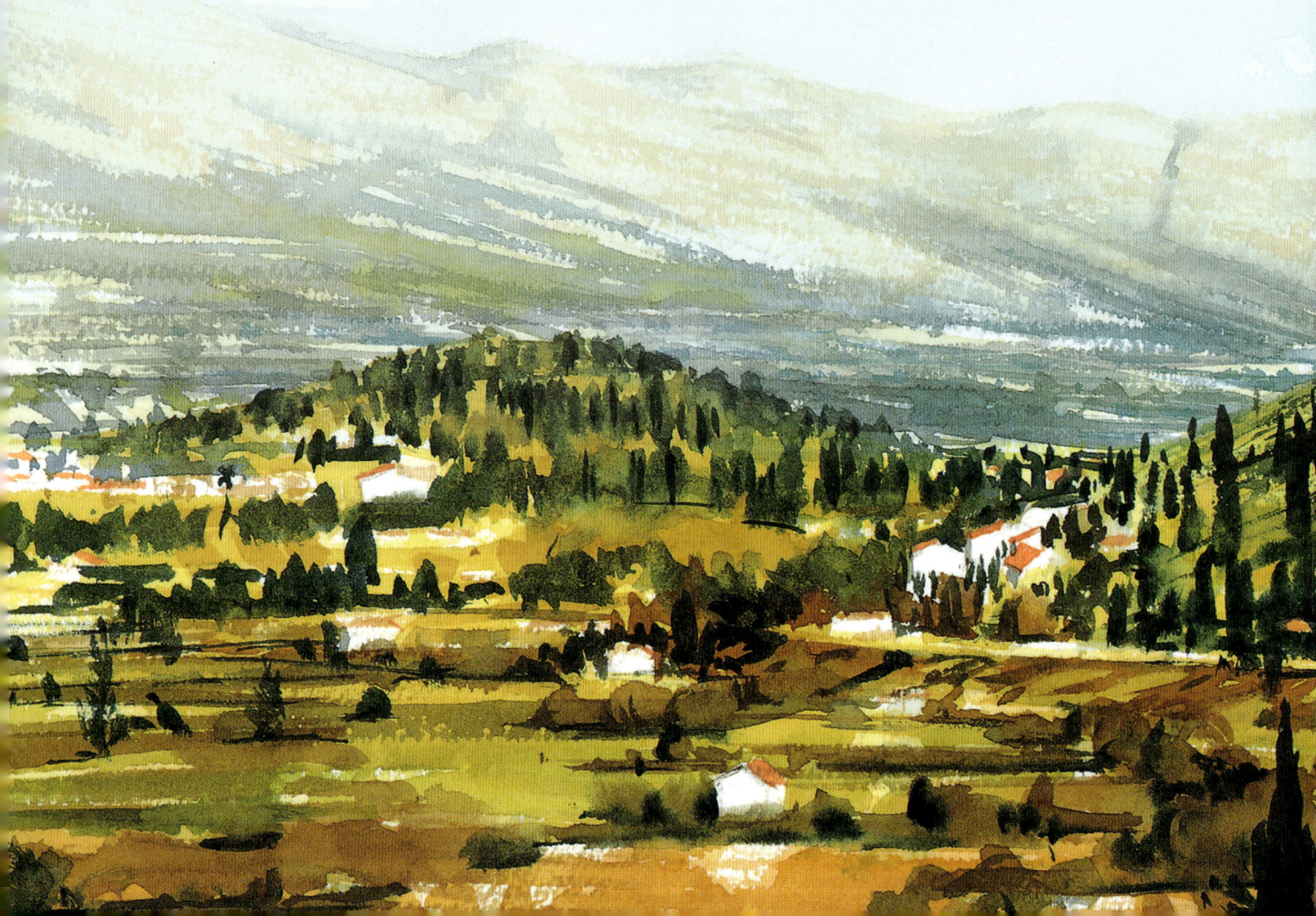

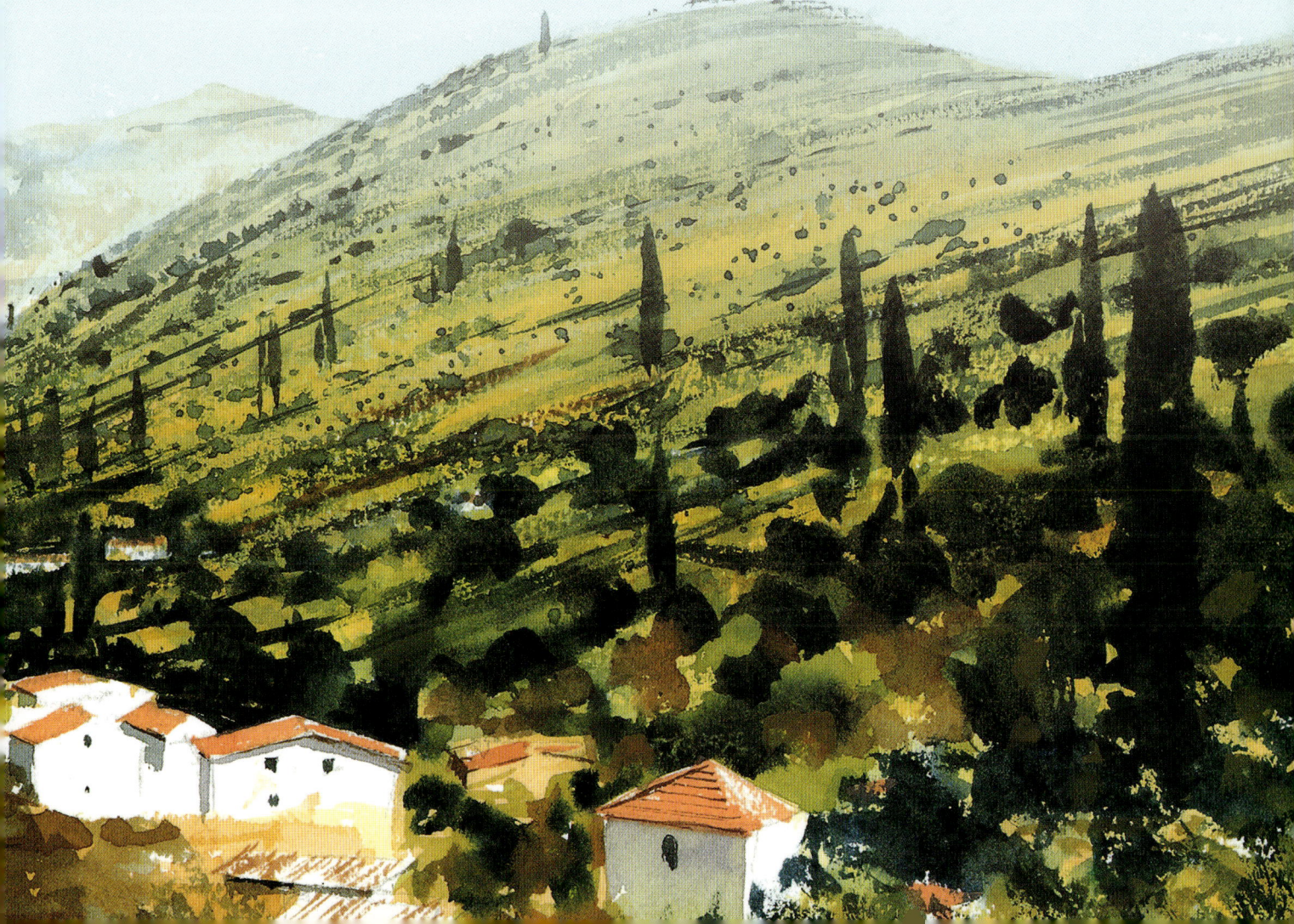

Introduction

Never forget, the results of your painting will always be better than you expect! This book can help. It is a reference book, which means you can go on finding new things almost indefinitely. There are many simple things in here, as well as many in-depth techniques. Your best qualification is your desire to paint. This is my best shot at helping you achieve this.

I'm putting my own lifetime's knowledge down in an understandable way and I hope it will serve you for a lifetime. In here is a vast array of different types of landscapes and ways of putting them down in watercolour. Some techniques are very simple – painting sparkling water, for example, or beach shingle, sky, snow and more. These will give you the freedom to paint what you want, how you want. Here are the tools, the means for painting what you choose. This is the book I wanted when I was struggling with my own painting. Use it to build your self-confidence, to strengthen and revitalize your work, or to get going for the first time.

It's a wonderful truth about the human brain that no matter its age or youth, it goes on learning. You may have wanted to paint all your life, but not had the time or opportunity to start. You may be a student at college or university and want to progress quickly. You could be starting out, or you may have a moderate level of experience. You may be an accomplished painter, even a professional artist or illustrator, and want to approach watercolour from a new angle. You may simply want to find some new techniques to add to those you already know.

There is something in here for you – have a look through the pages now and see what you can find. The information is easy to follow. It builds on what has gone before, but it is not bound by tradition. It will help you bring something different to show the world, your peer group, and your friends. Above all, this is for you, for your own art.

Stay positive – happy painting!

Joe

HOW TO USE THE CROSS-REFERENCE SYSTEM

Each project features a Techniques list, directing you to additional information on relevant techniques.

IN-DEPTH TECHNIQUE PROJECTS

Many projects deal with special techniques in depth, such as the painting rock techniques in 'Moorland rocks' (pages 36–37). Because they give so much detail on technique, they do not cover the project in steps. However, you can complete the painting shown by following the page numbers given in the Techniques list. This list takes you to projects which give information on how to paint skies (pages 54–55), distant landscapes (pages 34–35) and other subjects. With the help of these pages, you can go on to complete the 'Moorland rocks' project. By following these cross references, you will find many more techniques and applications to use in this, or your own, watercolour.

STAND-ALONE PROJECTS

There are also stand-alone projects, in which all the information for completing that painting is on those two pages. There are thirteen of these projects, an example being 'Fair weather' (pages 54–55). This has step-by-step photographs of each stage of the painting. Then there are further projects with steps for a key facet of the project, such as masking for the boat, the same type of masking also being used for the swans in 'Lake with swans' (pages 76–77). The Techniques cross-reference system is invaluable here. You don't need the Techniques to complete the project, but you will find additional insight into facets of this painting, or similar subject matter.

Example: The Techniques list in 'Fair weather' (pages 54–55) refers to 'Boat sailing on the sea' (pages 92–93). Then the Techniques list in that project refers to 'masking sea effects (surf)' (pages 102–105). Here you will find several illustrated techniques for painting surf, as well as a step-by-step project. From here you can find references for masked detail (pages 32–33), masked objects (pages 76-77) and saved light objects (pages 72–73 and 83).

CONTENTS AND INDEX PAGES

You can also check out the contents page (pages 2–3) as a quick reference guide, and the Index (pages 127–128), which has many techniques listed.

YOUR JOURNEY OF DISCOVERY!

You can turn from one technique to another, following the cross-reference system through the book from project to project. You could even start making your own notes as you extract more and more information. The Techniques cross-reference system enables you to travel through the book gaining knowledge on the journey.

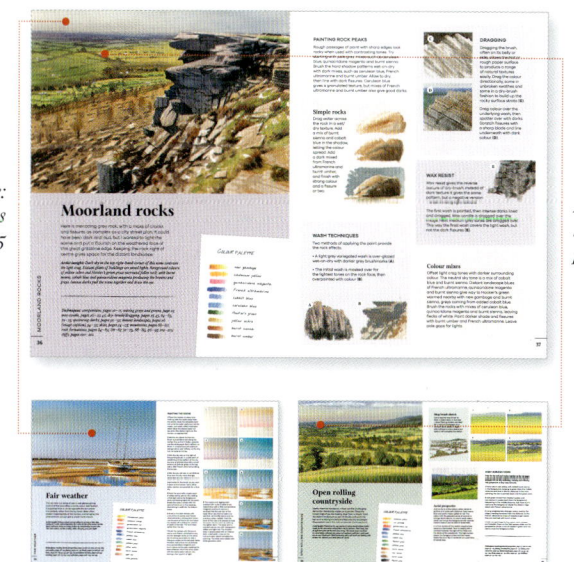

Skies: pages 54–55

Distant landscapes: page 34–35

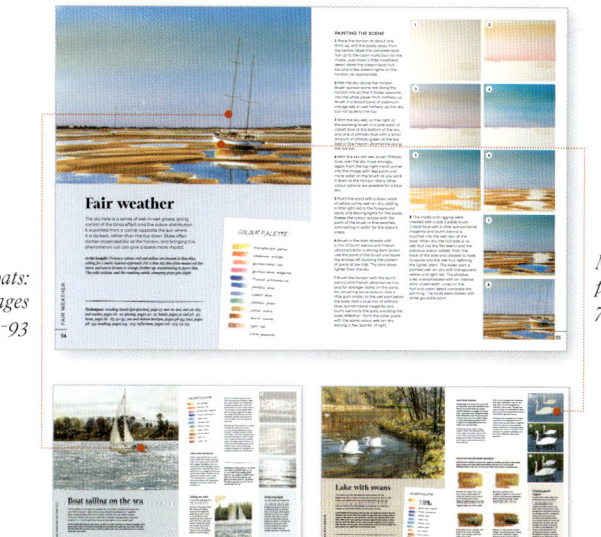

Boats: pages 92–93

Masking: pages 76-77

Materials

Excellent materials help, but you can still achieve good results without the best. Obtain what you are able to, and add as you go. Get top-quality paper and sable brushes if you can. If you cannot, substitute others. The same applies to the colours used for these projects if you do not have them all. If you are short of what you need, remember that many fine artists have lacked the best materials. Whatever you work with, have a positive attitude – your greatest asset.

PAPER

You need paper designed for watercolour painting. Watercolour paper is cheaper to buy by the sheet, but it is useful to have a pad at the ready for on-site watercolour sketching. Pads are also easier to carry and for storing finished paintings on the move. You may prefer to take a couple of boards with paper stretched by soaking and stapling down for painting outdoors, and I nearly always work this way in the studio too.

CHOOSING WATERCOLOUR PAPER

Watercolour paper comes in three surface types – hot-pressed or smooth, cold pressed ('Not') or moderately rough, and rough – with many variants of texture. A fine surface texture does not show in the finished painting, while a coarser rough surface is clearly discernible, but gives texture effortlessly. Most projects in this book are on rough surface 300gsm/140lb rough paper, or heavier paper with a Not (cold pressed) surface.

Use good-quality papers if you can; they are easier to work on and can give your painting a boost. Cotton fibre papers – known as 'rag' papers – usually perform well, and are often hard surfaced, but there are some good-quality papers based on cellulose fibres extracted from wood pulp. If you are masking, get one of the hard-surface papers. These will not rip, whereas soft papers rip when masked. I use a lot of Arches Aquarelle because it is does not rip.

The weight of the paper is a measure of its thickness, and hence resistance to buckling. I use a minimum weight of 300gsm/140lb.

STRETCHING PAPER

Watercolour paper is best stretched before use by soaking and sticking down to prevent it buckling or cockling. For years I used gummed tape to stick soaked paper to board. These days I staple paper because it never comes unstuck. Some artists do not stretch paper that is 425gsm (200lb) or more. I prefer to stretch all papers – even 850gsm (400lb).

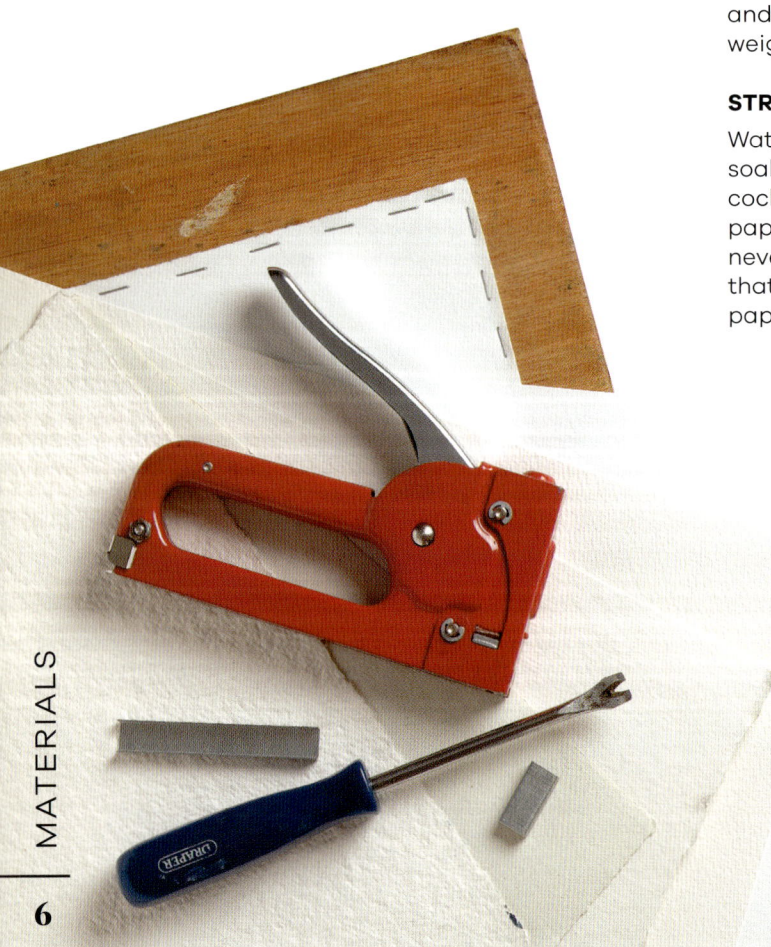

My preferred paper

There is a wide range of paper on the market and your style of painting will dictate to some extent which brand, type and weight you work on. I favour a 300gsm/140lb rough surfaced cotton fibre paper. I prefer to stretch all papers – even 850gsm/400lb.

BRUSHES

No other brush can match the qualities of a sable for painting. Pure red sable and kolinsky sable 'round' brushes – if made with top-quality fibre and put together by an excellent brush maker – are controllable, firm, point well, hold pigment and release it evenly, and clean in an instant when changing colour. The term 'round' means round when dry, pointing when wet. A kolinsky brush has a wider middle or 'belly' and returns to a point with a snap when flicked. It is sometimes the better performer, though more expensive, but it is better to seek well-made brushes of whatever type. The longer the fibre, the more expensive the brush. Be sure not to push the fibres or get masking fluid on your sable brushes.

I recommend at least two sable brushes – a size 2 or 3, and size 6 to 8. The number refers to the ferrule diameter.

My other brushes include squirrel mops, which are cheaper alternatives to sable, though I find them more difficult for detail work, because they are not as firm. For various techniques I use several brushes including a home-made woodcock-feather rigger, which makes the longest unbroken fine lines possible. I find a bristle 'bright' brush useful for lifting out small areas. I also use many other different shapes of brush – a fan, a goat-hair wash brush, and a hake. A toothbrush is used for spattering. For masking, a small well-pointing synthetic brush (size 2 to 6) can be used for masking in place of a colour shaper.

I do not put soap or masking fluid on sable brushes as they can damage the fibres. Soap used in brushes to protect them from masking fluid creates a problem. Soaps are likely to be alkali. Good watercolour paper has a balance of acid/alkali neutrality. There is a risk alkali will cause paper to go yellow in time.

To solve this problem, when masking by brush, I mask with inexpensive, small synthetic brushes, (around size 3), with good points. They can be cleaned more easily. They are cheaper to replace if they get ruined. Each time I finish masking, I wash them in water and squeeze them clean between my fingers and thumb. While masking I keep them brush end down in a waterpot just for this purpose. I don't want masking fluid residue in my painting water. I do this for a few minutes until I need them again. Never dump sables or any good-quality brush head down in water. When I have finished masking, I clean the brushes as well as I can for next time. It's OK to use soap at this stage, but not to protect brushes while masking with them.

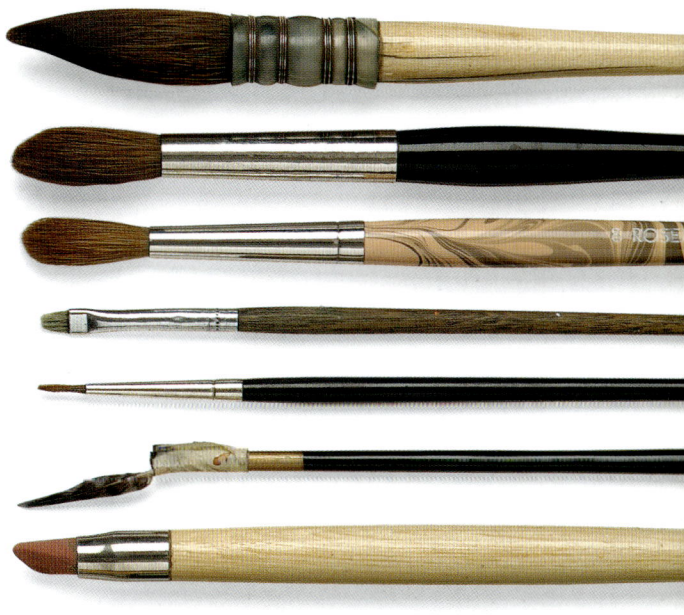

Mops, rounds, brights, feathers and shapers have various uses.

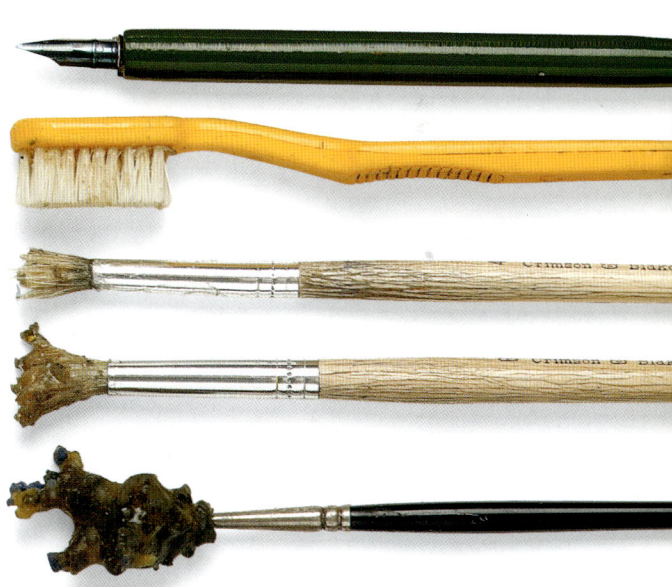

Use old brushes, a toothbrush or pen to apply masking fluid.

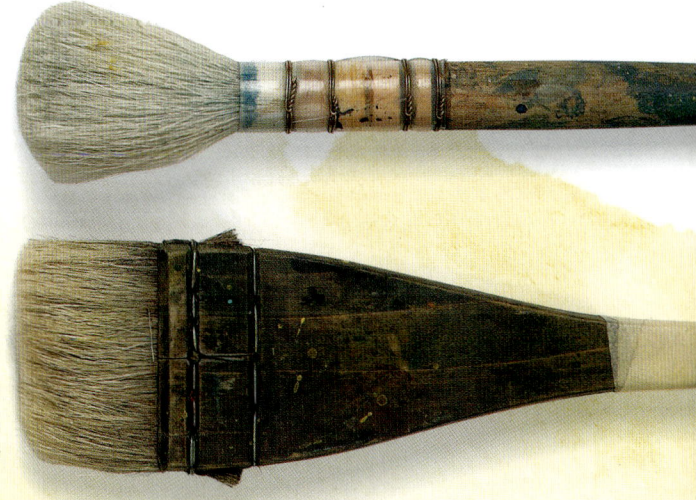

Apply water and washes with a goat-hair brush or hake.

PAINTS

Some artists use a limited palette, but I enjoy colour and I love trying new ones. I often like to balance strong bright colour with powerful tone, ranging from light or bright, to intense dark.

You can produce many of the colours perceived by the eye with just a handful of paints. A useful starter palette might consist of burnt sienna, burnt umber, cadmium lemon, French ultramarine, cobalt blue, Payne's gray and quinacridone magenta.

These seven colours will allow you to paint with a full colour palette. You can mix French ultramarine and cadmium lemon to make a good green. French ultramarine and burnt umber will give a dark grey or black plus greys and browns, while quinacridone magenta and cadmium lemon make a scarlet red.

The addition of other colours can extend your range and save mixing time.

USING BLACK

Payne's gray or another intense dark such as neutral tint allows intense darks, either on its own or mixed with other colours. I use these to get intense dark or blackness into my paintings, often in limited areas of intensity for deep shade or foreground texture such as on pages 80-81, or in linear markings such as dark streaks in mud banks on page 108. A mix such as French ultramarine and burnt sienna will not achieve the same strength. Without these darks, it can be impossible to achieve the intensity of dark, and the intense light by contrast. A variety of powerful black watercolour pigments are available. Enjoy experimenting for yourself. Strong black is successful where it is balanced with bright colour and intense light – often the white of the paper. An example is sunset over low tide on page 108.

Your initial palette

Buy good-quality paints, or student quality from major brands. You only need six, or eight, colours to start with; this small palette will help you organize as you discover the properties of different colours. Later add other colours you like.

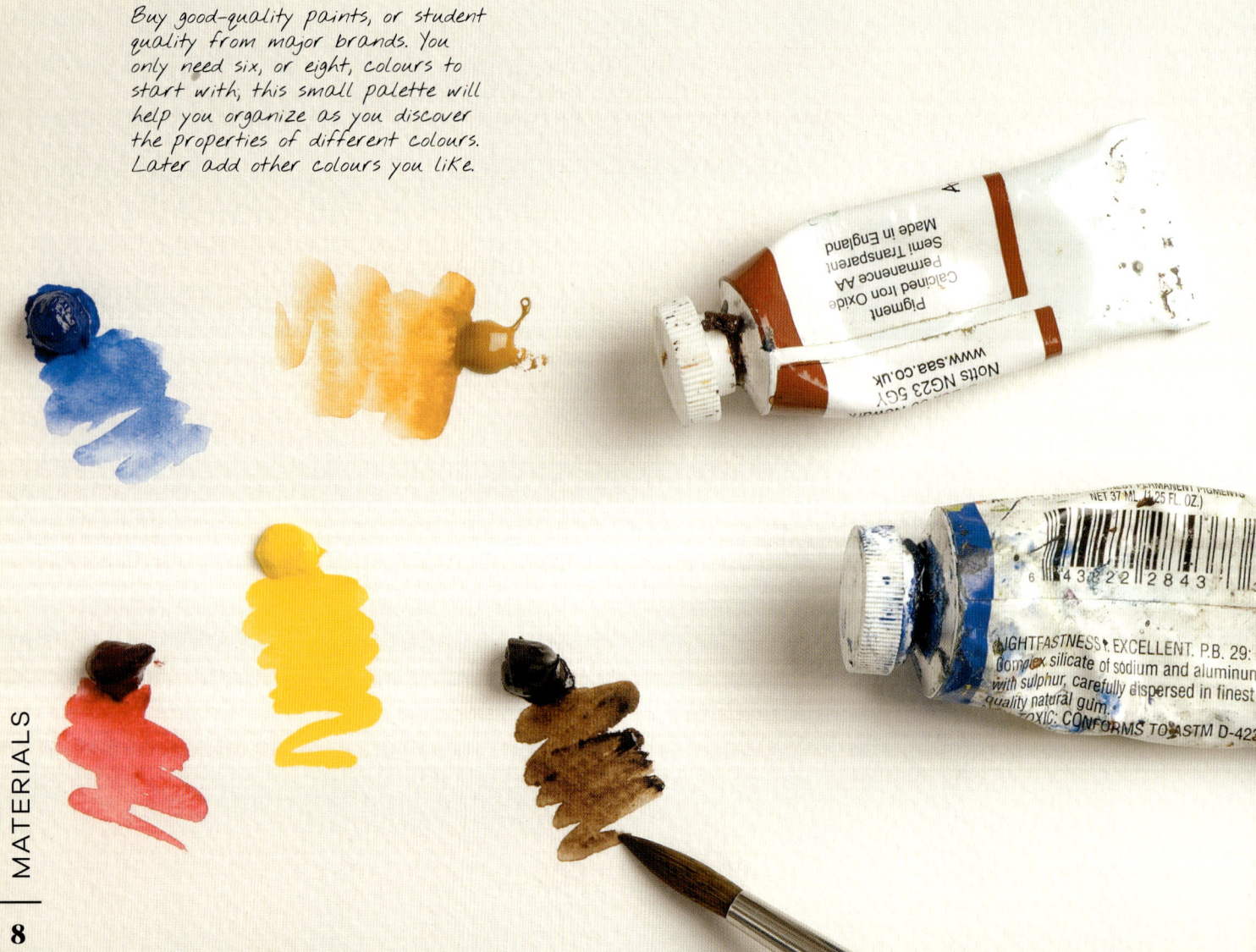

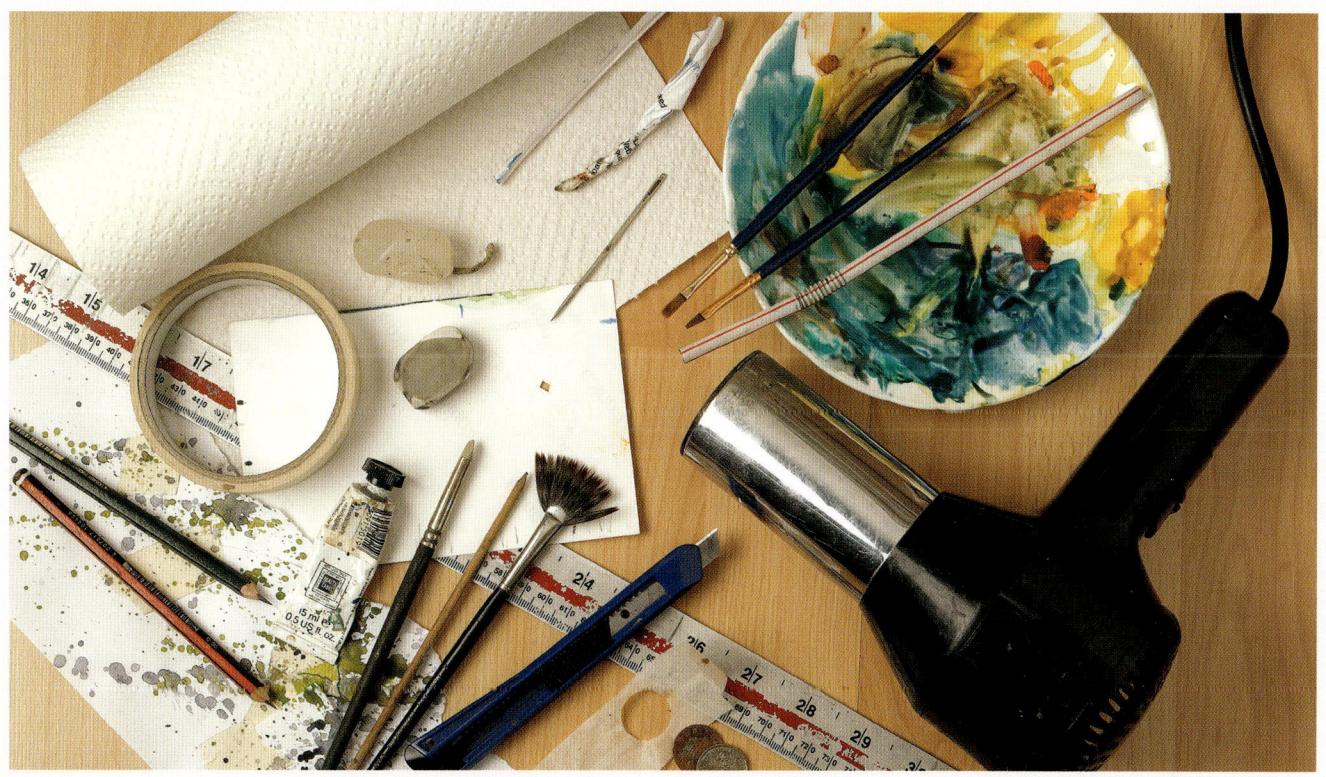

Found around the home

Items from your home can be used in your painting – here you can see masking tape, a steel ruler and craft knife, a hairdryer, kitchen paper and a saucer that works as a small palette. I use palettes with large, flat mixing surfaces. I have a collection of ordinary ceramic side plates from the kitchen – I can squeeze paint to the edges and mix many colours in the central area. The flat surface of china makes it easier to control these mixtures and work with large amounts of paint. Some palettes have hemispherical mixing wells, but I never use these. It's difficult to control the mixture and get the correct strength.

OTHER TOOLS AND MATERIALS

I am always discovering new techniques, and the tools used for different effects can be absolutely anything – a coiled-up piece of paper for masking, a laden seed head for spattering, a toothbrush for applying spatter or masking – it is just a matter of finding what works for the painting. You can use a vast array of ordinary items, such as kitchen roll, drinking straws and coins as stencil templates. Use a hairdryer if you need to dry areas of your painting quickly.

More specialist art equipment includes water sprayers, masking fluid, gum arabic and ox gall. A mirror is useful so you can see your work in reflection because it gives that vital second objective viewpoint – you can see instantly any creeping flaws in the work.

My paintings are generally exhibited in artificial light so I don't mind painting in it. You can use a daylight bulb if you wish, but remember that your paintings will look different under changing lighting conditions – often less colourful.

MATERIALS FOR TEXTURES

- Keep old brushes for dry-brush effects.
- Use an old toothbrush to spatter paint or masking fluid on the paper.
- Sprinkle coarse salt on a damp wash to create 'salt stars'.
- Squirt water from a sprayer before or after applying paint.
- Dab paint on or off with a sponge.
- Rub candle wax over the paper.
- Scratch out with a knife.
- Add gum arabic to slow the spread of paint – ideal for super-wet puddles.
- Spatter water from your fingers for texture.
- Dab masking fluid on with bunched up torn kitchen roll.

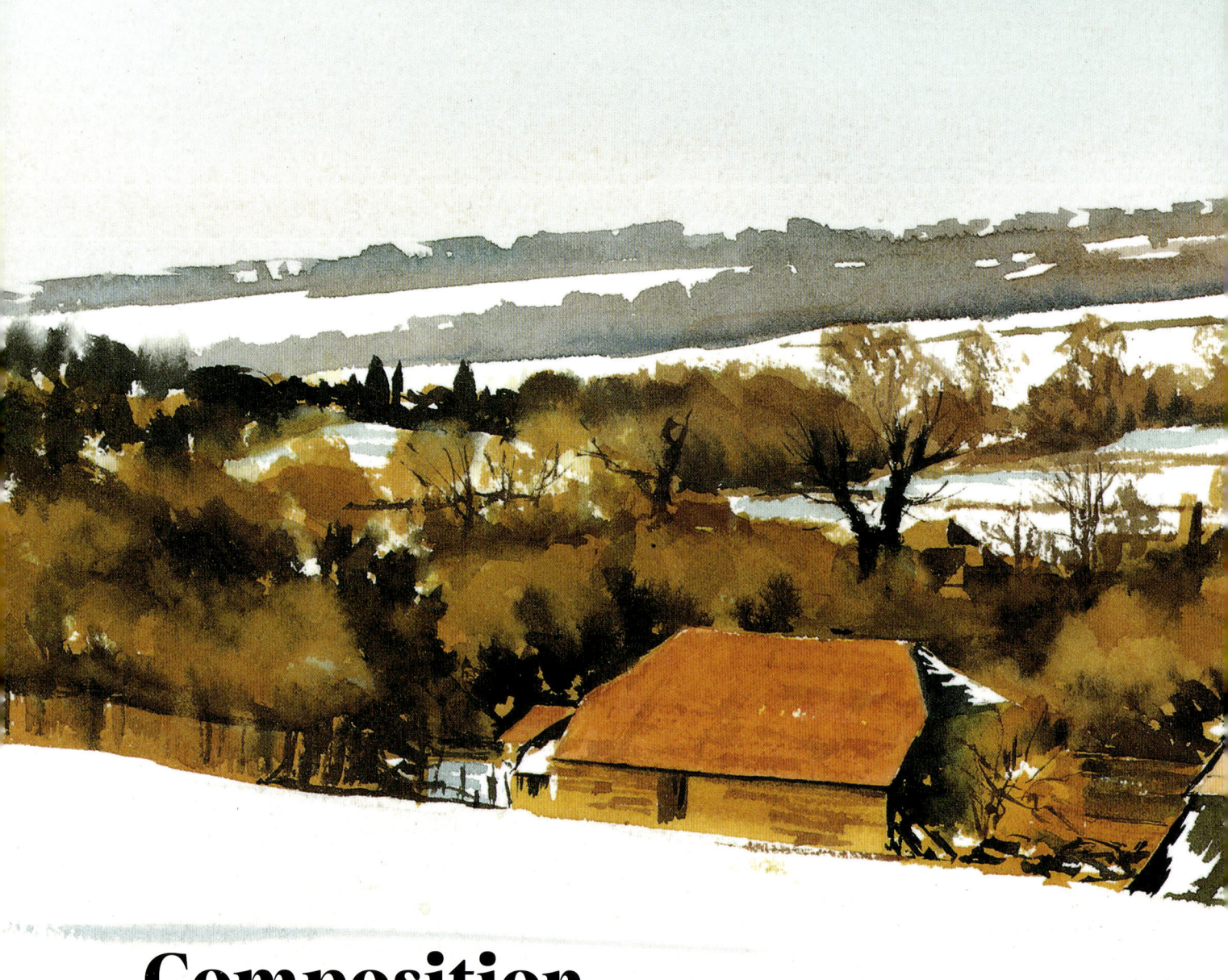

Composition

Why is it that one image looks great, while another does not? This is largely down to composition, and there are certain guidelines that can help you compose any subject into something visually truthful and pleasing. Planning is the key, so ask yourself questions: Where is the focal point? Where will I put the horizon? What is the best aperture shape? Answering these questions will help you produce a good composition with ease.

THE POINT OF INTEREST

Keep the focal point away from the middle of the composition – if it is in the centre the image will appear very static. Likewise, make sure that the horizon does not divide the painting into equal halves. These guidelines can be broken, of course, but only when you know how to use them.

USING GUIDELINES

One way to place the main parts is to divide the horizontal and vertical edges of the image into eighths. Place a line across for the horizon at three-eighths or five-eighths depending on whether you want it high or low. Place a vertical line for dividing masses at three- or five-eighths. Draw within these lines.

In this river bank scene (**A**), the horizon line is around five-eighths of the way up the image. The dark mass of trees to the left, and its reflection, forms a vertical about three-eighths in from the left (see pages 80–81).

HIGH HORIZON

Raising the horizon in the image removes some of the sky, emphasizing the height of the view by forcing the eye onto the land below. This has the effect of lengthening the horizon, giving a sense of breadth and scale. Even when the image is about sky, information can be contained in the short space above the horizon line.

A high horizon (**B**) increases the sense of distance and gives a deep foreground (see pages 36–37).

LOW HORIZON

With a lowered horizon, the foreground drops out of the frame and pushes the viewer's gaze into the distance and sky, producing a sense of space.

A low horizon, as in this low tide scene (**C**), emphasizes a tall summer sky. The horizon placement is massively influential in the outcome of the composition (see pages 54–55).

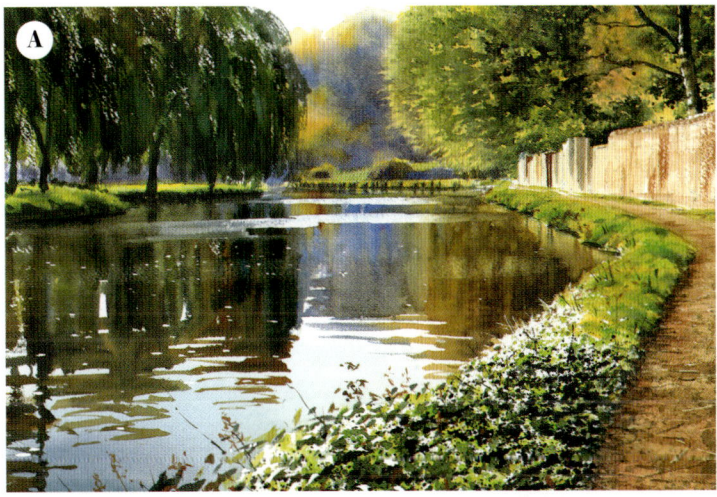

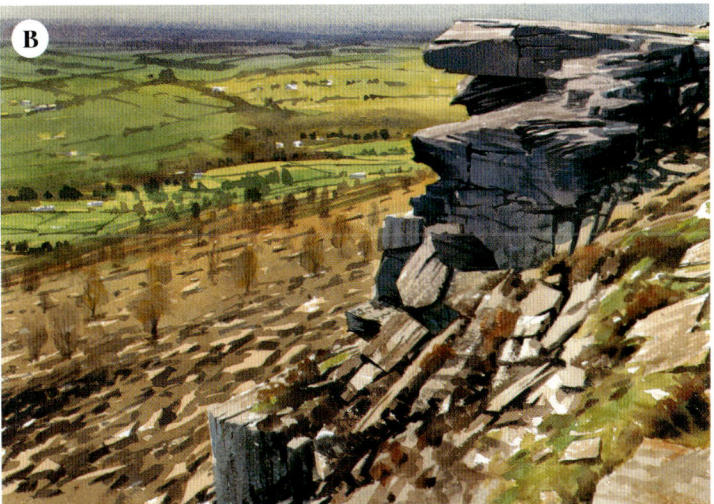

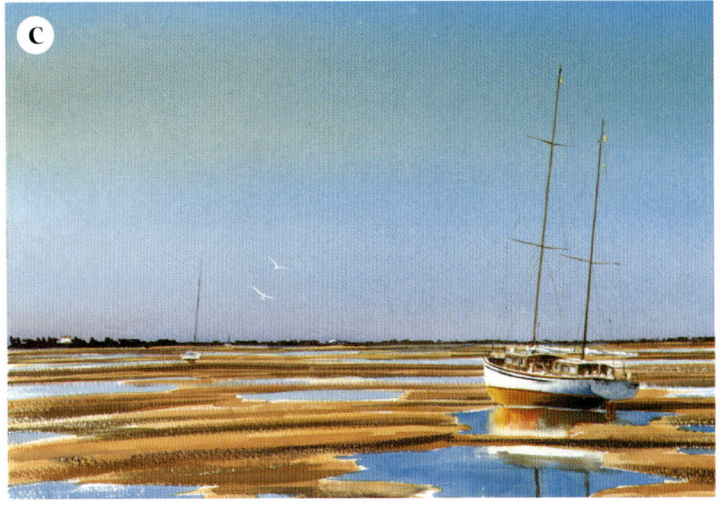

Formats

Choose a shape to suit your subject – portrait, landscape, panorama or square. The shape can help you solve compositional problems such as how to create impact or how to avoid including certain areas of the scene. When subject matter is short, a portrait format works well; for a landscape, a numerical aspect ratio of 'five up, by eight along, give or take a little', perhaps wider, gives sufficient breadth and space. For drama, or to remove a troublesome foreground, try a panoramic format. To put emphasis on the main subject you could try a square. No potential shape is off limits. Here are some examples of the effects of different crops on one scene.

CHOOSING THE RIGHT CROP

This painting is based on a photograph taken by mountaineer Chris Bonington. This is the original painting, with the mountain offset slightly and with the far shoreline acting as a horizon placed a little way above the centre. With any subject, the artist should consider possible formats and the placement of the main focal areas. The coloured frames here show a variety of possible crops to consider instead of the traditional landscape format, all of which retain the main focal area – the mountain, highlighted in green.

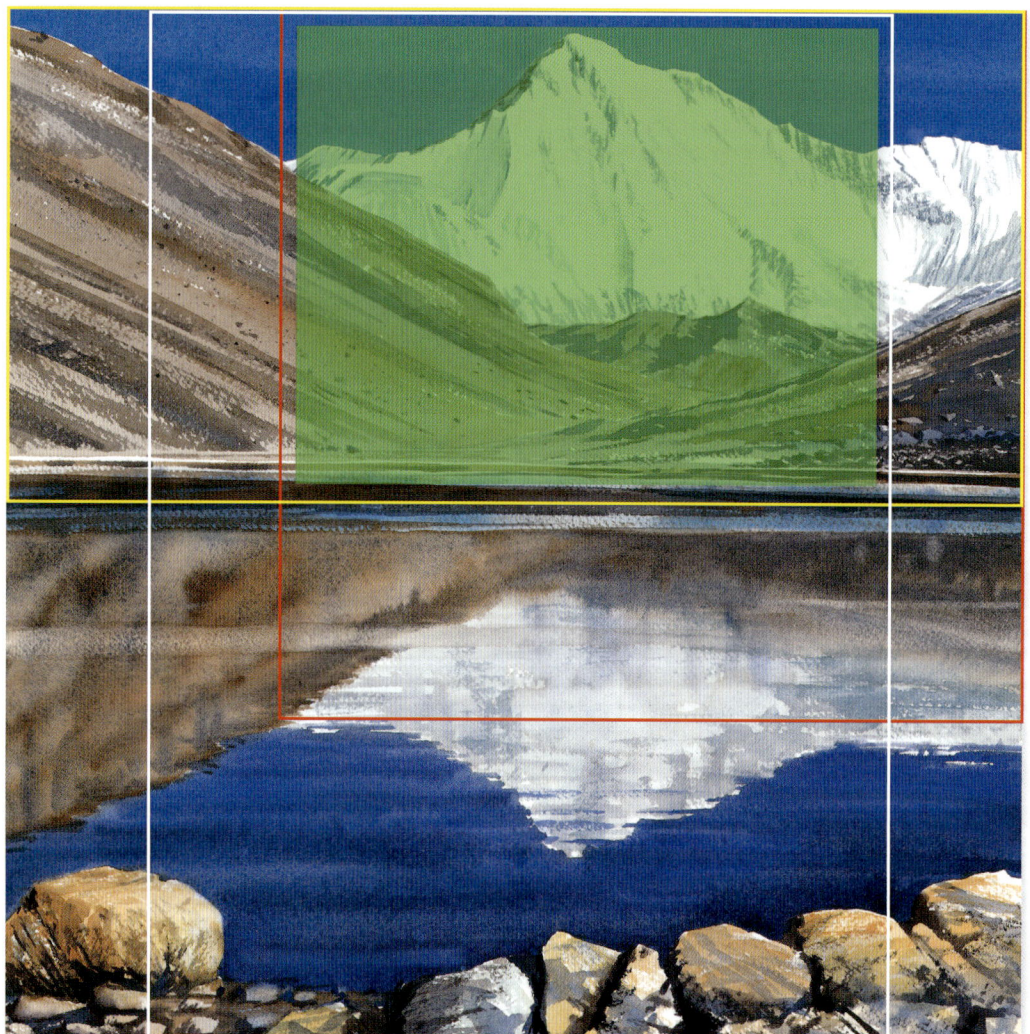

— square
portrait
— panorama
focal area

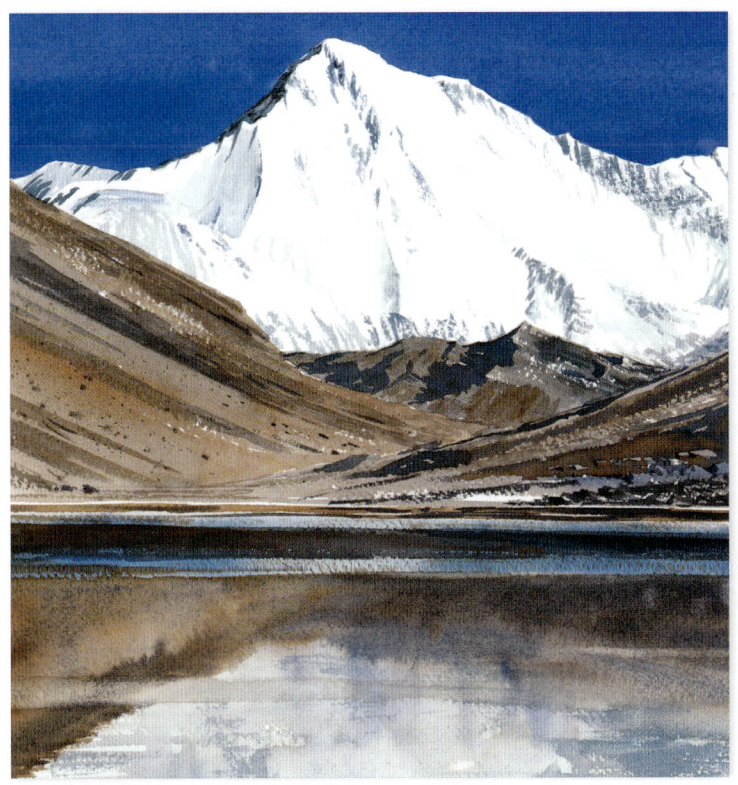

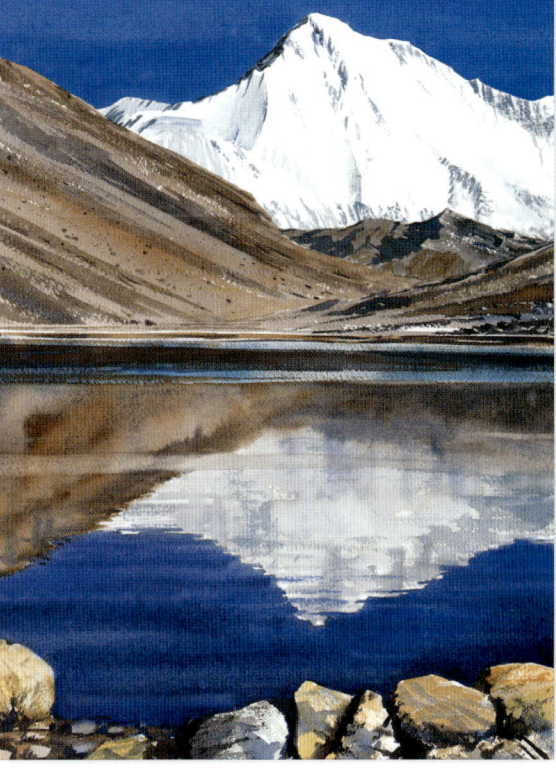

Square

By cropping in on the snowcapped mountain, emphasis is placed firmly on the subject matter. The low horizon leaves enough room for the lake but allows the mountain to dominate.

Portrait

This format conveys virtually all the same information as in the original square format but it emphasizes the height of the mountain rather than the breadth of the landscape.

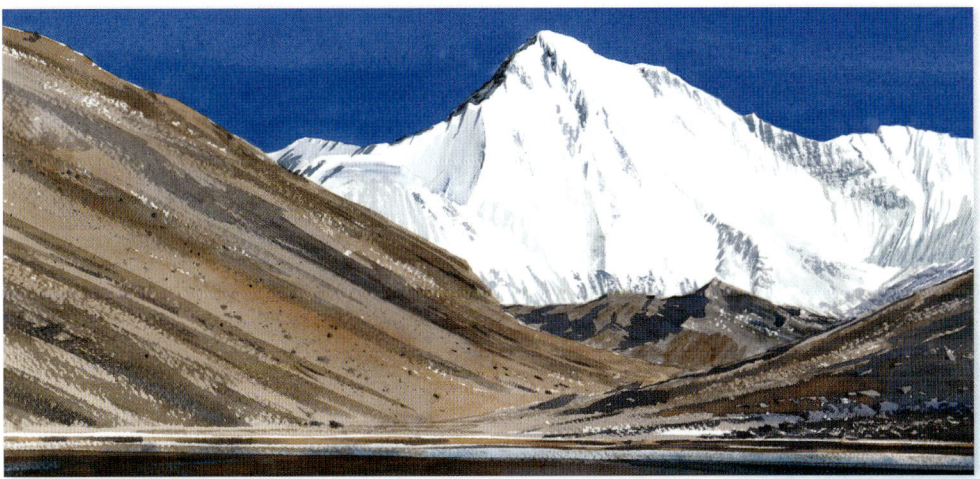

Panorama

The entire width of the image is used and the foreground is removed, emphasizing the drama of the long ridge. This format can be used to remove troublesome foreground detail.

Tonal composition

Tone is the combination of light, shade and colour that provides the lightness or darkness of a pigment on the paper. Paintings are defined by light and dark contrasting patterns of tone, which can run the full range from intense dark to the white of the paper.

A tonal pencil sketch can help you sort out lights and darks, and help you make sure that the separate parts of the painting contrast each other in an appealing way. It is often helpful to produce a tonal plan with a maximum of three or four different tones to check that a painting will function visually before proceeding to a painting.

USING MONOCHROME

Work with one colour only to visualize the tone on its own – a good exercise is a monochrome painting in about four different strengths of tone plus white. If it does not work in black and white, it will not work in colour and conversely, if it does work in black and white, it is more likely to work in colour.

Tone before colour

The sunset scene shown on page 108 uses brilliant colour, but it would not work without the massive tonal range from white to dark and intense shade, demonstrated below. With the tonal plan set, any number of different colour options would have succeeded. Tone comes before colour and is crucial.

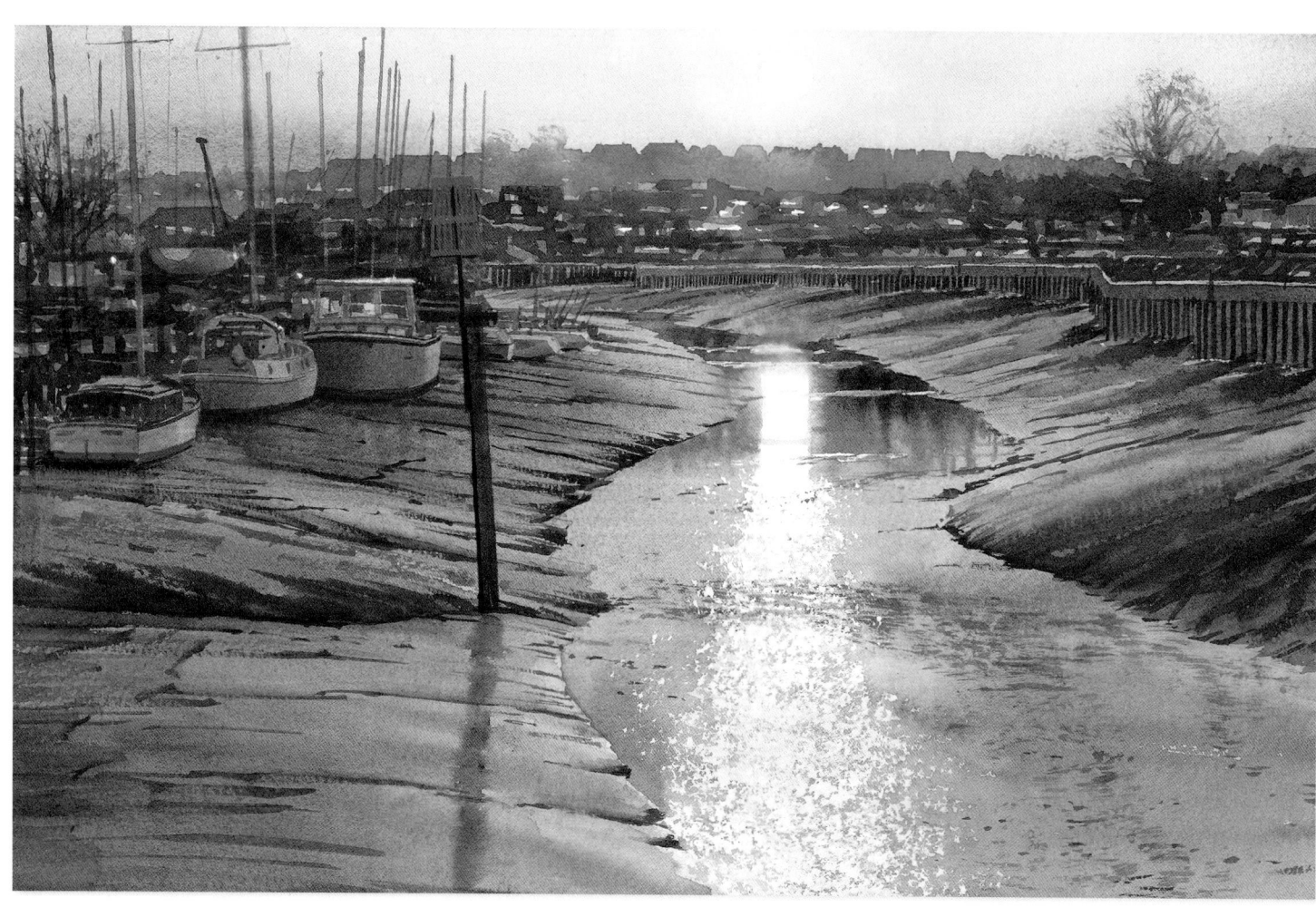

X FACTOR

Two ways to create zest and zap, giving your painting that 'X factor'.

1) A TRICK WITH LIGHT

Reserve light with a limited area of paper white.

The sparkle on the estuary painting (see page 108) is reserved by masking. Reserve a very limited area of the lightest white as white paper, then start the painting. You will notice that only a small area of the glinting reflection is white. Paint everything else. Some washes may be very pale, such as sky. The reserved or protected area appears very bright because the entire surrounding painting has tone, even if only pale. Plan a limited area of white paper. Protect this zone. You can get the glint on metal, (pages 30 and 52), the sparkle on water, (pages 42 and 108), and other effects in this book. This gives it some zest and zap – the X factor.

2) A COMPOSITIONAL CHANGE

Boost composition to create impact – a way to do this.

Placing major elements well away from the centre creates another X factor. These elements are the focal point – the horizon, skyline and important objects. The lake painting, here and on page 82, features an extremely high horizon, creating a strong dynamic composition. Foreground trees are situated well to the left. The boat is to the right and above the horizontal centre-line. This extreme off-setting can add impact. The serenity of the painting hides the power in the composition – this is a secret of watercolour. Use extreme placement of its elements to add X factor to the composition.

The sparkling water painting on page 108 has a very high horizon. The focal point of the estuary is near the centre of the horizontal axis, but the more visually significant sun-glare reflection is moderately to the right. It was enough to place only the horizon at an extreme, high position. I often use these X factor methods to give it some zap.

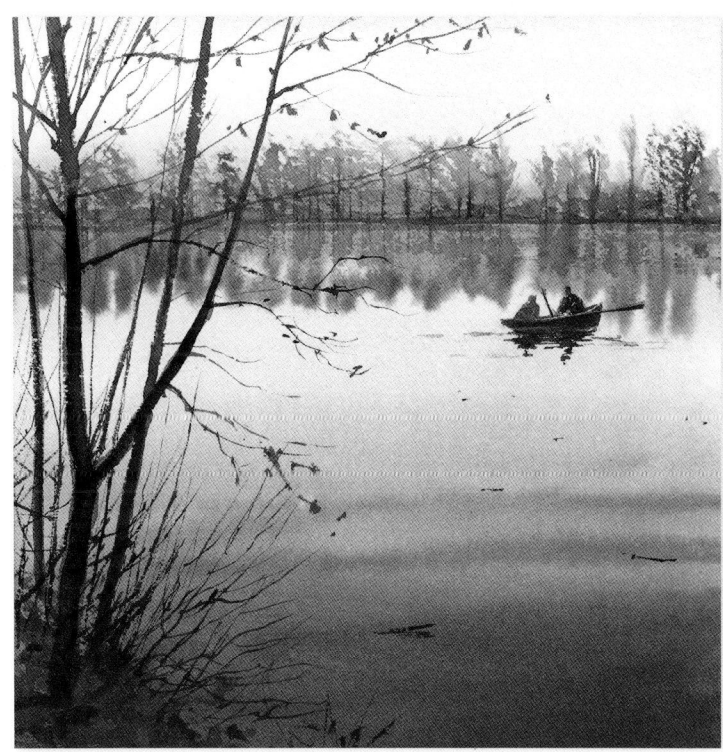

Focal contrast

Sky and water are basically the same light tone in this lake scene, but the foreground water is graduated to dark. The distant trees and reflection are a mid tone, the foreground trees are dark. Notice how your eyes keep returning to the boat, a dark tone on a light area, which produces maximum contrast.

Energize the skyline

The skyline is the line defining the upper part of the land against the sky – a vital element. Be creative. The sparkling water image has an urban skyline with an irregular pattern of roofs interrupted by masts and trees. The lake image has a skyline of trees, interrupted by spaces which counteract uniformity. Change a repetitive, uniform tree line to a ragged and windblown one (when appropriate). Vary heights and spacings between trees; avoid symmetry. Water can be dragged by brush, and paint can be flowed from its point.

My landscape

My native UK has a gentle landscape with less industrialized forestry. It is informal, very pleasant to observe, with infinite complexity – a vast wandering 'patchwork quilt' of fields and woodlands often spread over undulating topography. Flatlands are in the minority but are often a great natural sprawl. I convey this in my skylines.

Perspective

Perspective allows the artist to place three-dimensional objects in the two dimensions of a piece of paper. Without a basic understanding of the laws of perspective it is virtually impossible to draw a landscape that looks realistic. Even when a landscape is devoid of straight lines, the artist still requires a basic understanding of perspective to render the scene correctly.

LINEAR PERSPECTIVE

Parallel lines appear to meet at a single point as they pass into the distance. In reality they carry on as parallel, as with railway lines for instance. A system for easily working out the effect of perspective on objects was developed centuries ago. It allows you to plot converging lines to represent the diminishing of objects with distance, and is known as 'linear perspective'. It can be used as a framework to plot all the elements of your painting.

THE VANISHING POINT

The vanishing point is the point where parallel lines disappear from view. A receding horizontal line disappears where it touches the horizon, and in conventional landscape painting the horizon is at eye level.

All horizontal lines on objects located above your eye level project upwards toward you from the horizon; for example, the tops of doorways. Lines below you, such as pavements, project downwards toward you from the horizon. When an element in your painting is not horizontal, such as a street running up or down hill from you, then the vanishing point is not located on the horizon, but is either above or below it. However, buildings on that same street, with a few exceptions, are likely to be horizontal, so each one will have to be projected with lines leading to the horizon.

A universal language

Perspective can be likened to the language of drawing – without language it is difficult to communicate anything at all.

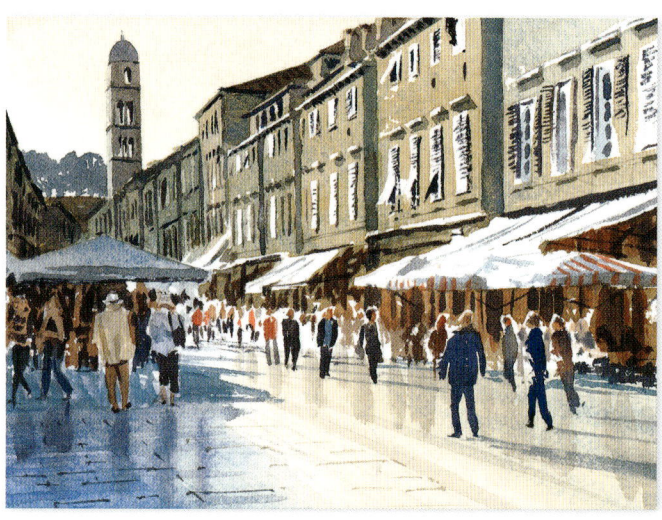

Maintaining the principles

Perspective is seldom simple. The street rises gently and the foreground left side is higher than the right, the building angles vary, and the vanishing points differ but are close together. The viewer is just above head level, so nearby heads are lower, and distant ones higher. The frontages of the shops are lost in street clutter, so lower perspective lines disappear, but the principles still apply.

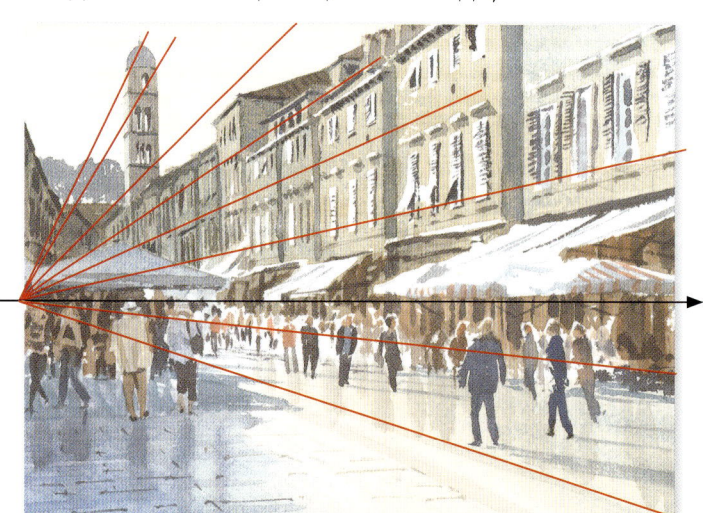

theoretical horizon ⸺

perspective lines ⸺

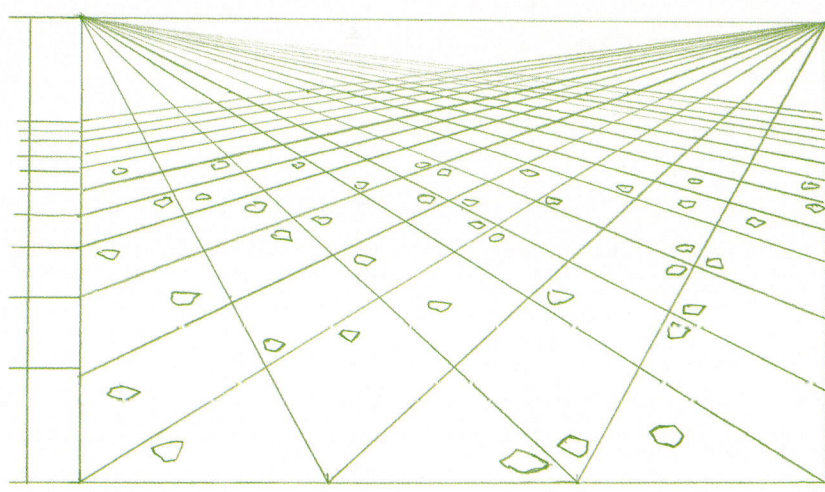

Making a grid like this enables you to superimpose perspective over a random distribution of objects. By placing objects in different positions in each box, making a random choice for each, you can still follow the principles of perspective in recession.

The bar alongside shows how distances of equally spaced lines reduce as they recede. You can use this diagram as a reference when considering the perspective of your own subject matter.

THE VANISHING POINT

A single line extended from a house will locate the vanishing point on the horizon for all other lines in that elevation. When all of these lines are projected from this vanishing point, they automatically agree with each other. Establishing the position of the building, and working out a single line to the horizon using guesswork enables you to produce a correct perspective drawing, even if your drawing is wrong in other respects.

LOCATING FURTHER VANISHING POINTS

When more than one elevation of a building is visible (for example, the side of the house at right angles to the front), another vanishing point is required for the second plane. Parallel lines along the elevation will point to a different position on the horizon – a vanishing point for that elevation. Finding where one line from the building crosses the horizon will enable you to locate a vanishing point.

Objects exist in three dimensions, so a third vanishing point is often required. If you look upwards at tall buildings you will see that vertical lines also recede. They converge towards a vanishing point up above. A vertical vanishing point above the scene was used to project the Golden Gate Bridge on page 120.

The vertical vanishing point may sometimes be down below instead of up above. This is the case if you are above the subject, perhaps looking down a shaft or viewing a scene from a helicopter, for example. Guesswork is often sufficient to plot the vertical perspective.

PEOPLE IN PERSPECTIVE

People on the same level and of a similar height to you share your eye level. Because of being on your eye level, their eyes will be in the same horizontal plane along the horizon. By drawing their heads along this line, no matter how near or far, and their bodies in proportion, your drawing of them will obey the laws of perspective. Shorter people will be drawn lower than the horizon line and taller people higher.

RECEDING BANDS

Surfaces or planes narrow with distance. Though these may be broad swathes, they resolve into thinner and thinner bands as they recede in the image, as with a field pattern or mud banks on an estuary. Making wide objects narrower the further away they are helps them conform to the principles of perspective and gives an illusion of distance – see this effect on page 54.

AERIAL PERSPECTIVE

Colour cools and becomes paler with distance. So to give a feeling of recession in your pictures paint distant areas bluer and use warmer colours for the foreground. This is described in more detail on page 35, where the effect of aerial perspective is demonstrated in a long-distance painting of countryside.

Washes

The wash is the building block of watercolour – a swathe of colour brushed onto paper. Watercolour is transparent. Light passes through the pigment onto the paper and bounces back; the white paper imparts light. Watercolour depends on this transparent effect of pigment, paper and light. A potential problem with watercolour is a lack of strength in the finished result because paint always dries much lighter. This can be overcome by using more colour in washes, or by overlaying washes, even washes of the same colour. Colours can be built up by overlaying them in transparent washes, by mixing the colours, or a combination of both.

There are two basic types of wash: wet-in-wet, where the paper is wet and colour added; and wet-on-dry, where paint is applied to dry paper.

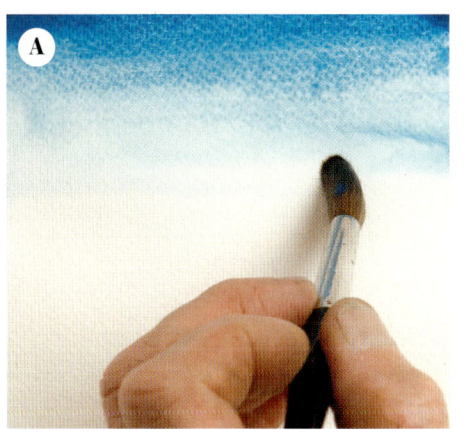

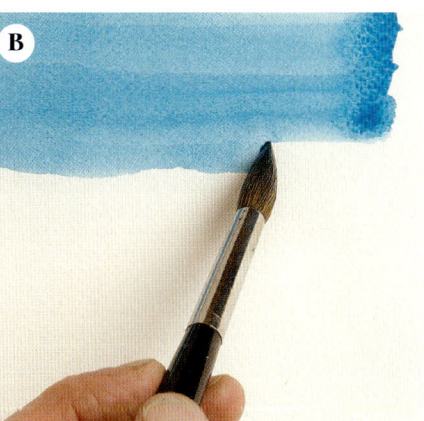

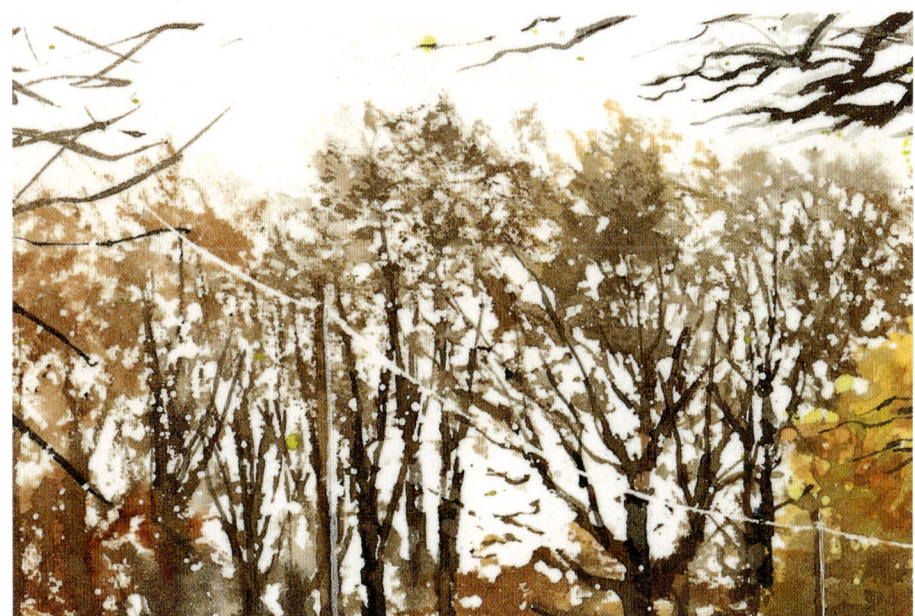

WATER FEATHERING

This is a variation of working wet-in-wet. Apply water by dragging it across the surface of the paper with the belly of the brush (see page 7), dragged sideways, leaving a stippled wet-on-dry texture of water on the surface. While it is still wet, brush a line or stroke of colour through this water-feathered area. The colour spreads and diffuses into the wet and dry water-feathered pattern (**C**). This technique is useful for many textures including a winter-woodland tree canopy.

First, masking fluid was spattered from a toothbrush and dried, to create random pattern sky-holes. Then water feathering was used to capture the look of the distant tree canopies in this autumn landscape (**D**) (see page 112). Effective realism can be achieved by combining techniques such as water feathering, with masking.

WET-IN-WET

I use wet-in-wet for smooth skies. Washes are glazed, or overlaid one above the other, building colour and tone. The colours can be applied one after the other wet-in-wet. For slightly greater control dry between each application, and rewet the paper before applying the next wash. Wet-in-wet washes can be graduated – in a gradient from dark to light, or flat and even all over.

First mix plenty of colour with water. Next wet the area to be covered and add the colour. Smooth effects and transitions of colour are attainable (**A**).

WET-ON-DRY

Mixing colour with water and applying it to dry paper is the simplest form of watercolour painting. With the paper dry, the colour can be controlled to leave whites or areas of underlying colour left unpainted.

For a smooth wet-on-dry wash, mix the colour and apply it in successive streaks, one below the other. With a slight tilt on the board, the colour will flow down into each new streak and form a smooth, even colour (**B**).

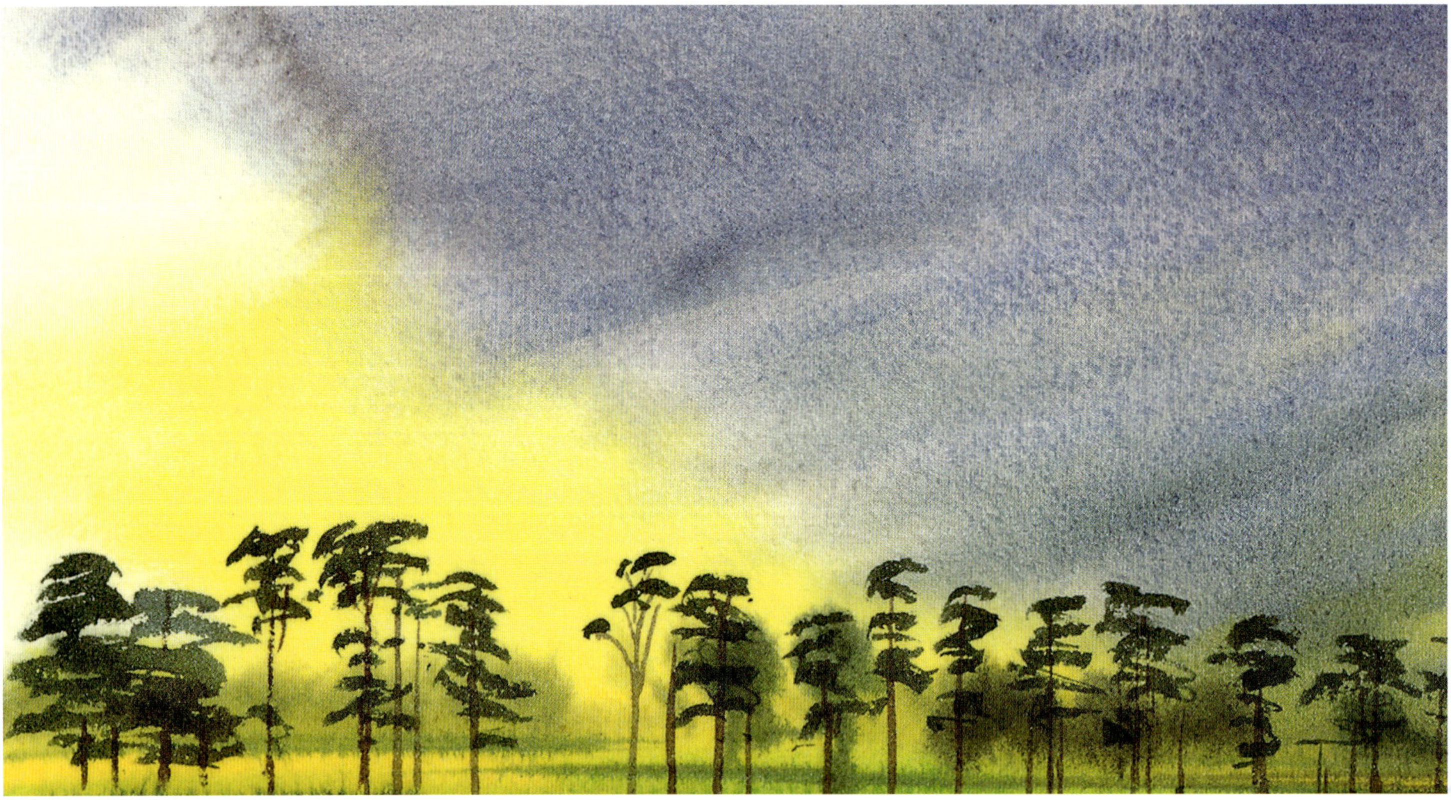

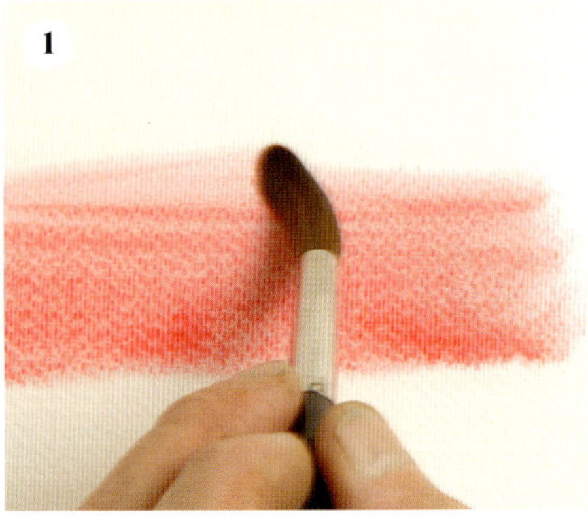

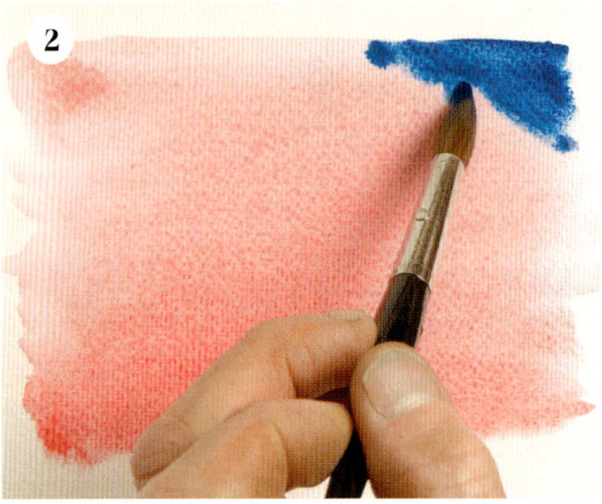

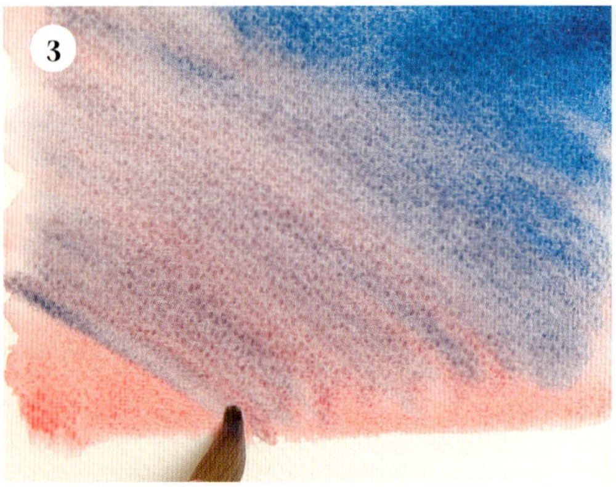

GLAZING

Watercolour paintings can be built by 'glazing' or overlaying colours. When overlaid, colours alter, but remain transparent. Subsequent coverings can cover some areas, leaving others unaltered.

1 Wet the paper and 'let in' colour, brushing it onto the wet paper.

2 While still wet apply the next colour, as shown here, or dry it, rewet and apply the colour wet-in-wet.

3 A transparent 'glaze' of colour allows the underlying wash to be seen, and the two colours combine.

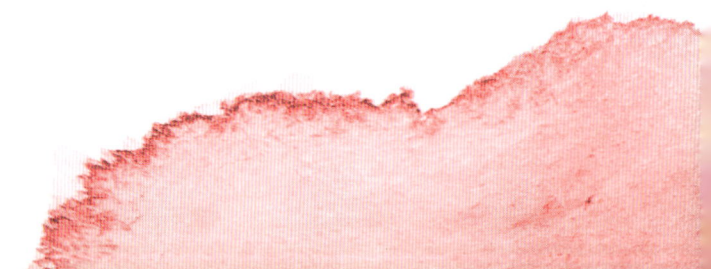

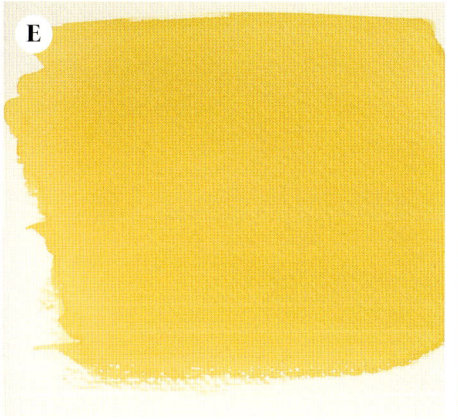

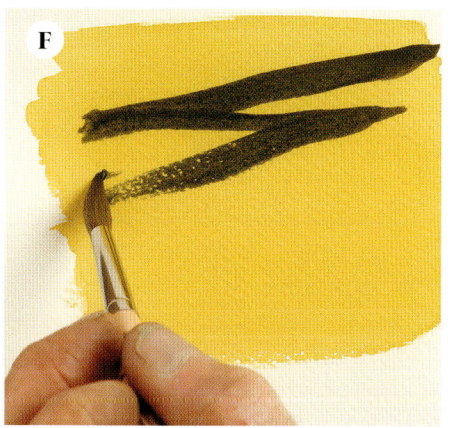

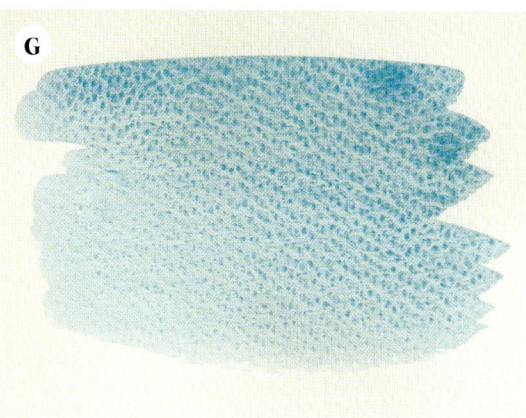

FLAT WASH

Applying a wash to dry paper is an effective way of tinting an area ready to start painting over it – such as a sky, field or foreground foliage. The colour can be easily applied flat – the water smooths the flow of colour.

Apply a mix of colour – here cadmium lemon, phthalo green and burnt sienna – on dry paper or wet-on-dry (**E**).

BRUSHMARKS

Colour can be applied from the tip of a brush or by any other means over unpainted paper or onto a wash of colour. When applied on dry colour, as shown, the focus is sharp; on wet paper it is soft.

The drier the paint is on the brush, the more the colour breaks up, creating texture (**F**).

GRANULATION

Useful for texture, granulation, a grainy effect, appears from certain pigments such as cerulean blue, cobalt blue, cobalt violet, manganese blue, manganese violet, raw sienna, burnt umber, ivory black and others. Manganese colours and cerulean blue are best. French ultramarine produces a similar and beautiful gathering effect of colour, sometimes called flocculation.

Mix cerulean blue with plenty of water. Brush it on. The granulation is formed by the heavy pigment gathering in the dimples of Not and rough paper (**G**).

MIXING COLOURS FOR WASHES

Precise colours can be attained by mixing them together thoroughly with water before applying. Greys mixed from two colours can be biased slightly toward red or blue on the palette, for a warm or cool grey, then applied pale with a watery mix.

This warm grey, mixed from cadmium red and cerulean blue, has granulated slightly (**H**).

Colour

A colour wheel presents colours simply; here it shows spectrum positions of mixes and tube colours used in this book. Three primary colours create all colours, including the three secondary colours, but even large numbers of pigments cannot duplicate pure colour perfectly. Primary and adjacent secondary colours produce beautiful third rank or 'tertiary' colours. If you don't have the right colour, you can often mix your own. For example, one of the yellows I have used is new gamboge, made by Winsor & Newton. You can substitute this particular warm, transparent yellow for a yellow mix of your choosing.

PRIMARY COLOURS

The inner circle of the colour wheel shows the primary colours: red, yellow and blue.

SECONDARY COLOURS

Secondary colours are shown on the second round of the colour wheel between the primary colours of red, yellow and blue. Secondaries can be mixed from adjacent primary colours.

TERTIARY COLOURS

Mix secondaries with the adjacent primary colour to make the tertiaries. Alternatively use an appropriate tube colour as shown on the colour wheel.

Most of the colours used in this colour wheel are from the Winsor & Newton range of artists paints. The exceptions are marked as follows:

*Schmincke paints
**Society of All Artists (SAA)
***DaVinci Paints

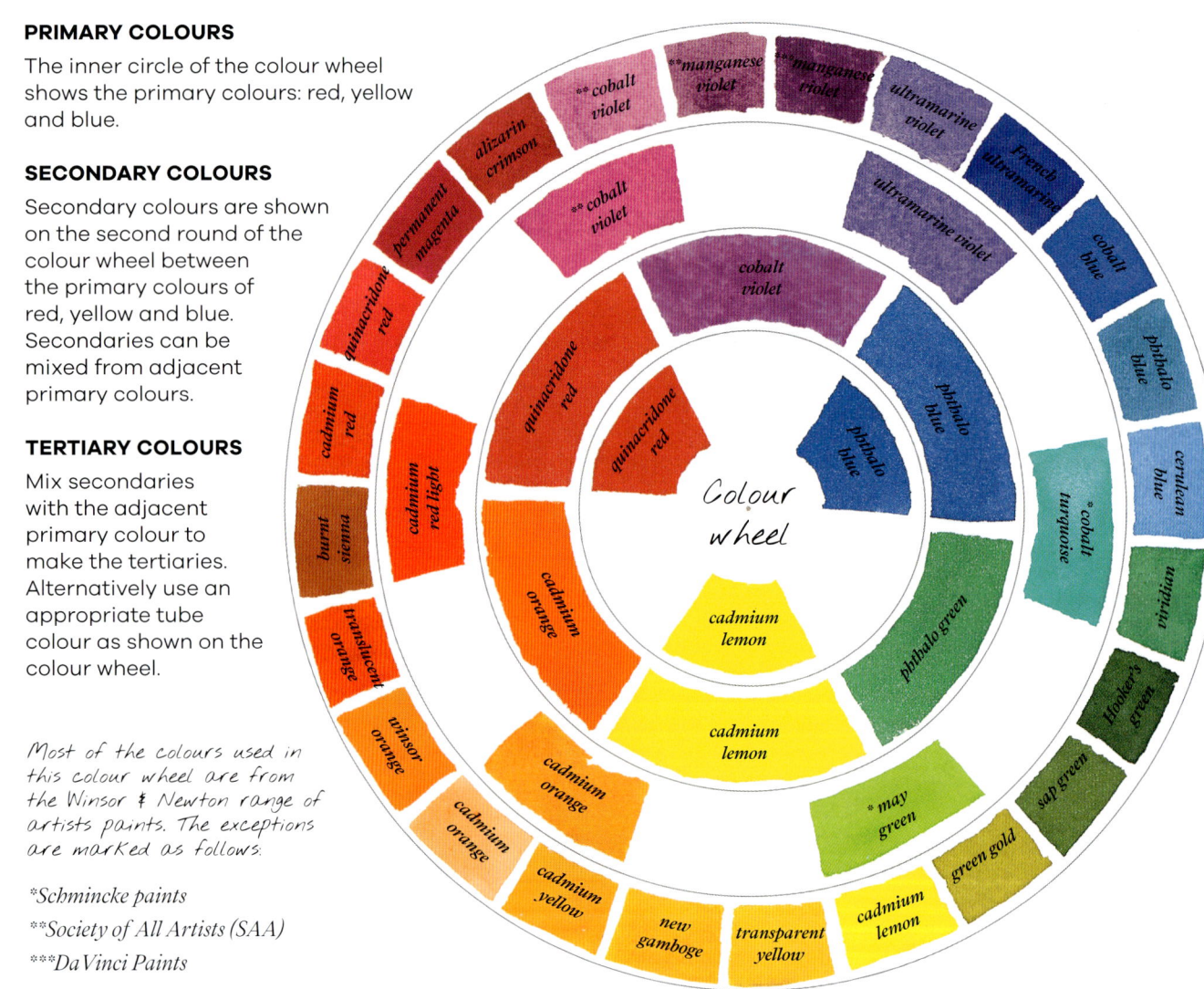

FURTHER MIXING

Gradations of colour can go on more or less indefinitely. The fourth round of the colour wheel shows appropriate tube colours for this stage, but if you prefer you can mix these from a smaller range of paints. From this stage you can go on to mix even more variations as well as mixing paints from other areas of the colour wheel to produce some wonderful muted colours like the greys and greens in the sample mixes (see Mixing colours, page 23).

MIXING COLOURS

There are many tube colours, but for greys and greens it is often best to mix your own. Beautiful greys, the key to mature watercolour, can be mixed with two or three colours.

GREYS AND DARKS

Useful colours from transparent greys to intense darks may be mixed from pairs of opposite or complementary colours. The resulting mixes can range from warm red or brown through neutral to cool blues. On the right are a few examples but there are many more possibilities you can explore. Observe the middle three rows for the most neutral greys. You can create virtually any colour you see, by mixing grey, and adding grey to brighter colours.

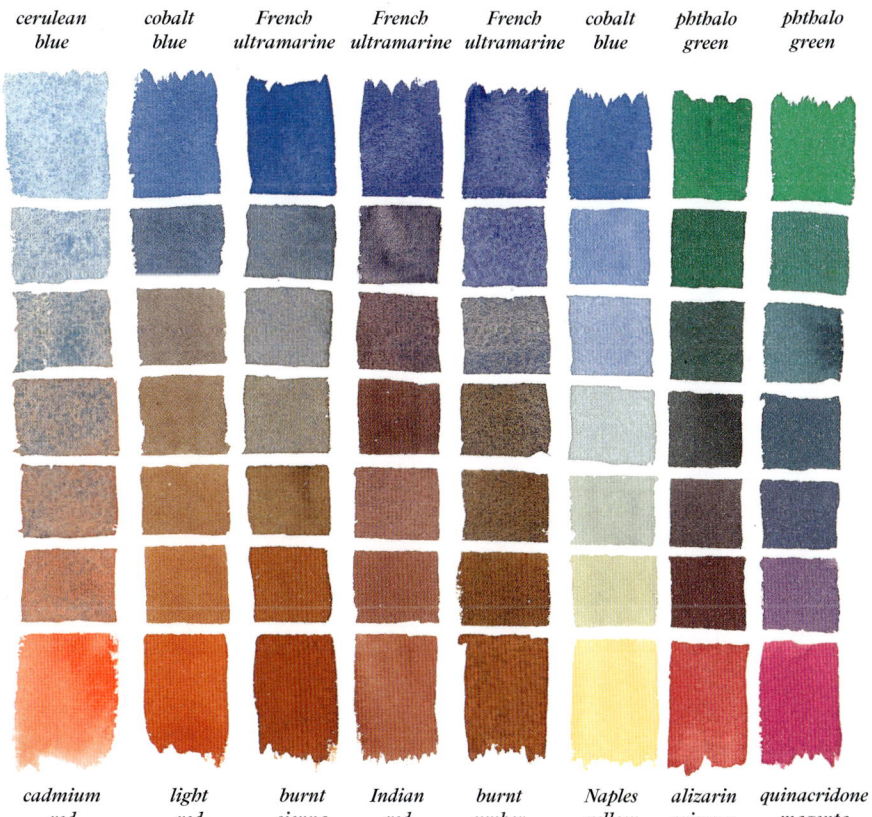

Mixing greys

Here is a selection of possible mixes for greys. Opposite or near opposite colours on the colour wheel can be combined in differing proportions for warm, cool or dark greys.

GREENS

There are more greens than any other colour. Greens of nature are seldom pure, hence the need to mix other colours. The general principle is to start with yellow, adding small amounts of tube green or blue, and tinting with other colours. If you work the other way around, starting with the darker colour, you will find you need to add a lot of yellow to the mix in order to make a difference, and you may never succeed. If it goes too green, start afresh on another palette, rather than try to change it. You can add this colour into your yellow on a fresh palette, or use it later for darker green.

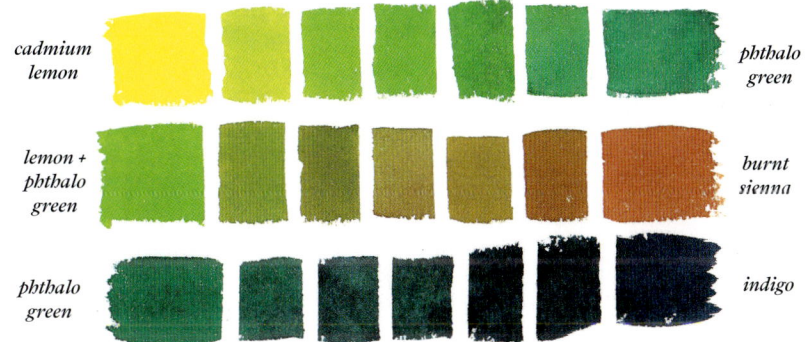

Mixing greens

Here are three green mixes. Some basic foliage greens can be mixed by adding a little phthalo green to cadmium lemon. Add burnt sienna to the mix of cadmium lemon and phthalo green to create a range of warm leaf greens. If you want a darker green, mix phthalo green or a mixed green with indigo.

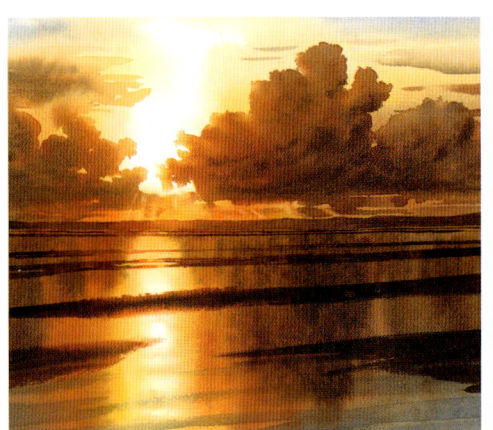
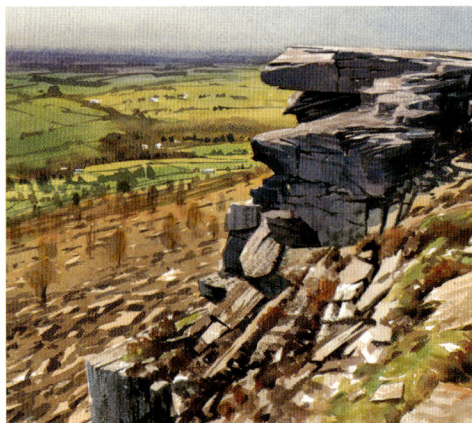
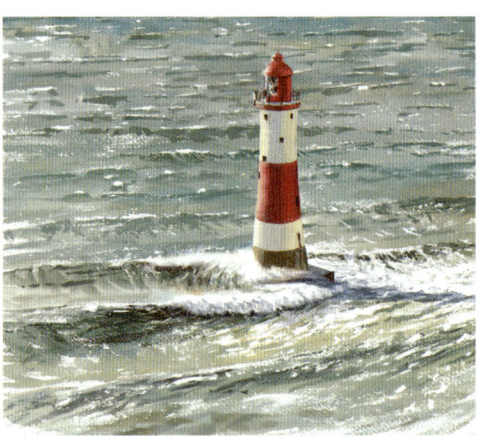

Paint 50
LANDSCAPES

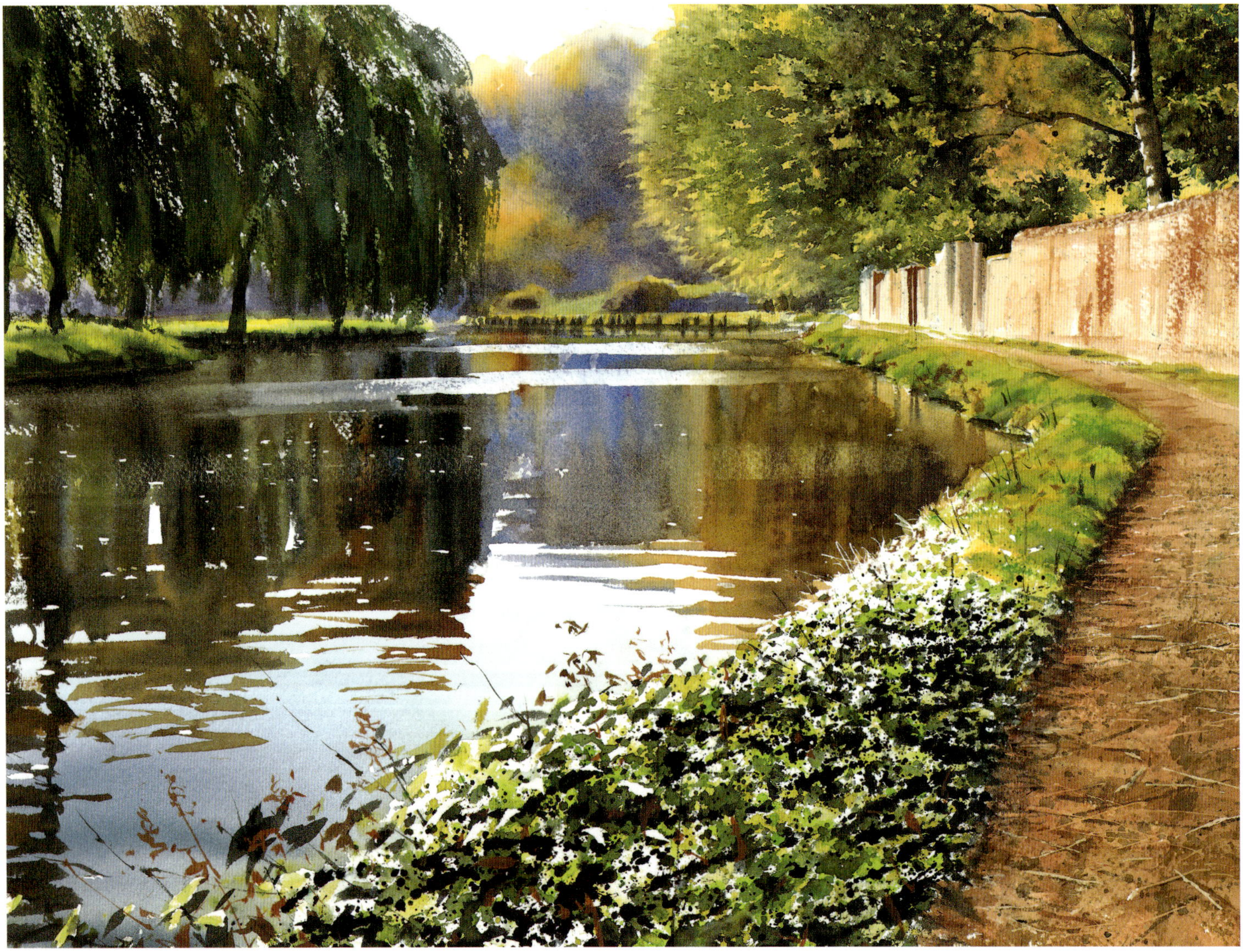

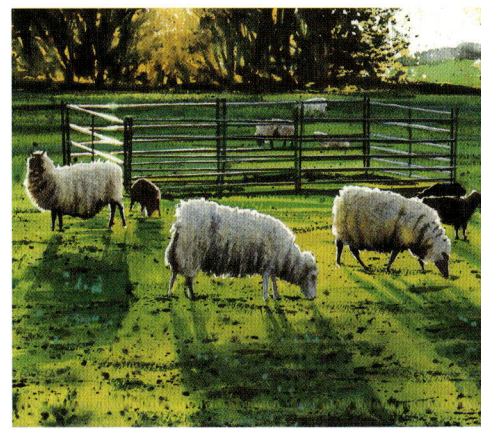
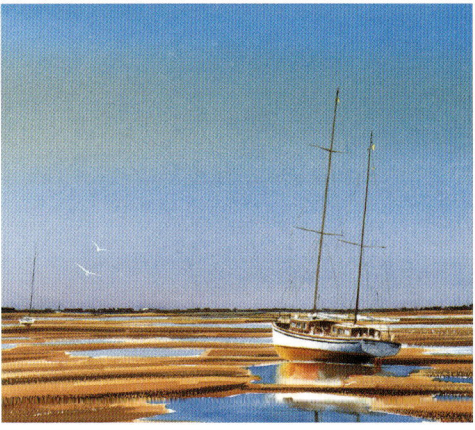
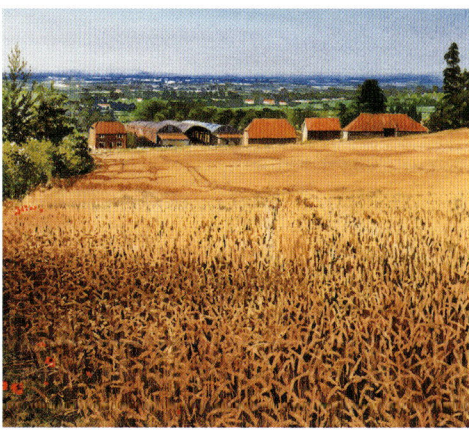
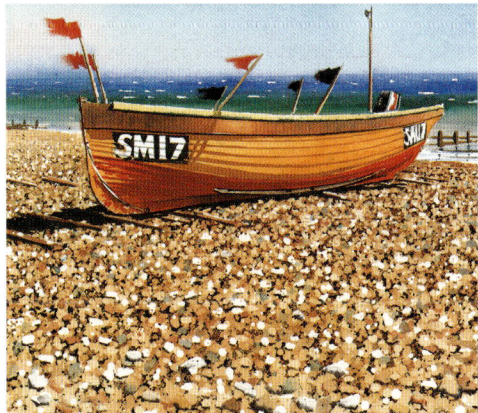
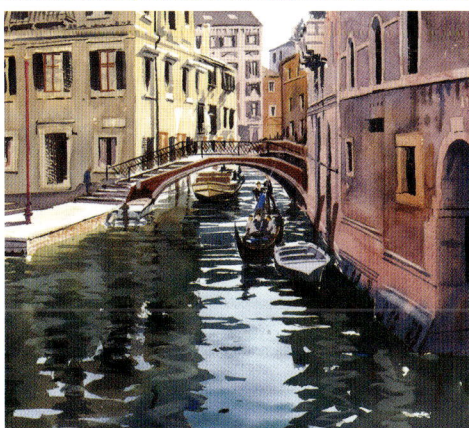
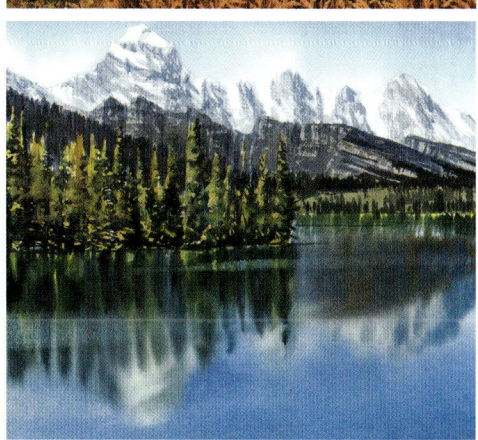

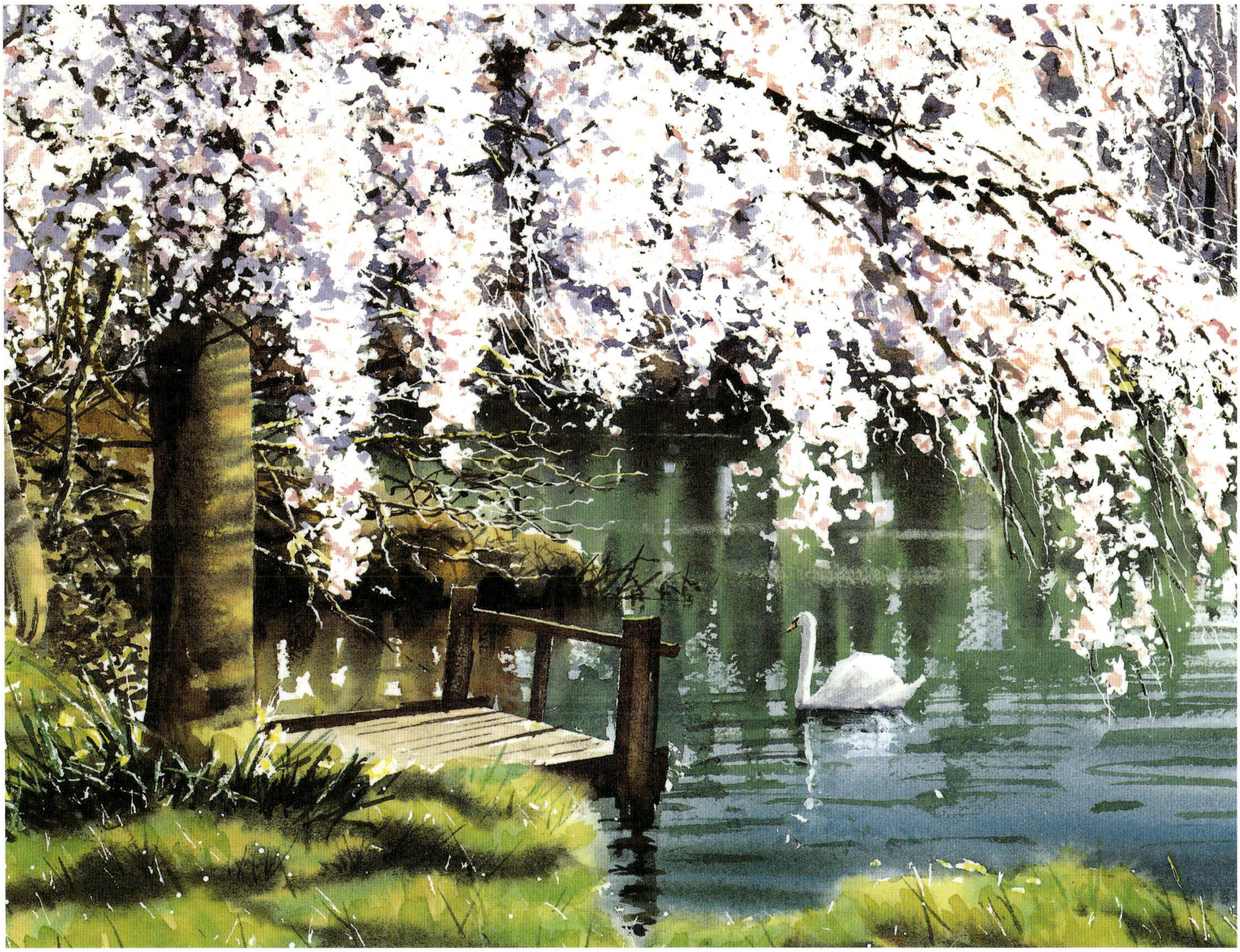

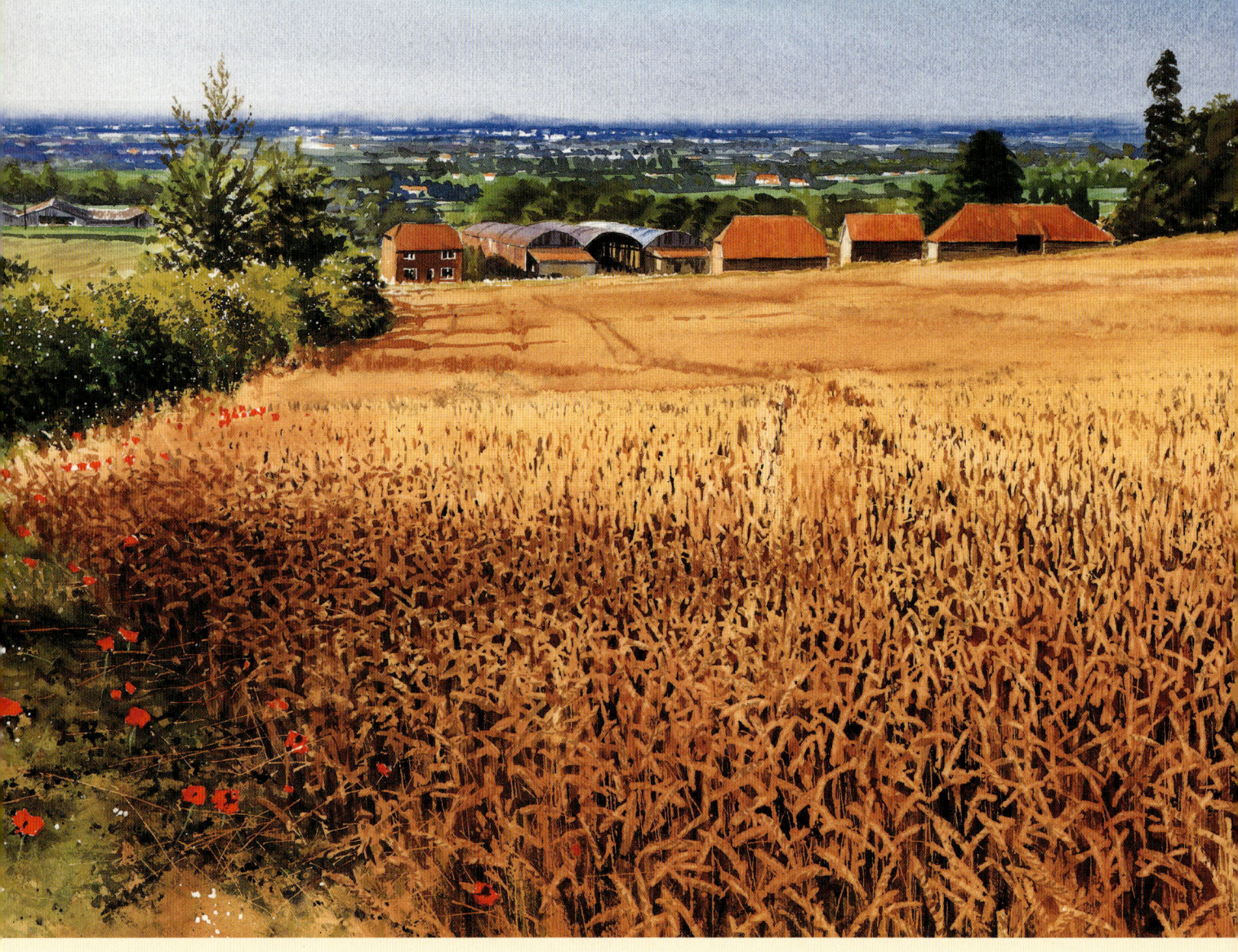

Field of wheat

A sea of wheat stalks as far as the eye can see presents a complex pattern that diminishes with perspective. The challenge is to create detail, but not lose the overall feel, including foreground, distance, texture and recession, all on a bright sunny day. Create light on the land by contrasting it with tone in the sky.

Artist insight: Distance is created using aerial perspective, with cool colours far away, and warm colour in the foreground. Distant colours are ultramarine blue with a little quinacridone magenta. Foreground colour is burnt sienna, greyed for shade. The fields behind the buildings are Hooker's green with cobalt blue. Distant darks are burnt sienna added to ultramarine blue. The left distant field is raw sienna greyed with cobalt blue. The hedgerow is new gamboge, burnt sienna and Hooker's green. The roofs were cadmium red tinted yellow ochre. Darks are ultramarine blue and burnt sienna. Lights in the hedge were toothbrush spattered, foreground poppies were masked.

COLOUR PALETTE

- new gamboge
- cadmium red
- quinacridone magenta
- French ultramarine
- phthalo blue
- cobalt blue
- Hooker's green
- yellow ochre
- raw sienna
- burnt sienna
- burnt umber

MASKING WHEAT

The masking technique adds realism, allowing you to paint wheat, as shown, and other cereal crops and grasses.

1 Paint the field with a mix of raw sienna and cadmium red, adding burnt sienna in the foreground. Mask the wheat heads with a colour shaper (see 'Colour shaper'). Mask a few wheat stalks with a dip pen.

2 Brush on a mix of French ultramarine and burnt sienna, leaving a few rough lights. Brush roughly vertical strokes for texture, fewer as you get more distant. Drag on a dry brush for some texture.

3 Brush intense darks of burnt umber and French ultramarine into the foreground, including dry-brush work, leaving some lights. When the paint is dry, remove the masking.

4 Paint some seeds in the heads of the foreground wheat, and dry-brush over them to give texture. Brush shadows across the field with a mix of burnt umber and French ultramarine.

Techniques: aerial perspective, page 17; washes, pages 18–21; mixing greys and greens, page 23; fields, pages 28–29; distance and open landscape, pages 34–35; skies, pages 54–55; buildings (houses), pages 40–41; buildings (farm and barns) in the landscape, pages 114–115.

Colour shaper

A colour shaper is like a brush, but the tip is made of silicone rubber in a limited range of shapes including angled, tapered and flat chisel. Colour shapers were originally designed for manipulating pastels as a type of replacement finger, but they are also brilliant for applying masking fluid where you want a sharp line – on a tree, for example. The masking fluid just peels off the colour shaper when dry.

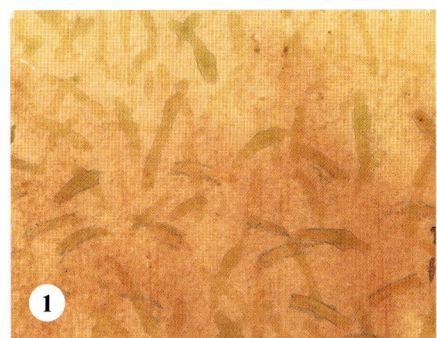
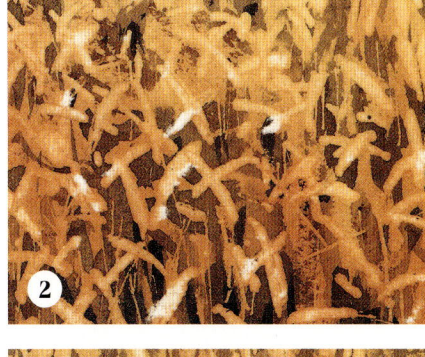
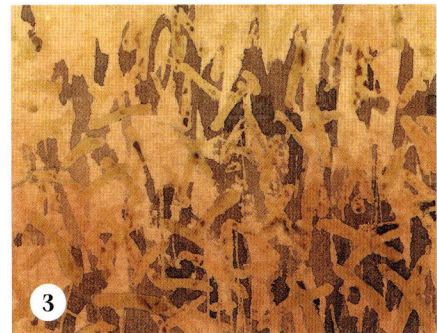
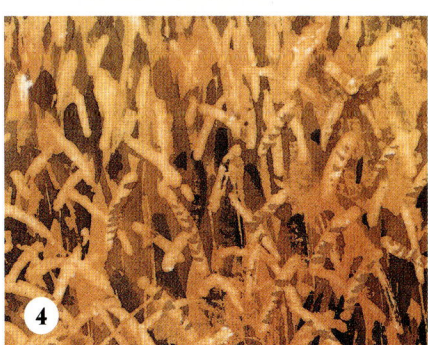

Techniques for painting wheat

With an underlying wash in place, you can use a variety of techniques, including masking. Vertical dry brushstrokes imply the wheat texture. A candle rubbed over the surface and overlaid with a darker wash reveals the paler wax-resist texture. Brushstrokes can be applied for the stalks themselves or the spaces between them. Try brushing in strokes of water, then strokes of colour.

Wash.

Dry-brush.

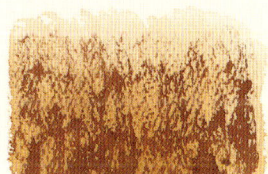

Dry-brush on wash.

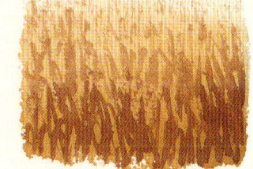

Brushstrokes on wash.

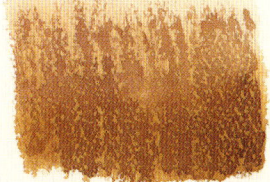

Wax candle over wash, then dry-brush.

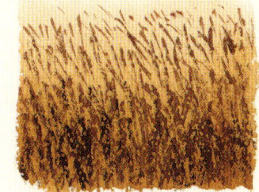

Wax candle over wash, then brushstrokes.

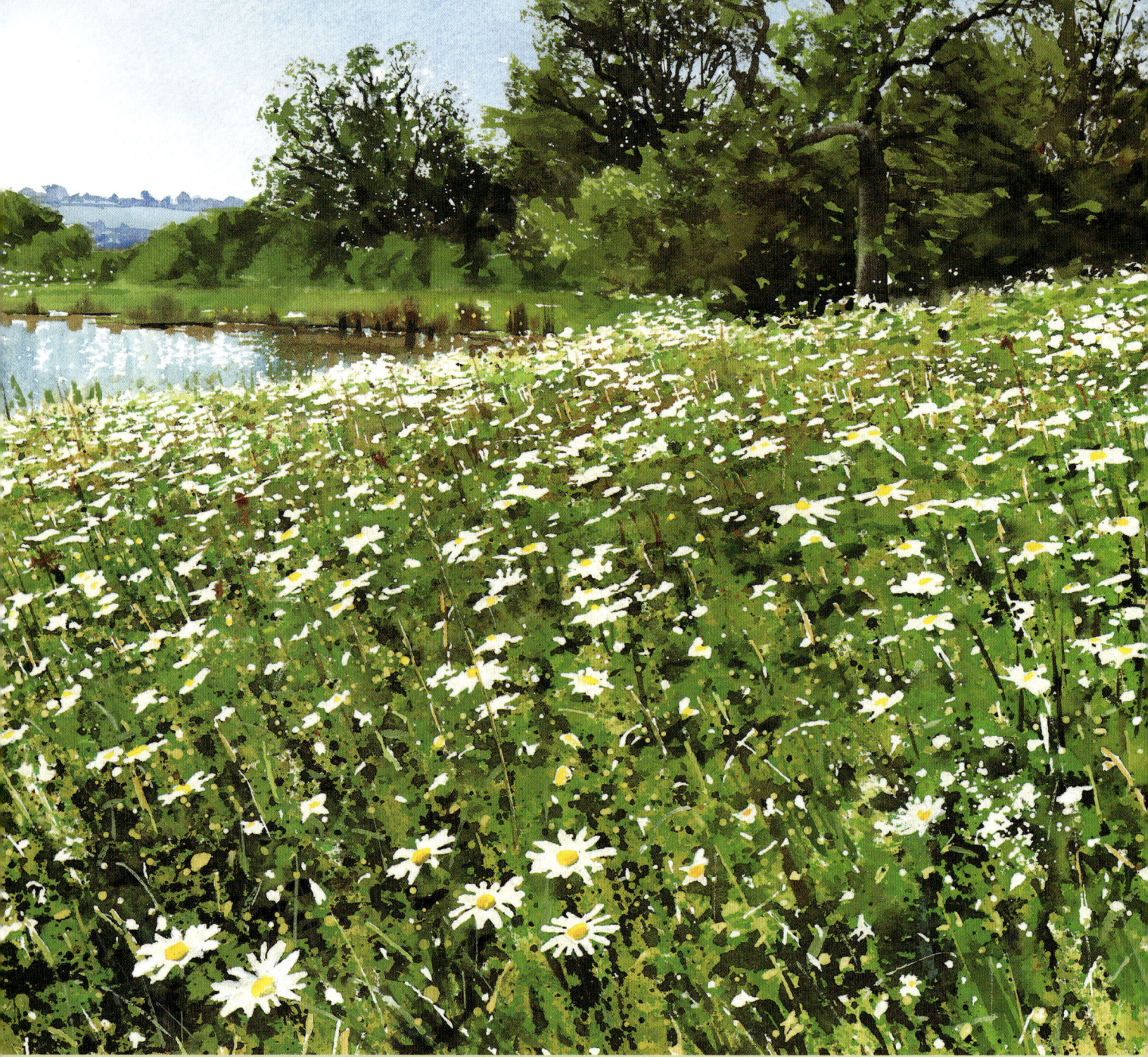

Wildflower meadow

A flower-filled meadow is an explosion of colour, tonal variation and movement where a myriad of tiny shapes collide and dance. You can convey the confusion of a field of flowers by using simple processes such as masking and spattering, overlaying the separate techniques. Paint abstract shapes, even in the foreground, and describe just a few daisies in more detail.

Artist insight: When planning the foreground texture of a meadow, think in terms of broad diagonal lines that define underlying form – deeply slanting and long in the foreground, shorter and flattened off in the distance. Practise a few pencil lines on scrap paper to get the feel of perspective in the distance. Masking fluid was spattered from a toothbrush over the woodland. Tree greens were applied with a lot of cadmium lemon, burnt sienna, phthalo green and dark greens with added ultramarine blue and burnt umber.

COLOUR PALETTE

- cadmium lemon
- quinacridone magenta
- French ultramarine
- cobalt blue
- phthalo green
- burnt sienna
- burnt umber
- white gouache

PAINTING DAISIES

Each daisy petal can be a single stroke made with a colour shaper. Only a few daisies are drawn completely; the rest are just marks, perhaps with a hint of petals. Here, the sun is slightly ahead and to the left, so the flowers are flattened, except in the foreground where the viewer is right above them. Paint the centres with cadmium lemon, adding a little half-moon accent round the edge of the white in a muted green from the palette.

Toothbrush spattering

Dip the toothbrush in the masking fluid and bang it on your hand, bristles facing down. For fine texture, drag your thumb across the bristles. For a field of flowers, spatter larger blobs in the foreground, keeping them fewer and wider spaced. Work from the foreground into the distance so that the droplets get smaller with perspective. Follow diagonal lines back into the meadow as you spatter, from bottom to top.

1 Mask a few daisies in the foreground. Then use single strokes to mask distant flowers, making them larger as you work nearer, and keeping them ragged and unevenly spaced. Spatter a few daisies with a toothbrush dipped in masking fluid (see 'Toothbrush spattering' for guidance). Mix a yellow green glaze from cadmium lemon and a little phthalo green, adding burnt umber to warm it. Brush this colour over the daisies.

2 Spatter more masking fluid over the meadow. Mix darker versions of the yellow green, some brighter greens, and some dark greens using burnt umber, French ultramarine and a little phthalo green. Working from the bottom up, spatter water from the point of a large brush, aiming at ragged blobs of water, with dry spaces between. Vigorously spatter the greens into the water areas.

3 When dry, spatter with water. Spatter dark colour in, deep and jagged in the foreground, smaller in the distance. Spatter lighter colour in – burnt umber on its own, and mixed with cadmium lemon. When dry, brush in a few vertical marks for weeds and stalks. Allow to dry, and remove the masking fluid. Lightly remodel the foreground daisies with a little white gouache.

Techniques: flowers in perspective, page 17 (see grid); tree canopies, page 19; tree sky holes, pages 30–31, 112; mixing greens, page 23; distance, pages 26–27, 34–35; masking bluebells, pages 44–45; masking blossom, pages 48–49; skies, pages 54–55; grasses, pages 76–77; foliage (foreground and trees), pages 80–81; dark greens, page 80.

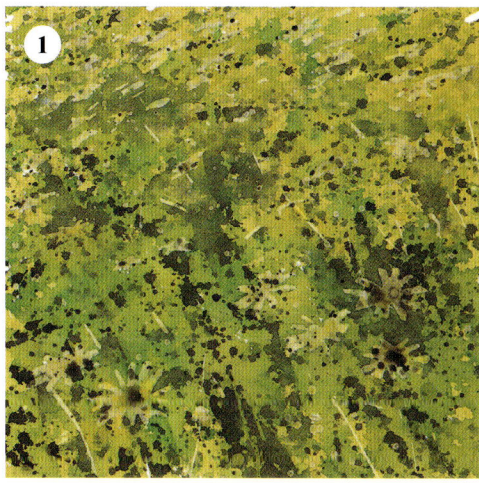

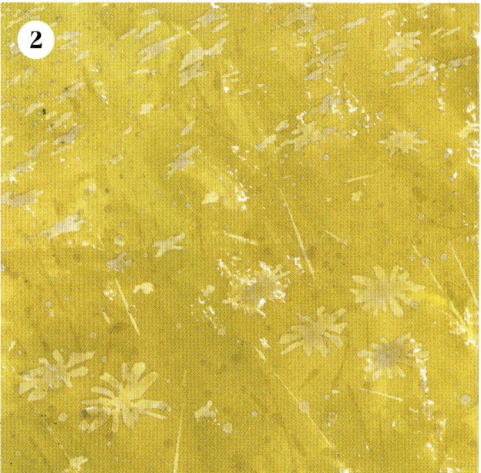

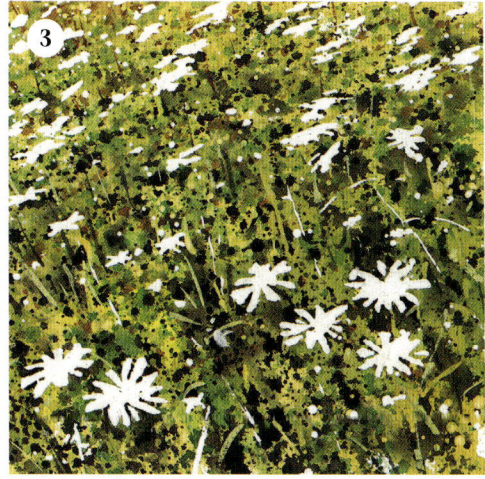

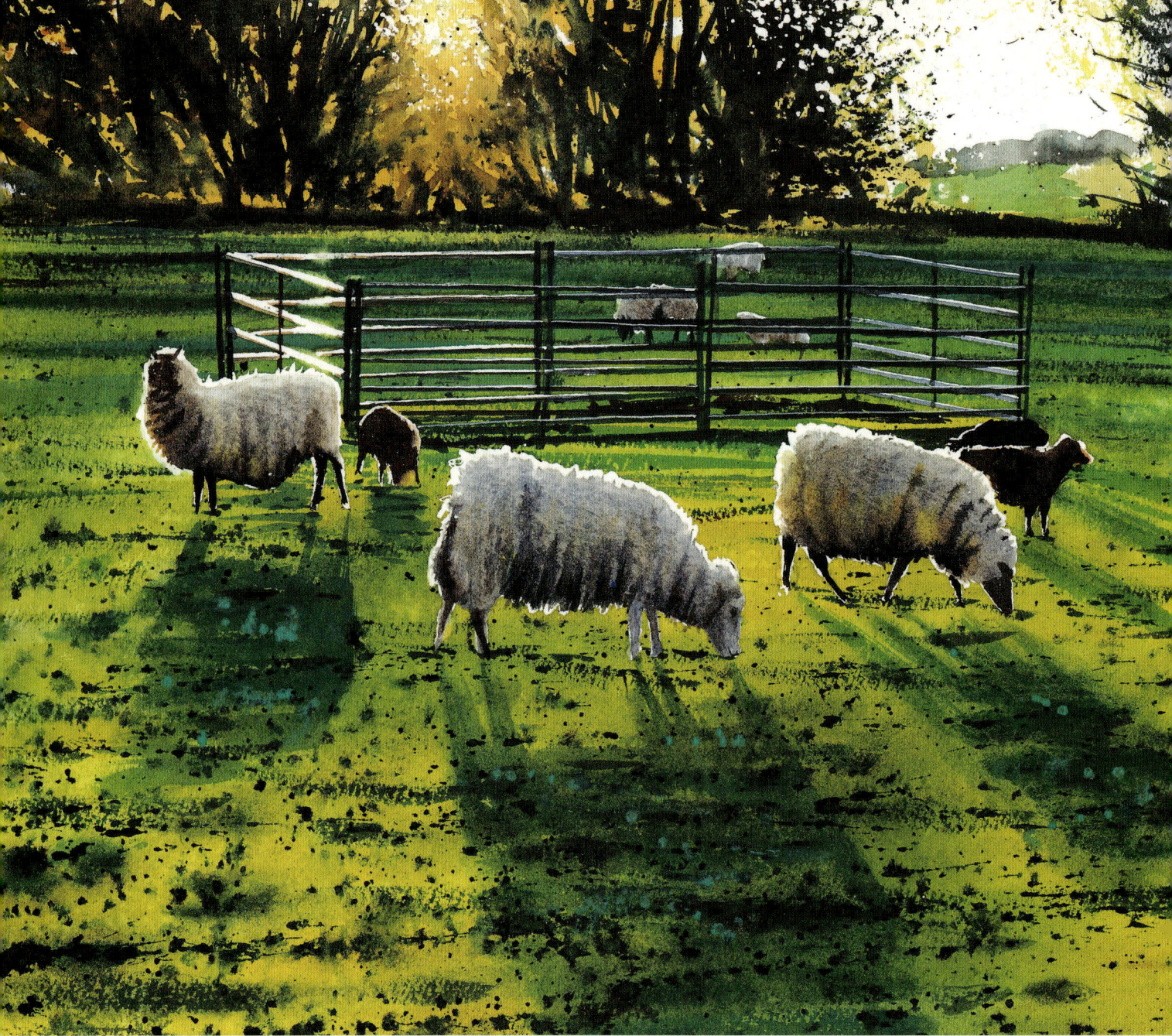

Sheep in pasture

Splitting the pasture into two greens – a warm yellow, orange green and a cool dark blue green – gives the effect of looking into the sun. Masking the sheep and pen means you can work the field very roughly across. Painting the darker pen bars across the lighter ones while they are masked enables you to paint a complex sequence more easily.

Artist insight: To create texture, use a pointed sable brush and strong dark paint to spatter horizontal layers one above the other, starting at the bottom. The brush should point along the paper's length. As the brush load diminishes, texture gets finer with smaller droplets higher into the painting and therefore further away, creating texture in perspective. Experiment by banging the brush firmly on an object such as a roll of tape to get directional spatter.

COLOUR PALETTE

- cadmium lemon
- new gamboge
- translucent orange
- French ultramarine
- cobalt blue
- cobalt turquoise light
- phthalo green
- Indian red
- burnt sienna

PAINTING THE SCENE

1 Mask the sheep and pen bars, plus any other lights.

2 Brush new gamboge wet-in-wet onto the field, and paint translucent orange and a little phthalo green over it, with burnt sienna soaked into the foreground. Paint shadow greens with a mix of cadmium lemon, phthalo green and burnt sienna.

3 Brush cool greens horizontally. Spatter darks mixed from Indian red, French ultramarine and phthalo green. Darken shadows wet-in-wet with a mix of phthalo green, Indian red and French ultramarine. Brush new gamboge and a warm green mix onto the tree area, and use phthalo green for the distant field.

4 Paint the distant woods with a mix of cobalt blue and burnt sienna. Wet and strengthen the shadows with the Indian red, French ultramarine and phthalo green mix. Spatter these darks across the field. Brush cobalt blue over the orange-green trees. When dry, spatter water, then brush and spatter dark colour; hold up the image and spray the field with water droplets from a sprayer for texture. Paint the unmasked sheep pen bars with a French ultramarine and Indian red mix.

Techniques: wet-in-wet, pages 18–21; tree canopies, pages 19, 112; mixing greys (for sheep), page 23; toothbrush spattering, pages 28–29, 98–99; foreground grass, pages 38–39; sun effects on field, pages 52–53; light glints and sunset, pages 62–63.

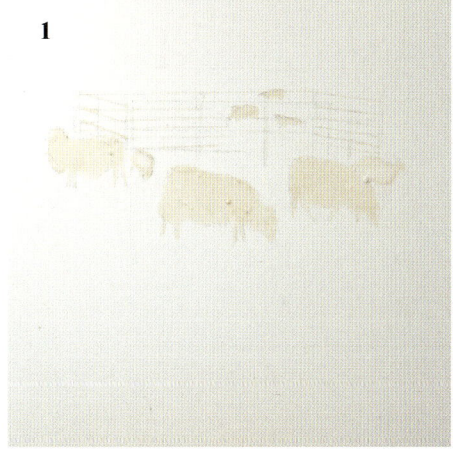
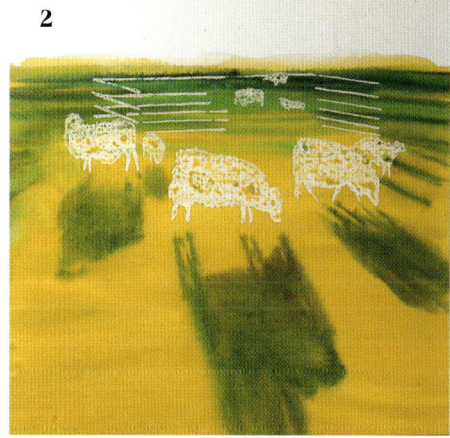

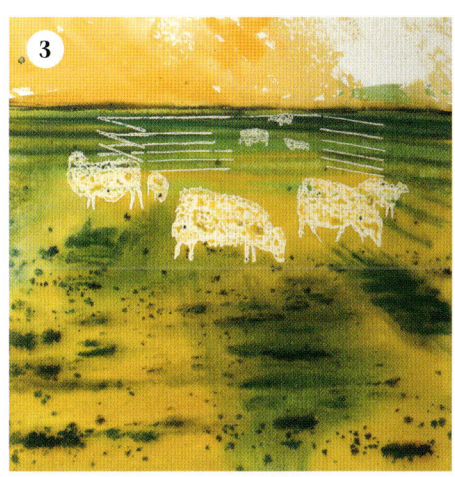
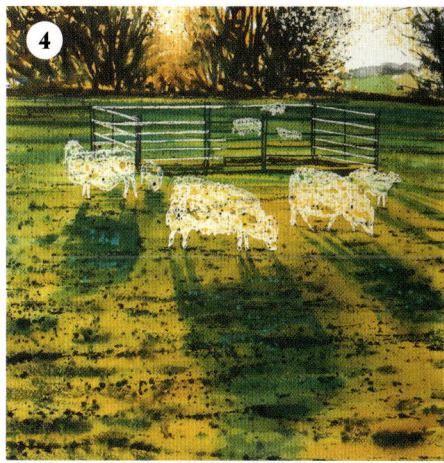

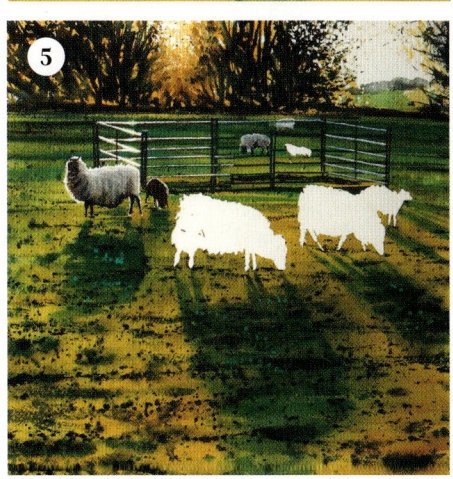
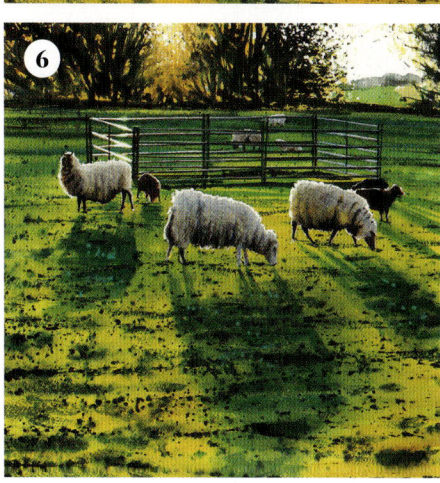

5 Finish all the darks on the pen with a mix of French ultramarine and Indian red. Remove all the masking. Touch in the under-shadows of the sheep pen bars with cobalt blue and a little burnt sienna. Re-mask the edges of the nearest sheep and apply cobalt blue and burnt sienna. Run Indian red and French ultramarine into the wool wet-in-wet from the point of a brush for the wool effect.

6 Touch in the remaining sheep, including the black ones. Give the pen bars a final directional up and down scrub to achieve the rays of glinting light. Finally, spatter a little cobalt turquoise light into field shadow areas.

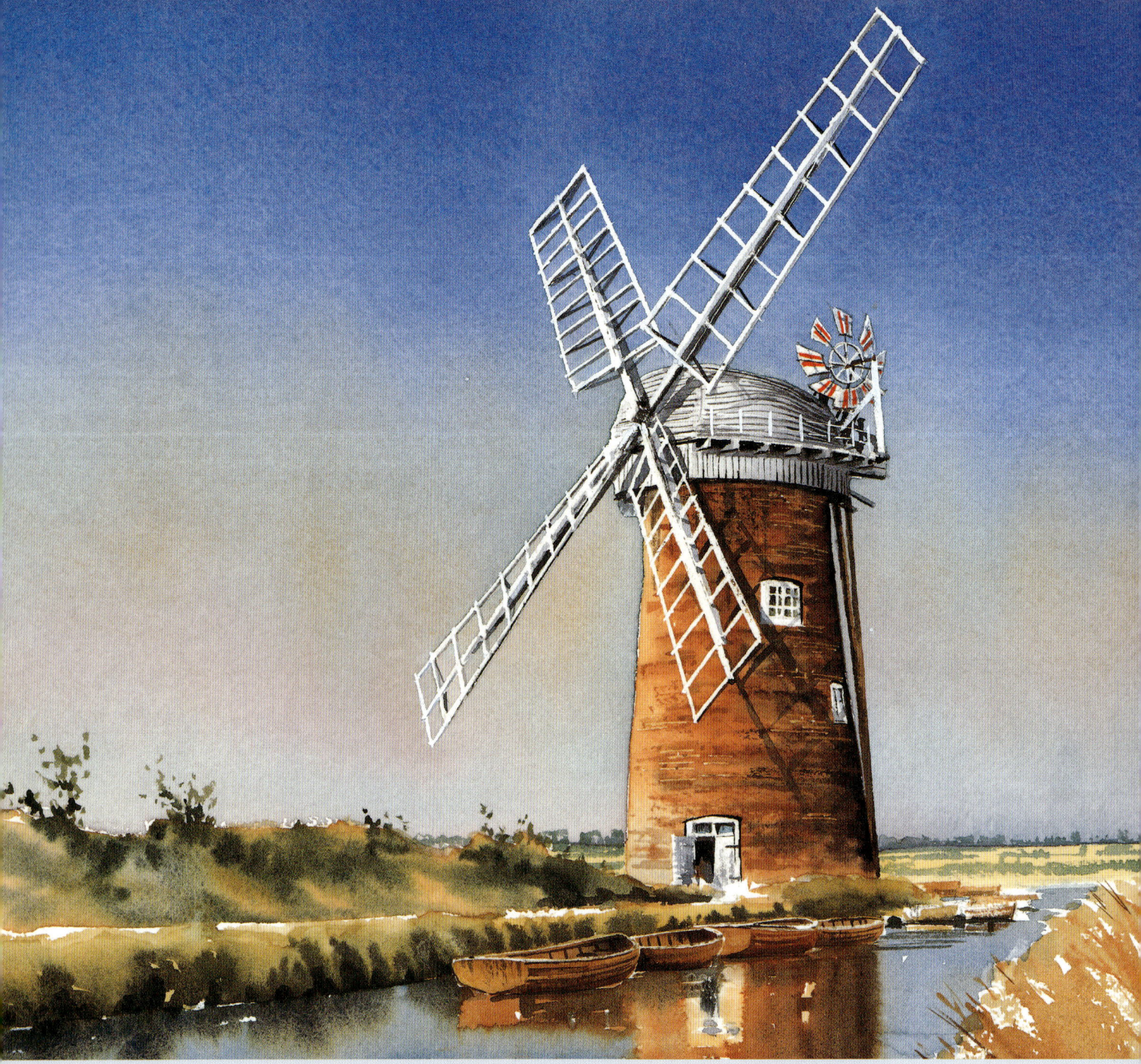

Marshland windmill

It is a challenge to draw and paint a windmill close up like this. Problems diminish with distance. A windmill's sails twist through fifteen degrees from their centres to their ends. Although symmetrical, one pair is mounted above the other, so they are not in the same plane. But although few of us are aware of these technicalities, the amazing visual mind can recognize when something is wrong, even without knowing why. So, get the drawing right and your painting will have integrity and appeal to the viewer. Truth is beautiful but often difficult to depict. This is why it is worth taking the trouble to get it right.

Artist insight: Everything above the water was completed first, the boats left as white shapes against the bank. Later, the darker parts of the sails, the shadow across the tower, the distant landscape and details on the boats and tower were added.

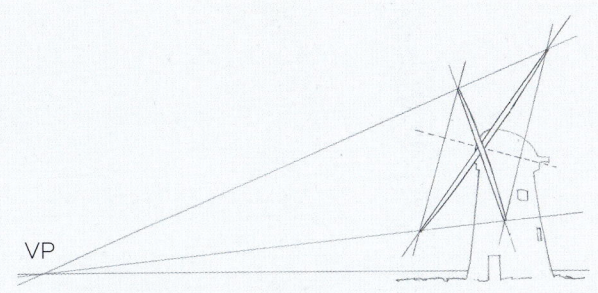

Drawing windmill sails

From a vanishing point (VP) on the horizon, draw a line across where the bottom of the sails will be. Run two parallel lines up from the line for the sides of the sail area, then complete a backward-tilting box with a line for the top of the sails from the VP. Draw an 'X' between the box corners.

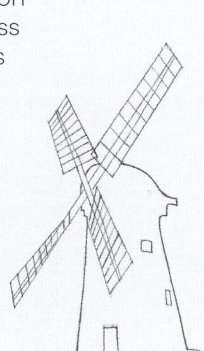

Building up a tower

First paint the sky around the tower. Wet the body of the tower, avoiding the windows, brush in the first colour from left to right, and let the wash dry. Rewet the paper and add the second colour, again from left to right. Use a darker colour for the shade on the left. Wet the cap and add a very pale wash from the shadow side, then add the details to the cap and windows. Lift the paint for the doorway.

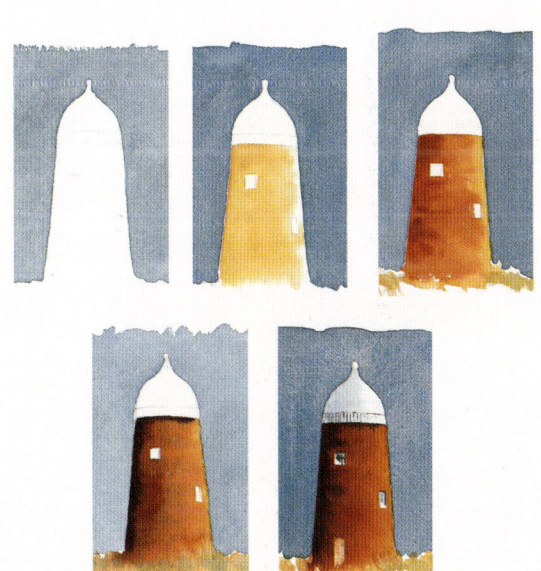

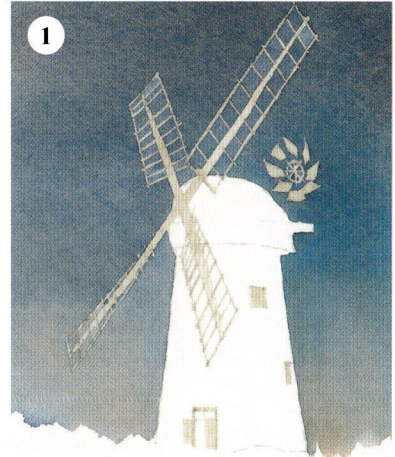

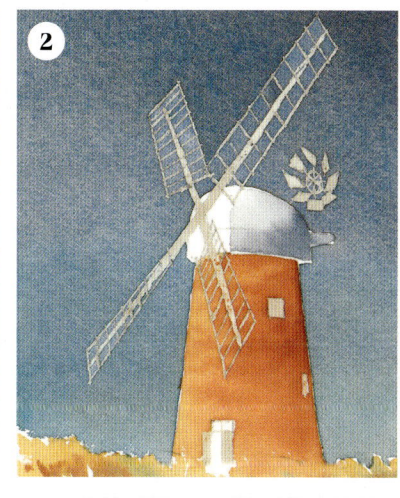

PAINTING THE WINDMILL

1 Mask the sails and fantail, the top window frame and slats, the bottom window and the door. Wet the sky area and add the sky colours. Allow to dry.

2 Paint the first wash for the tower, going over the masking fluid and out to the edges, and add the foreground mixes. Once dry, apply the colour on the cap.

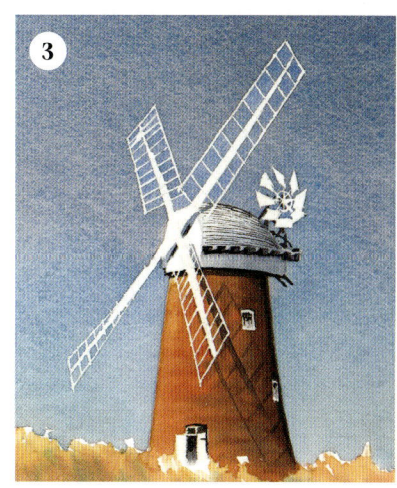

3 Apply the shadow to the side away from the light. Remove the masking fluid and add the details of the cap, fantail, windows and door.

Techniques: washes, pages 18–21; masking, pages 26–27, 46 47, 104 105, 120 121; foreground washes (similar), pages 26–27, 100–101; distant landscapes, pages 30–31, 34–35; tower (lighthouse), pages 104–105; skies, pages 54–55; lifting, pages 66–67, 90–91, 93, 111; water, pages 66–67, 80–81, 82–87; grasses, pages 100–101; brickwork, pages 116–117.

COLOUR PALETTE

- cadmium yellow
- cadmium red light
- alizarin crimson
- French ultramarine
- phthalo blue
- cobalt blue
- cerulean blue
- raw sienna
- burnt sienna
- light red
- Indian red
- neutral tint
- white gouache

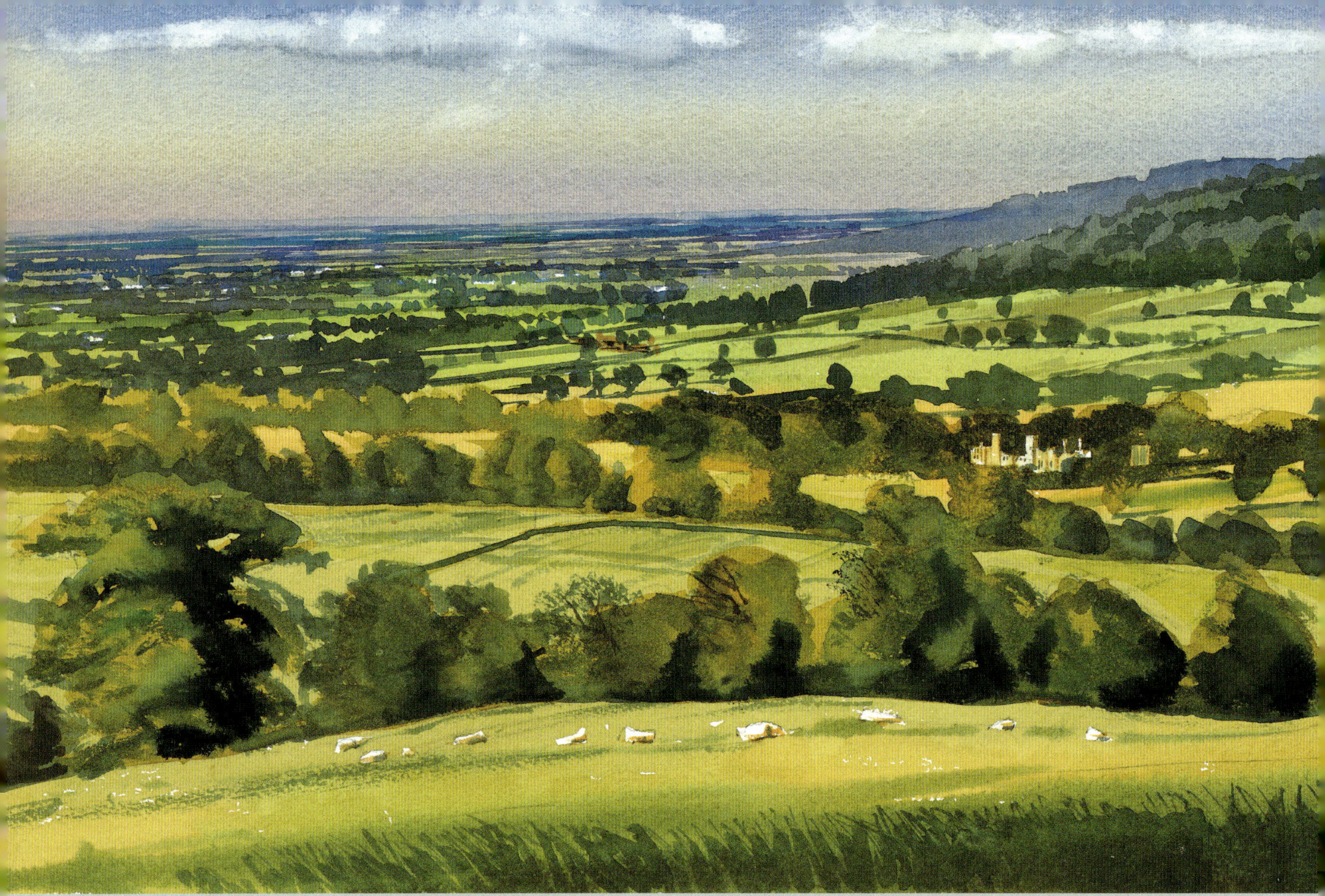

Open rolling countryside

Depth, distance and space – these are the challenging demands a landscape makes on a painter. Place the horizon high if you are looking down from a height. Treat the distant landscape as part of the sky and paint the two as one, letting the distance fade into the landscape. Progressively warm the colours towards the foreground.

Artist insight: Painted on site, any number of colours would achieve similar results for this view across countryside to the far distance. Work loose, keep the light tones pale and the dark tones strong. The manor house and sheep are saved whites, with pale raw sienna and touched in with dark underneath wet-in-wet. Clouds were 'lifted' by wetting with a soft brush and dabbing with kitchen roll. Add pale grey shade below the clouds.

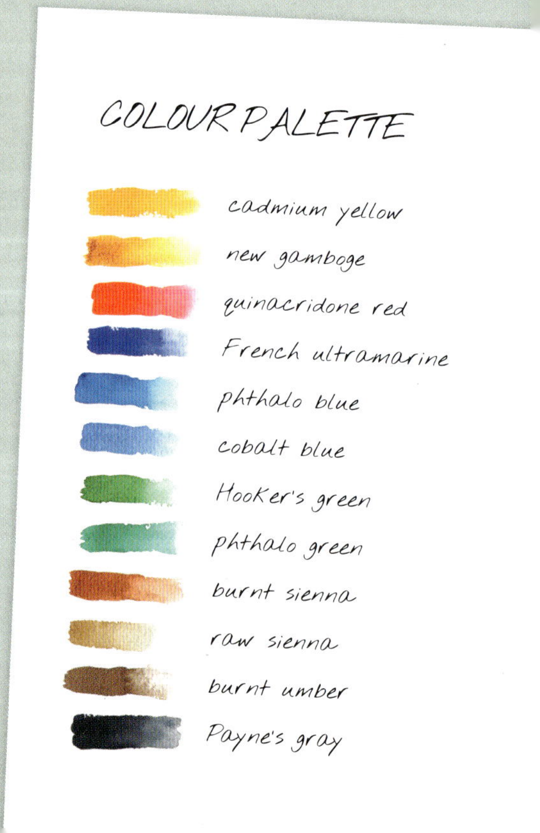

COLOUR PALETTE

cadmium yellow

new gamboge

quinacridone red

French ultramarine

phthalo blue

cobalt blue

Hooker's green

phthalo green

burnt sienna

raw sienna

burnt umber

Payne's gray

Mop brush sketch

Use a squirrel mop brush to dash a scene down in minutes – loose flowing strokes are ideal for a natural landscape. As a monochrome sketch it might also indicate a snowy scene, but colours will complete the sketch.

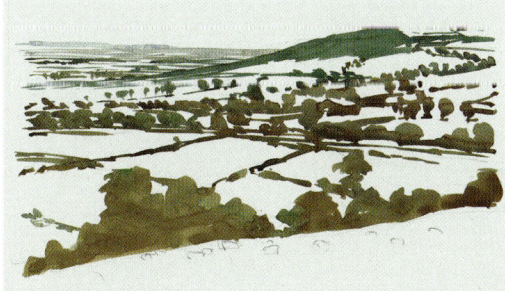

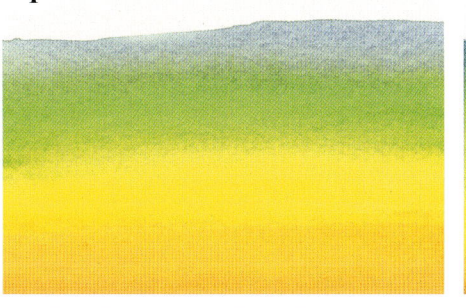

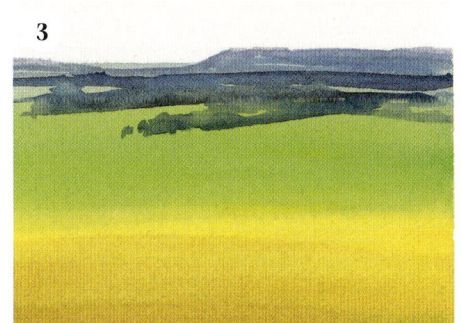

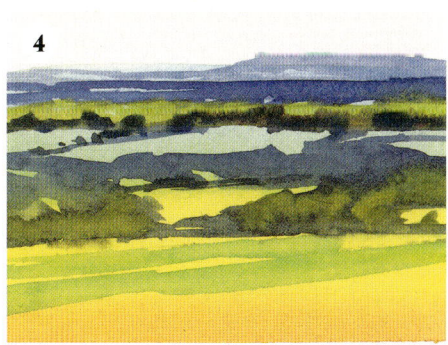

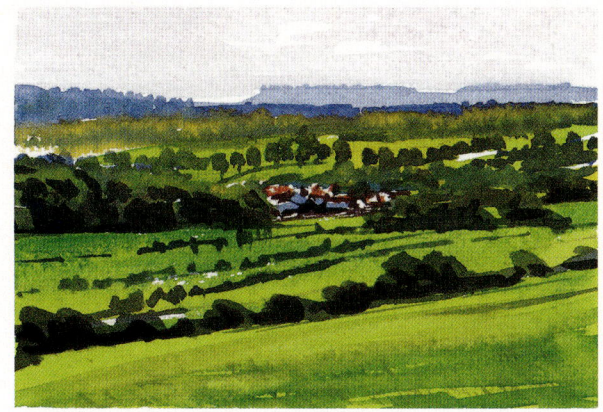

Aerial perspective

Just as sky is a blue colour, colour tends to go blue as it pales with distance. Cool means blue and warm means yellow or red. The colour with the greatest sense of warmth is orange. Burnt sienna is a warm earth colour which can infuse the foreground with warmth. Distant colours can be blue or blue/violet.

In a final version of this sketch saved whites become a farmstead. Tone is helpful, with a contrast between the light of the fields and the darks of the woodlands. The high horizon places the foreground low and the viewer above the land. Sky is rendered as a pale tone of cobalt blue.

HIGH-HORIZON VIEWS

Paint the sky and land washes together on the wet paper, allowing them to blend and dry. Paint the distant pale passages wet-on-dry, darkening, warming and widening with perspective as they come forwards.

1 Paint wet-in-wet yellow, with added burnt sienna in the foreground, merging to green from the middle distance and blue in the far distance. In the main painting, the sky is painted down into the green area.

2 Add green mixed from Hooker's green and raw sienna in a pale wash from the foreground, deepening in the middle distance. Add more burnt sienna to the foreground. Model the distant ridge detail with French ultramarine.

3 Using progressively stronger colour, overlay the ridges, working forwards from the distance. As the French ultramarine strips of woodland get nearer they are warmed with burnt umber.

4 Add new gamboge to the nearer dark masses, and broaden them as the field spaces widen out for perspective. Brush a mix of Hooker's green and raw sienna onto the foreground field.

Techniques: landscape/aerial perspective, page 17; wet-in-wet, pages 18–21; glazing, brushmarks, pages 20–21; mixing grey and green, page 23; distant landscapes, pages 26–27, 74–75, 114–115; sheep, pages 30–31; skies, pages 54–55; buildings, pages 40–41, 114–115.

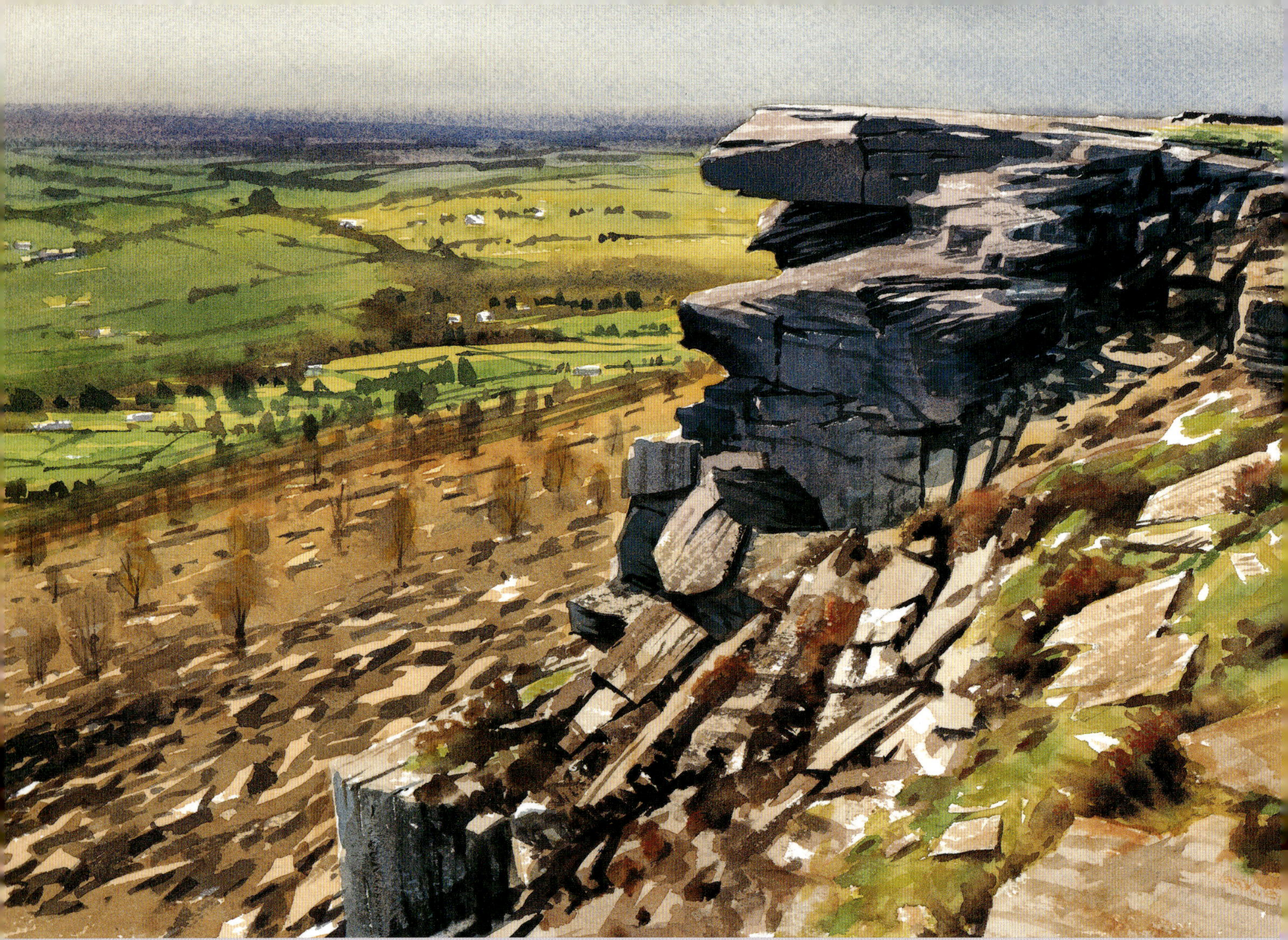

Moorland rocks

Here is menacing grey rock, with a mass of cracks and fissures as complex as a city street plan. It could have been dark and dull, but I wanted to light the scene and put a flourish on the weathered face of this great gritstone edge. Keeping the rock right of centre gives space for the distant landscape.

Artist insight: Dark sky in the top right-hand corner of this scene contrasts the light crag. Distant glints of buildings are saved lights. Foreground colours of yellow ochre and Hooker's green grass surround fallen rock, with burnt sienna, cobalt blue and quinacridone magenta producing the browns and greys. Intense darks pull the scene together and draw the eye.

Techniques: composition, pages 10—11; mixing greys and greens, page 23; wax candle, pages 26—27, 45; dry-brush/dragging, pages 27, 45, 64—69, 72—73; spattering darks, pages 30—31; distant landscapes, pages 26 (image caption), 34—35; skies, pages 54—55; mountains, pages 66—67; rock formations, pages 64—65, 66—67, 72—73, 88—89, 96—97, 102—103; cliffs, pages 100—101.

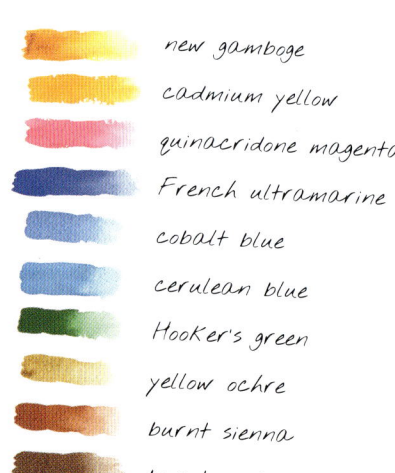

COLOUR PALETTE

new gamboge

cadmium yellow

quinacridone magenta

French ultramarine

cobalt blue

cerulean blue

Hooker's green

yellow ochre

burnt sienna

burnt umber

PAINTING ROCK PEAKS

Rough passages of paint with sharp edges look rocky when used with contrasting tones. Try starting with pale grey mixes such as cerulean blue, quinacridone magenta and burnt sienna. Brush the hard shadow patterns wet-on-dry with dark mixes, such as cerulean blue, French ultramarine and burnt umber. Allow to dry, then line with dark fissures. Cerulean blue gives a granulated texture, but mixes of French ultramarine and burnt umber also give good darks.

Simple rocks

Drag water across the rock in a wet/dry texture. Add a mix of burnt sienna and cobalt blue in the shadow, letting the colour spread. Add a dark mixed from French ultramarine and burnt umber, and finish with strong colour and a fissure or two.

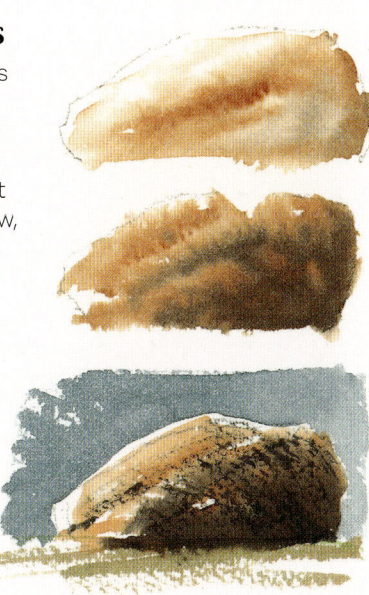

WASH TECHNIQUES

Two methods of applying the paint provide the rock effects.

• A light grey variegated wash is overglazed wet-on-dry with darker grey brushmarks (**A**).

• The initial wash is masked over for the lightest tones on the rock face, then overpainted with colour (**B**).

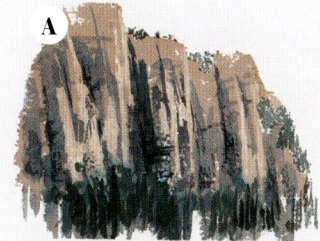
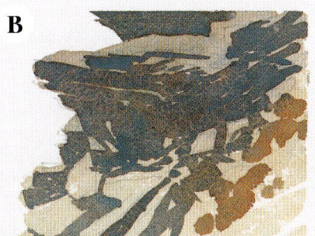

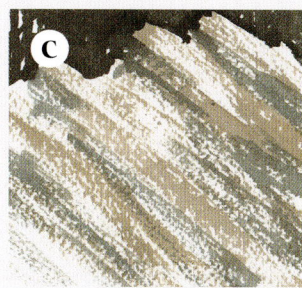

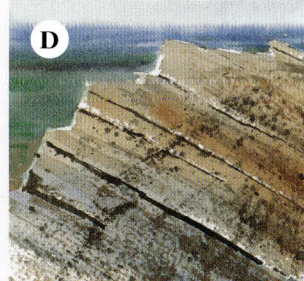

DRAGGING

Dragging the brush, often on its belly or side, allows the Not or rough paper surface to produce a range of natural textures easily. Drag the colour directionally, some in unbroken swathes and some in a dry-brush fashion to build up the rocky surface strata (**C**).

Drag colour over the underlying wash, then spatter over with darks. Scratch fissures with a sharp blade and line underneath with dark colour (**D**).

WAX RESIST

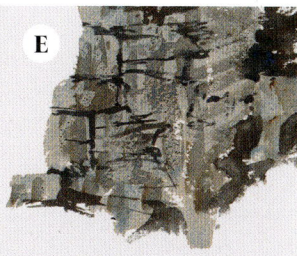

Wax resist gives the reverse texture of dry-brush. Instead of dark texture it gives the same pattern, but a negative version – a convincing light texture.

The first wash is painted, then intense darks lined and dragged. Wax candle is dragged over the image. Next medium grey tones are dragged over. This way the final wash covers the light wash, but not the dark fissures (**E**).

Colour mixes

Offset light crag tones with darker surrounding colour. The neutral sky tone is a mix of cobalt blue and burnt sienna. Distant landscape blues of French ultramarine, quinacridone magenta and burnt sienna give way to Hooker's green warmed nearby with new gamboge and burnt sienna, greys coming from added cobalt blue. Brush the rocks with mixes of cerulean blue, quinacridone magenta and burnt sienna, leaving flecks of white. Paint darker shade and fissures with burnt umber and French ultramarine. Leave pale gaps for lights.

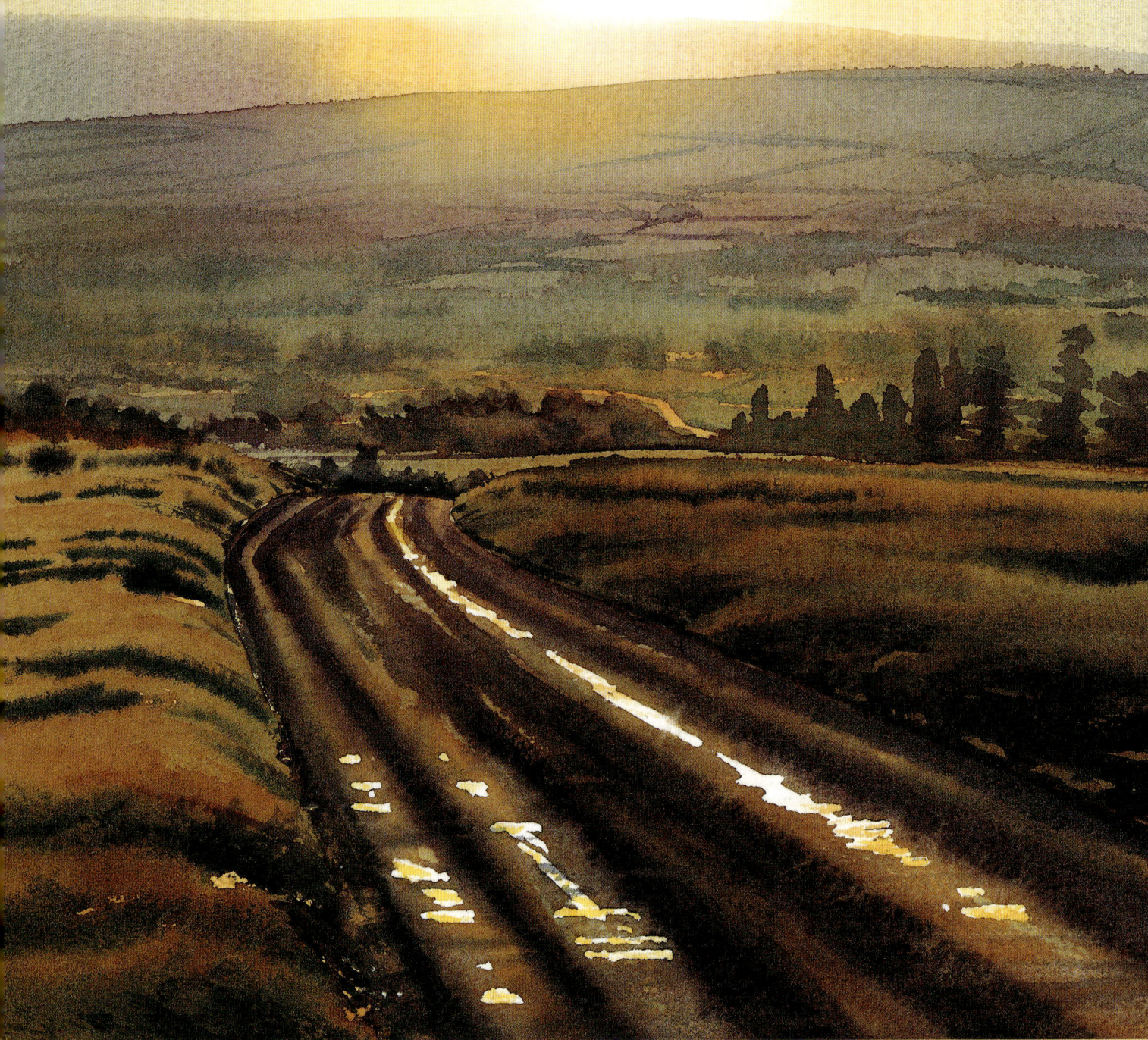

Golden landscape

What really matters in this landscape, flooded with the subtle, warm colours of sunset, is control of tone. The full range of tonal possibilities is explored, from white paper to intense dark. The warm orange-browns are dull in their own right, but work as a base for lights and darks to project the scene and make it glow.

Artist insight: *This scene is a succession of flat 'glazes' — evenly applied layers of colour allowed to dry before overlaying another. The colour consists of greys and darks, made from two opposing colours, crimson and green. The composition is simple, opening up endless possible variations; and the picture works visually because the road is offset and the image is divided horizontally into two unequal sections. The puddles were masked at the outset, and touched in with Naples yellow, and burnt sienna in places, saving some white for the sun reflections, after the masking was removed at the end.*

COLOUR PALETTE

- cadmium yellow
- quinacridone magenta
- phthalo green
- Naples yellow
- burnt sienna

Techniques: *composition, pages 10–11; tonal composition, pages 14–15; mixing greys, page 23; washes, pages 18–21; glazing, pages 20–21; sunlit grass, pages 30–31, 52–53; colour warming near sun, pages 52–53; sunset, pages 62–63; warm misty effects, pages 68–69; sunset skies, pages 108–109; puddles, pages 112–113.*

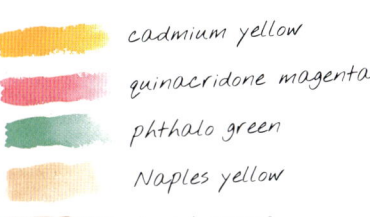

PAINTING THE SCENE

You can produce a wonderful glowing landscape with a limited colour palette.

1 Mask the puddles in the road using a colour shaper (page 27). Wet the paper. Apply a watery mix of Naples yellow, keeping it away from the sun area in a lost-edged wash.

2 Add warmer cadmium yellow and burnt sienna near the sun, saving white, shown here before it has spread smoothly on the wet paper.

3 With the paper wet, apply another mix of burnt sienna and cadmium yellow around the sun, reserving a yellow halo of the previous wash around the white. Apply a wash of burnt sienna outside and below this down to the foreground. Apply a grey of quinacridone magenta and phthalo green along this ridge and to the entire area below, keeping an outer halo of orange around the sun, all in soft-edged washes.

4 When dry, wet the sharp-edged ridge. Leaving a halo of underlying colour showing through below the sun, add a weak mix of burnt sienna and cadmium yellow, stronger further away, and then add this wash to the whole painting below the ridge. Follow with a red-biased wash with added quinacridone magenta around the edge of the glare. Outside this add a red-biased grey of quinacridone magenta and phthalo green, shifting this to neutral and darker further away from the sun, sideways and downwards.

5 The foreground wash is one with the halation wash. Brush intense dark streaks of phthalo green and quinacridone magenta mix for the tufts of grass into this, keeping these off the road. Brush the road with dark perspective streaks of this colour, which is also used for the distant trees when dry.

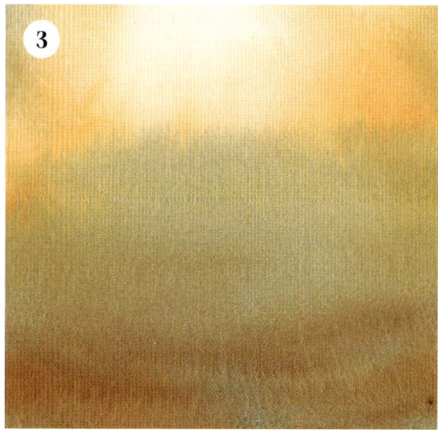

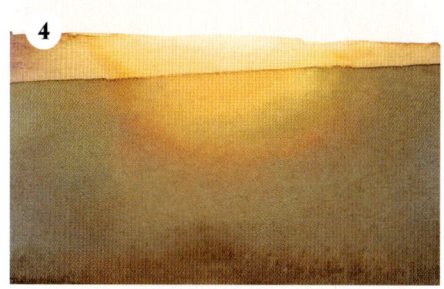

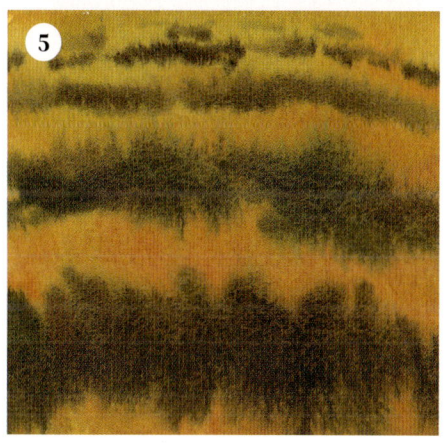

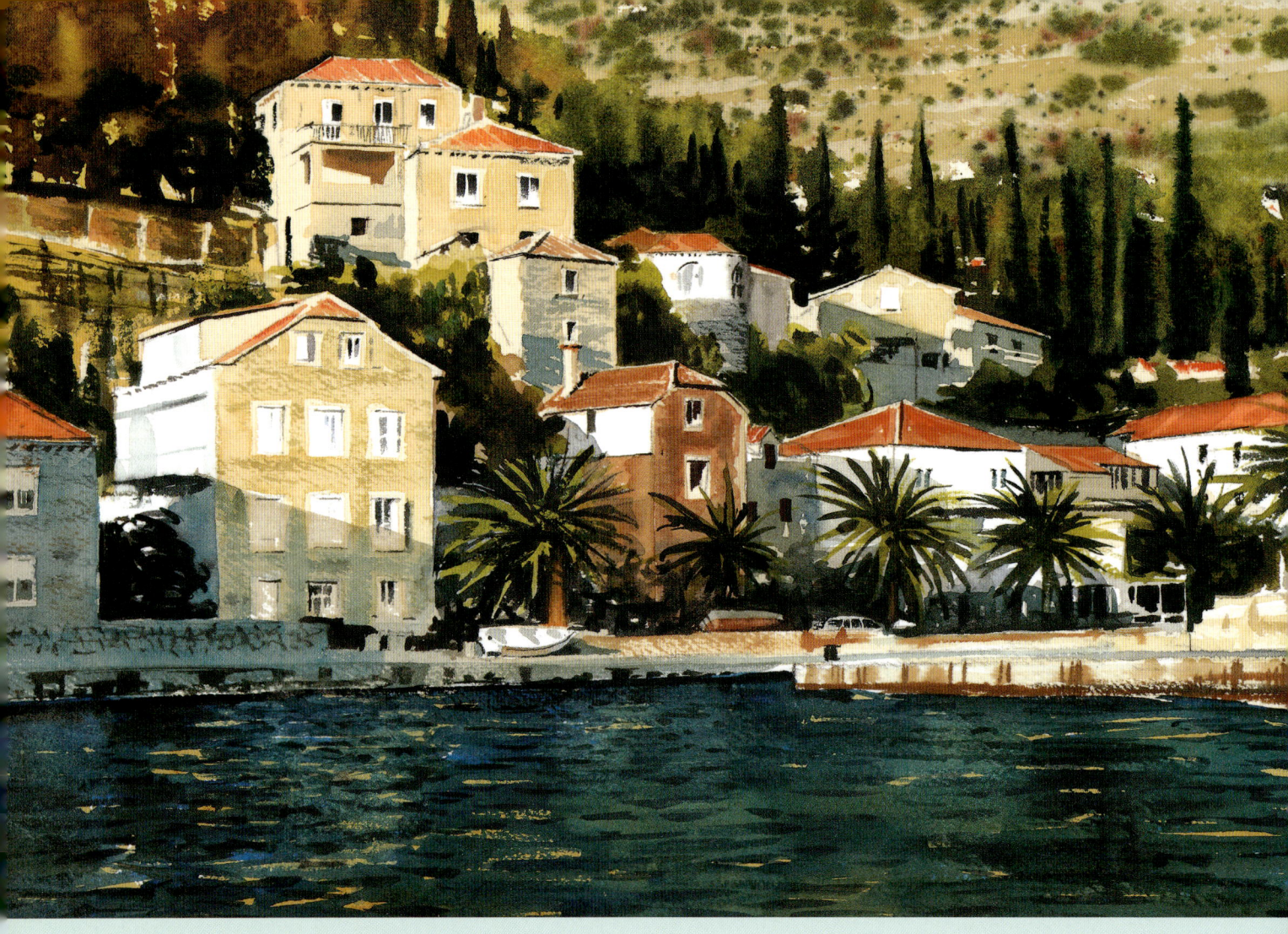

Mediterranean sunshine

You can capture sunshine without painting sun or sky. The effect on the land is constructed with saved whites and warm colours contrasted by strong darks. The pattern of buildings is defined at the outset, and the individual structures drawn as the painting progresses. The water was glazed with new gamboge then deep water washes applied. Note the warmth in the water and the yellow where the underlying glaze has been left to show in some of the ripples.

Artist insight: Think of a painting as a series of simplified paintings — each is a transparent layer painted over the previous layer. Mentally breaking the painting down into layers and working each one at a time in this way makes the process easier. Define foliage areas you want to work by wetting them and running the colours in and you will find that the water does the work for you.

COLOUR PALETTE

- cadmium orange
- cadmium red
- quinacridone magenta
- phthalo blue
- cobalt blue
- green gold
- phthalo green
- terre verte
- Naples yellow
- raw sienna
- burnt sienna
- light red
- Indian red
- indigo
- new gamboge

PAINTING A SUNNY LANDSCAPE

The colour mixes suggested here could be a reference for your own rendering of a sunny landscape.

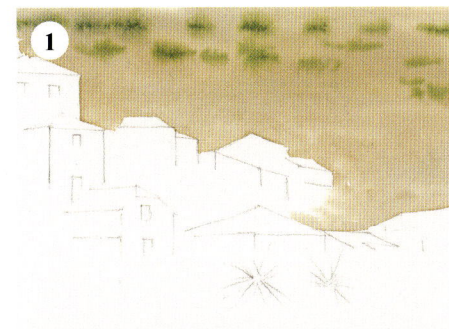

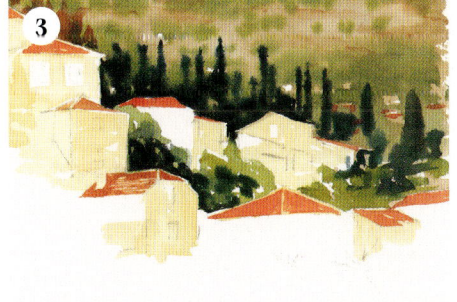
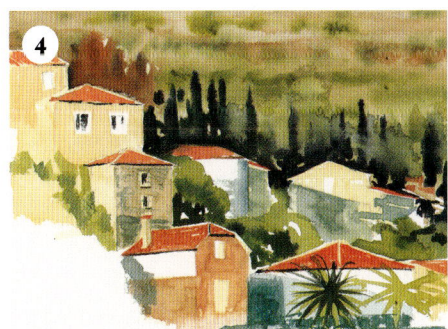

1 Try a mix of Naples yellow, cadmium orange and burnt sienna for the hill. Add patches of mixed green gold and terre verte wet-in-wet; this spreads for bushes.

2 Apply Naples yellow to the buildings, saving whites and add a pale wash of cadmium orange to the background. Apply your greens and run in a dark green mix of phthalo green and quinacridone magenta, and use these darks to contrast the buildings.

3 Build up the red roofs with cadmium red and Naples yellow, and add a little burnt sienna in places – groups of roofs are rarely the same colour. Use Indian red in the top corner to build up some of the warm, dark-coloured foliage.

4 Use phthalo blue and burnt sienna for shadows. For the masonry use a pale mix of cobalt blue, Naples yellow and burnt sienna. Use light red on the building face. Build up the mid and dark greens and shadows. Touch in the windows with indigo.

Techniques: water reflections, pages 66–67, 78–79, 80–81; saving lights in ripples, pages 82–83; buildings with reflections, pages 86–87, 122–123; buildings in compositions, pages 114–115, 118–119; windows, pages 118–119, 122–123.

SHARP-EDGED LIGHTS

The key to this image is to preserve sharp-edged lights in the buildings. Their edges are defined with wet washes. Flow strong colours wet-in-wet around them to create texture, along with tonal colour and variety. These loose, dark organic areas contrast with the sharp architectural ones. Much of the shadow is blue green, being lit intensely by the sea. Soft focus greens were created with terre verte, used for its spreading properties, but green gold and a dark such as indigo, or other greens could be used.

Painting the sea

If the sea is in your painting, as in the picture shown here, there are many ways of painting it, depending on the tidal state, lighting, wind conditions and so on (see pages 94–111).

The water here was created first with a wash of raw sienna, applied using horizontal strokes wet-on-dry, with a few white ripples left to suggest the play of light. This was overlaid with phthalo blue, leaving ripples in the underlying wash.

Once this base was dry, clean water was brushed on firmly in vertical strokes and soft, pale building reflections lifted out by dabbing with kitchen towel. Ripples of phthalo blue were added, and when dry, reflections added in indigo and a mix of indigo and phthalo blue.

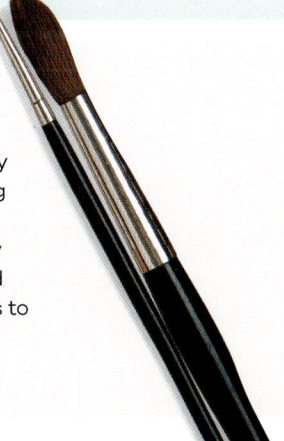

Choice of brushes

You can paint a scene like this with just two good-quality brushes: a size 6–8 round for the majority of the painting and a size 2 or 3 round for the detailing. Kolinsky sables are ideal because they keep a point well and hold plenty of pigment, which means that you can use a large round for a multitude of tasks, from laying background washes to painting brushes, trees and buildings.

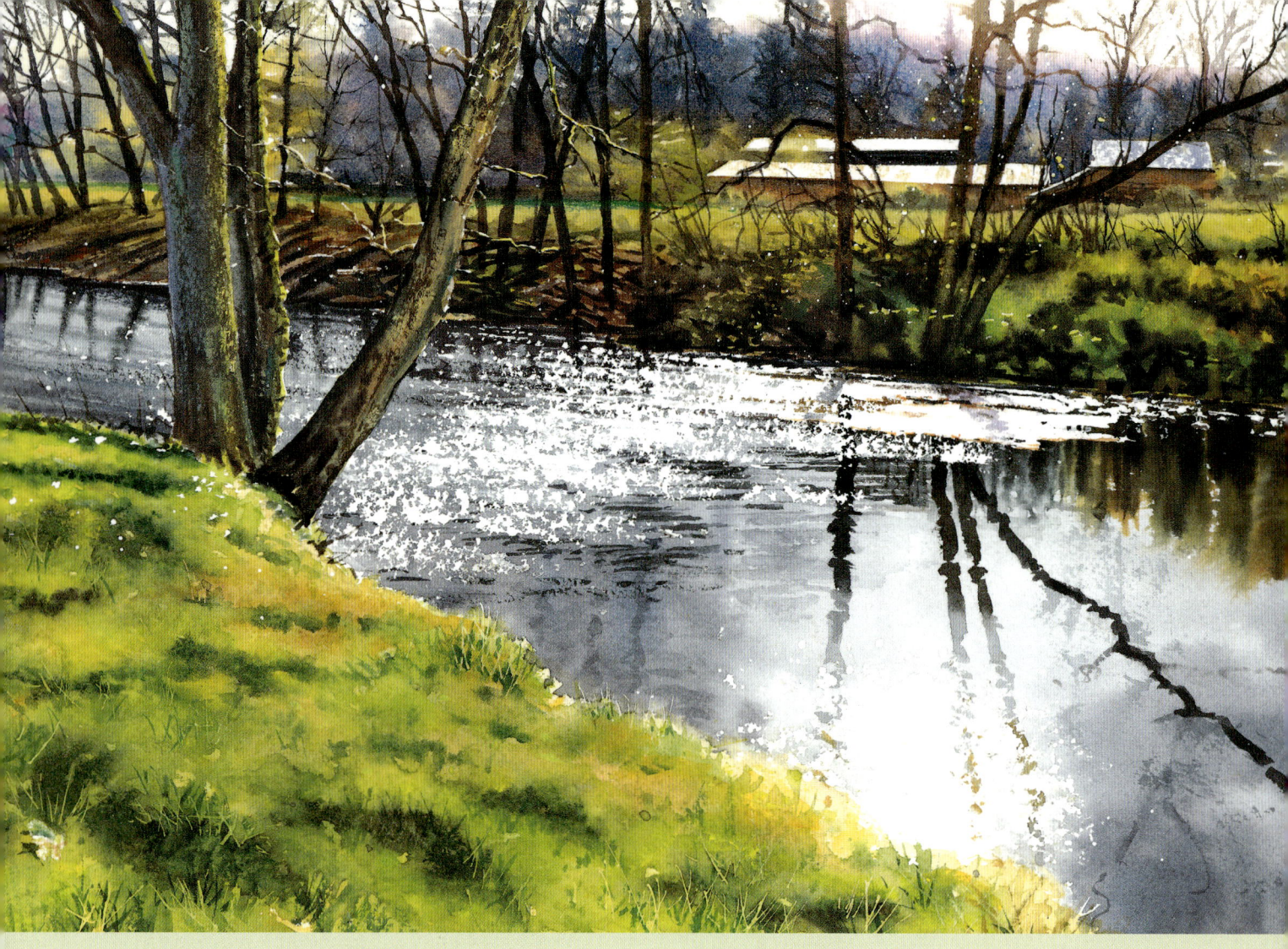

Trees by a river

The main feature in this river scene is the glint of light in the water – everything revolves around this. The theme of glinting light is repeated throughout the composition in the barn roofs, at the base of the tree and in the very light foreground water where glints from the high sun are just beginning to be reflected.

Artist insight: The mud banks were masked with a colour shaper. Water sparkles were created with a hog-hair brush as shown right. Sparkles of light were spattered from a toothbrush over the landscape. Trees on the far bank were water-feathered (see the Techniques list). Once the masking was removed, the large tree trunks were glazed with a yellow-green mix. A grey of cobalt blue and burnt sienna supplies shadows to the left of the trunks, and an intense dark mix of ultramarine blue and light red was stippled wet-in-wet with the brush point for dark texture in the shadow. Dark colour was dragged across the dry trunks for bark. Background darks were applied with mixes of quinacridone magenta, ultramarine blue and burnt umber. Washes of burnt sienna were applied to the river bank. Notice the paling of landscape and trees in the sunlit glare-area, with magenta added for heat. Grass blades were masked with a dip pen over the green grass colour, then when dry, over-painted with Payne's gray added to the green mix for a dark green.

COLOUR PALETTE

cadmium lemon

quinacridone magenta

French ultramarine

phthalo blue

cobalt blue

phthalo green

burnt sienna

burnt umber

light red

indigo

Payne's gray

PAINTING RIPPLES

Reflections often ripple downwards in a series of horizontal and vertical steps. Let them flow loosely off the point of the brush. Brush them in a series of loosely painted straight strokes, getting longer as they get nearer. Rather than copying the exact shapes, work fast and let the brush produce the shapes naturally.

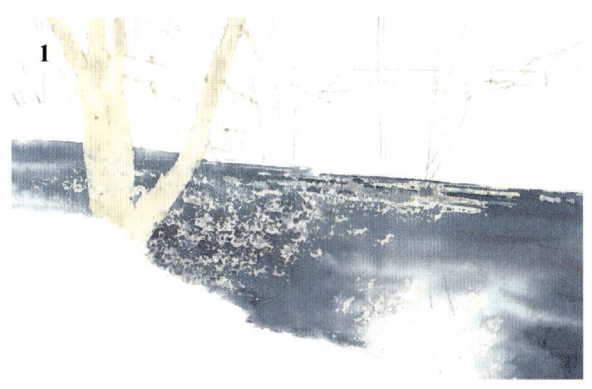

1 Mask the sparkles with a hog-hair brush. Paint on diluted phthalo blue and indigo, with cadmium yellow, burnt sienna and phthalo green in the background.

2 After the darks are brushed into the background, lightly brush in ripples of the water mix wet-on-dry.

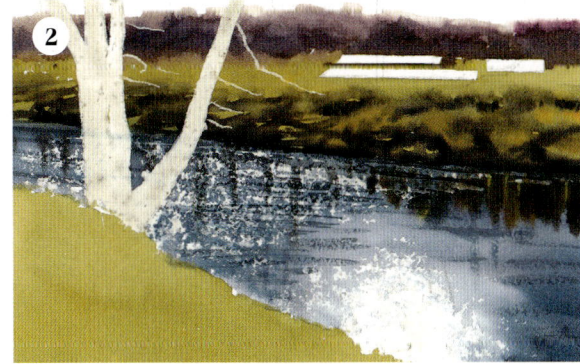

3 Brush in the water mix in a pattern of darker blue ripples, and then the tree reflection in a series of ripples, both wet-on-dry. Keep both colours light around the sun sparkles. Remove the masking.

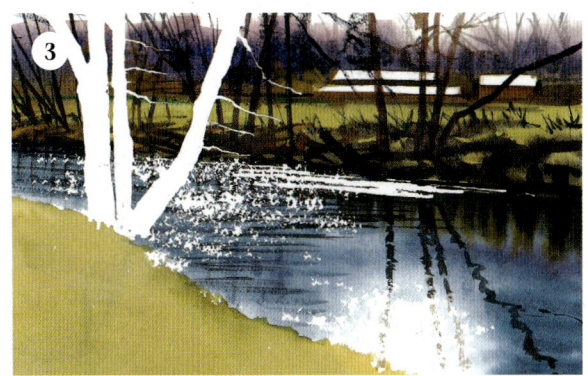

Techniques: masking sparkles, pages 78–79, 90–93, 108–109; mixing greens, page 23; dry-brush, page 27; tree trunk shadows, page 47; water (lakes), pages 66–67, 82–83; water edge grasses, pages 76–77; water (rivers), pages 78–81, 84–85; water (harbours), 86–87; water (tree reflections, puddles), 112–113; water feathering (trees), pages 19, 62–63, 112–113.

Masking to create sparkle on water

Sun sparkle on broken water can be achieved by wax resist on rough or Not watercolour paper, but masking gives a more interesting visual effect. Apply masking fluid using a hog-hair brush, with the fibres slightly splayed outwards. These three sparkle patterns were made by dabbing masking fluid gently downwards with the brush held vertically so all the fibres touch the paper separately.

I buy new hog-hair brushes or use older ones, it doesn't matter as long as the fibres are free of old masking fluid. Just dip the tips in the masking fluid. Then dab them gently downwards to get many separate marks from the individual fibres, rather than one large blob. After you dab each mark, rotate the brush so similar texture markings don't repeat themselves. You can also rotate the brush on the paper for interesting textures (**A**). When the masking fluid is dry, brush on colour. You can also streak dark colour through, wet-in-wet or wet-on-dry.

When the masking fluid is removed the flow of colours is revealed (**B**). The glints of light contrast with the darker wet-in-wet colours of the bank and meadow behind.

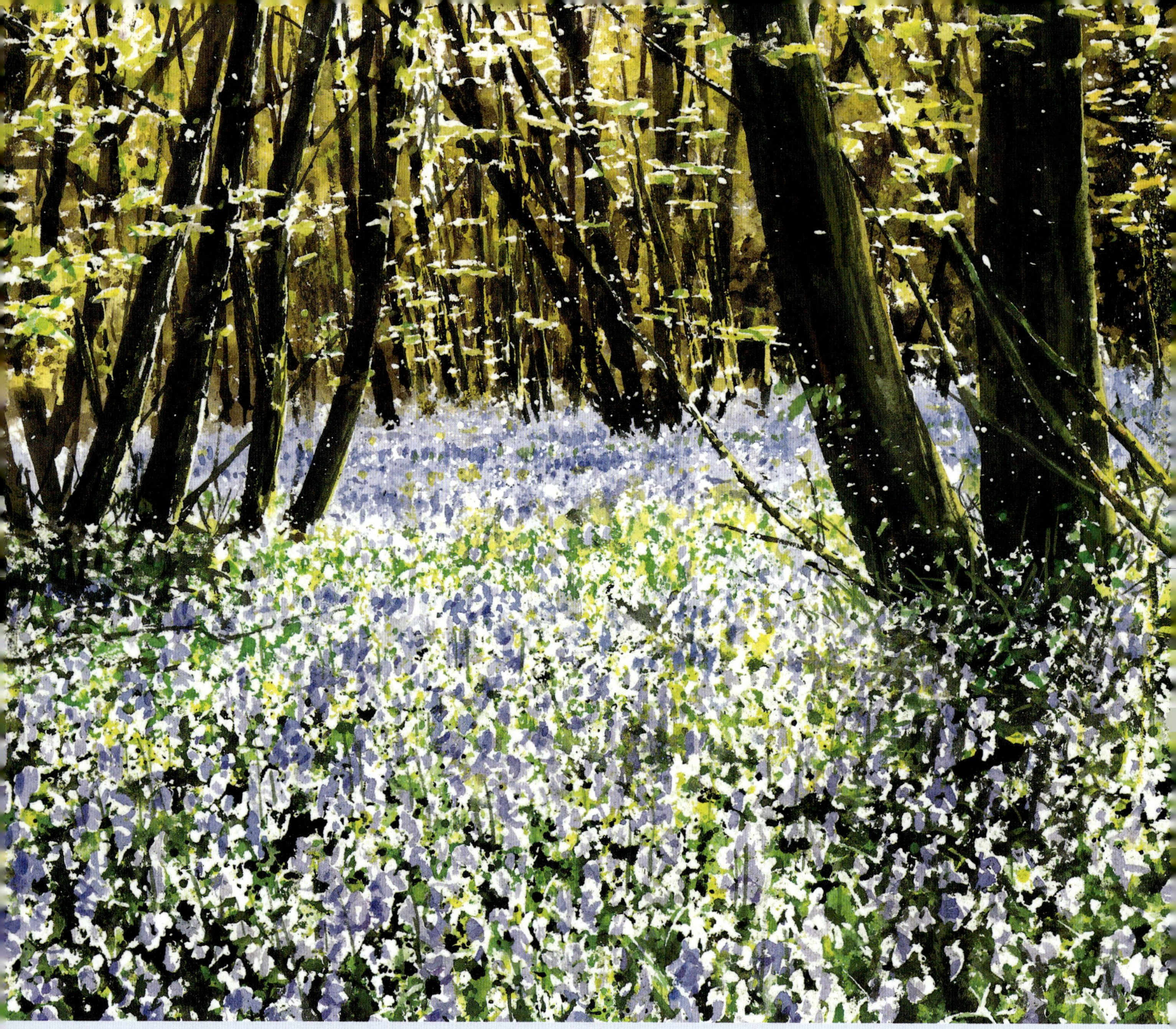

Bluebell wood

Bluebells in a forest – a texture, a blurred swathe of colour, a shroud of sky draped on the woodland floor – but how do you paint them? The answer lies in how your visual mind decodes the amazing prospect of thousands of individual bluebells. This scene shows how to paint not just bluebells, but the effect they create.

Artist insight: The bluebells were loosely touched in with a clear blue violet mixed from cobalt blue with a little quinacridone magenta, followed by a darker mix. Save plenty of whites as the forest floor is shimmering with light. You can model darks around some of the bluebells, but be careful not to overdo the effect. Horizontal leaf shapes were masked across the woodland before applying colour; then touched in with yellow/green when unmasked.

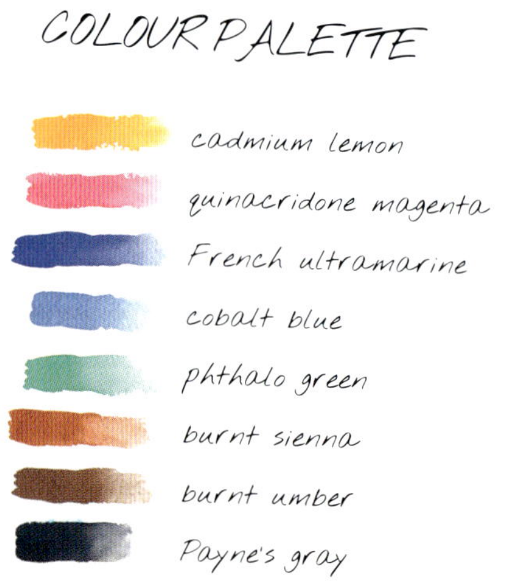

COLOUR PALETTE

cadmium lemon

quinacridone magenta

French ultramarine

cobalt blue

phthalo green

burnt sienna

burnt umber

Payne's gray

Wax resist technique

An alternative way of painting bluebells is to gently rub a wax candle on rough or Not watercolour paper. The wax leaves the dimpled surface covered in a texture of clear wax and unwaxed paper that becomes apparent only when wet colour is applied.

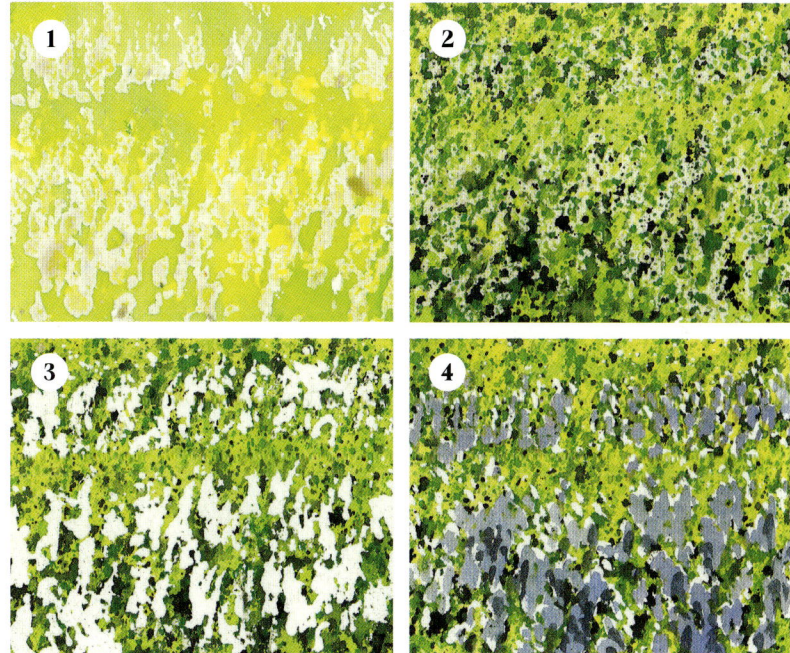

Wax candle rubbed on white paper, colour applied on top.

Wax candle rubbed over the bluebell colour.

Wax candle applied firmly over bluebell colour, with more colour applied on top.

PAINTING BLUEBELLS

Masking is a convenient way of saving whites, and also gives a beautiful result. An old ruined brush was used here. Other ways of painting bluebells include wax resist and dry-brush.

1 Mask the bluebells using many upward strokes. Cover the forest floor with larger marks in the foreground; smaller and closer packed further up the painting. Spatter masking with a toothbrush from above the foreground into the distance for diminishing spatter size. Apply pale colours.

2 Brush in the distant woodland floor with a mix of cobalt blue and quinacridone magenta (see the main image). Use scrap paper to protect this area and spatter darker versions of the green mix. When dry, spatter intense dark of this with added French ultramarine and burnt sienna.

3 Remove the masking fluid, leaving the whites for the bluebells.

4 Touch in the bluebells with the cobalt blue and quinacridone magenta mix. Add some Payne's gray marks for intense darks.

Techniques: mixing greens, page 23; meadow texture, pages 28–29; trees, pages 42–43, 52–53, 62–63, 78–79; winter trees, pages 46–47; masking flowers, pages 28–29; masking blossom, pages 48–49.

PAINTING THE TREES

They don't need to be tidy. After painting the woodland floor, mask vertical highlights and a few leaves, with the brush used for masking bluebells. Spatter some lights with a toothbrush. Mask the light edges of the trees, but not the trees themselves. Paint the trees and woodland area with a mix of a lot of yellow and some brown with a little green. Drag brush for long straight marks. Leave light areas in the sky. Mask more leaves and paint all the darks for the trees and branches. Use burnt umber and ultramarine blue mix for the trees and Payne's gray for stronger darks. Remove the masking. Touch in some of the leaves, and some tree edges with the woodland yellow, brown, and green mix.

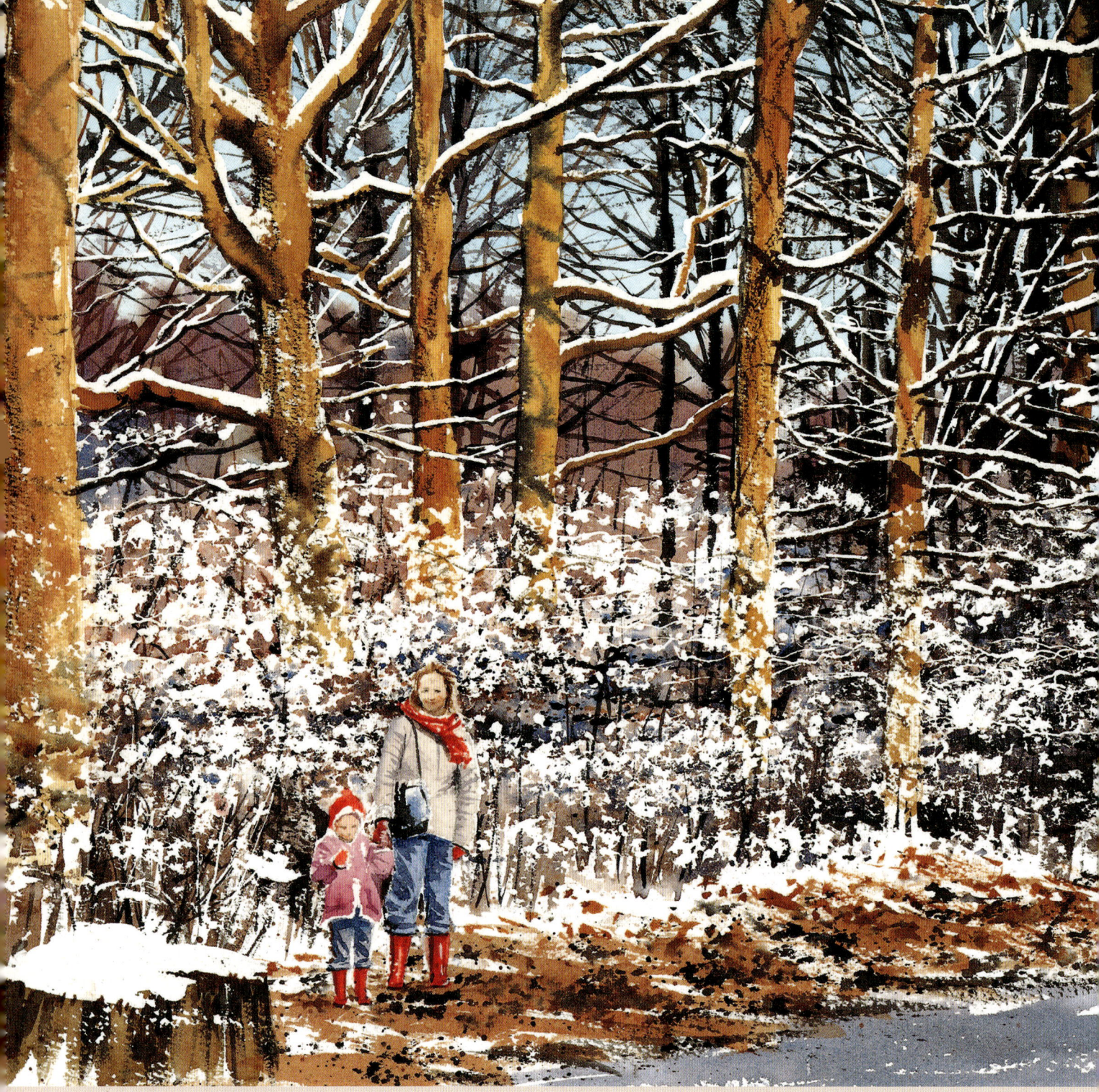

Winter trees

Here is a labyrinth of snaking branches in a woodland canopy. Masking allows you to paint an apparently complex scene with ease and also gives snow-clad branch effects. The branches may appear to be curving, but the underlying structure is of a series of straight lines changing direction suddenly – this is the key to drawing convincing trees.

Artist insight: The figures were masked and touched in with greys and scarlet lake – a small amount of red can give any scene a lift. Snow on the bushes was masked with a hog-hair brush and branches with a pen nib. Some of the texture was spattered and the road was painted with a grey of cobalt blue and burnt sienna. Knife scratch marks on the stump created the bark effect.

COLOUR PALETTE

scarlet lake
permanent magenta
French ultramarine
phthalo blue
cobalt blue
yellow ochre
burnt sienna
Indian red

These colours can be substituted with others. For example, a bright red such as cadmium red can be used in place of scarlet lake.

Techniques: brushmarks, page 21; washes, pages 18–21; rough-brush masking, pages 50–51; skies, pages 54–55; masking trees, pages 42–43; scratching out, pages 36–37, 58–59; trees, pages 78–79; figures standing, pages 94–95; figures in action, pages 106–107; snow, pages 114–115; snowy detail masking, pages 116–117.

MASKING TREES

Masking is more than just a method to make painting easier. It renders exquisite textures and marks, and is a creative technique in its own right.

1 Mask the trees using a colour shaper and allow to dry naturally. Wet the sky and paint it with phthalo blue. Ensure the colour dries evenly and is not 'panelled' into compartments of different intensity.

2 With the masking still on, paint the background trees. Useful colours are mixes of permanent magenta, burnt sienna and French ultramarine, and intense darks of French ultramarine and Indian red.

3 Remove the masking and re-mask the snow on the tops of the larger branches only. Add a mix of burnt sienna and yellow ochre to the branches and darks of French ultramarine and Indian red.

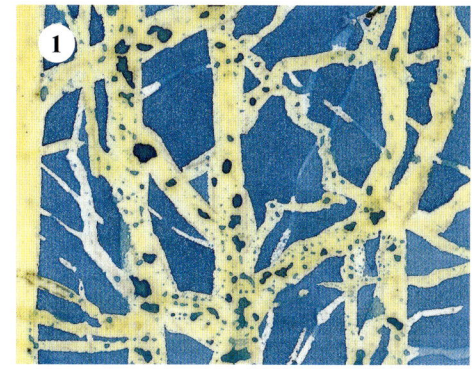

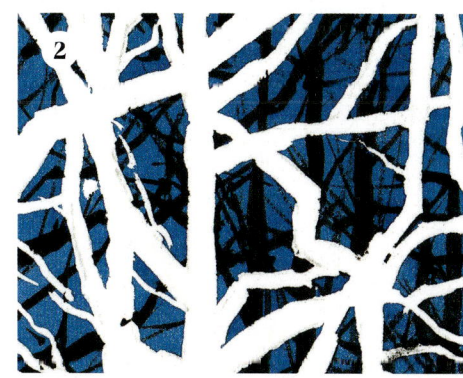

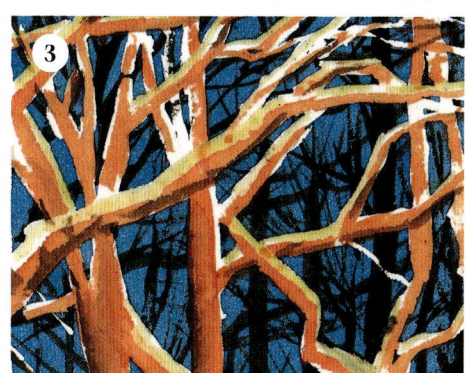

SHAPING TREE TRUNKS

You can control a watercolour event to create an impact. The event here is simply the passage of colour across wet paper. Here it is used to 'light' a tree and give it body.

1a Wet the trunks and brush a burnt sienna and yellow ochre mix wet-in-wet from the shadow side, letting it spread across.

1b Add more burnt sienna to the shadow side, and streaks across the trunks. Add French ultramarine and Indian red for the dark sides and drag branch shadows of this across.

1c Deepen the colour and let it dry. Notice the curving strokes for shadows describing the form of the trunks.

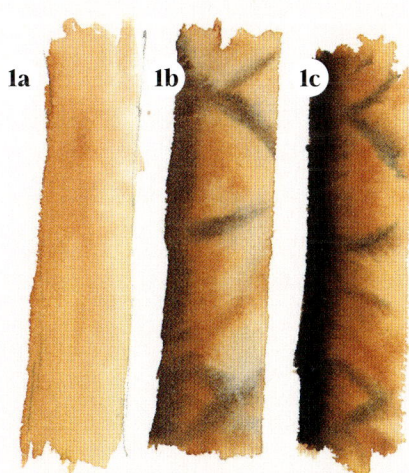

Mixing greys

A range of subtle greys can be mixed with three colours, such as French ultramarine, permanent magenta and burnt sienna. This mix can be shifted between orange, red, maroon, violet and blue with mature greys in between. Start with blue and when you add the other colour do so cautiously, as French ultramarine is easily greyed.

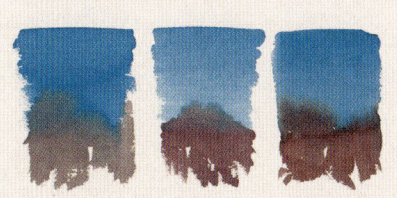

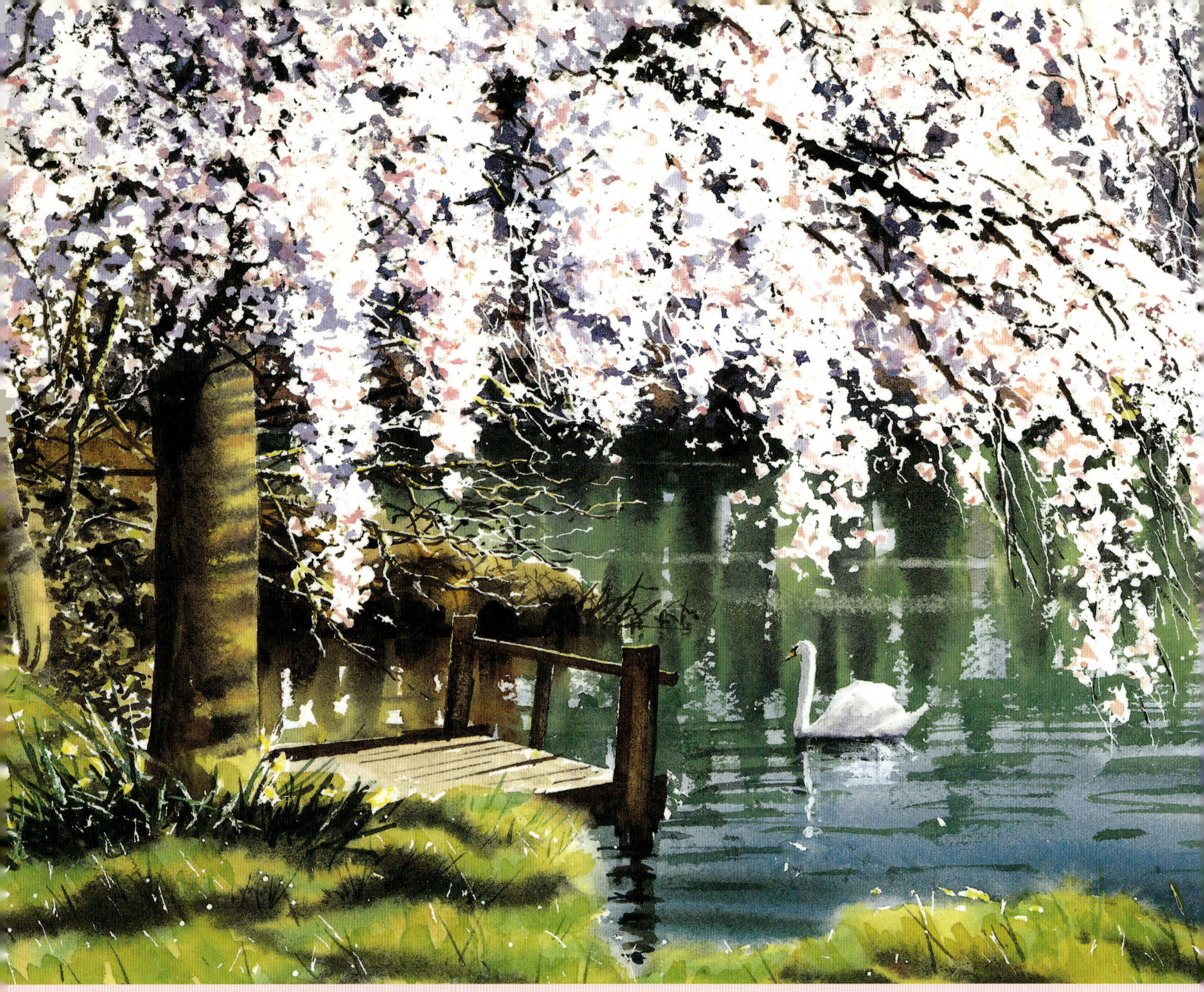

Spring blossoms

Painting blossom is easy – most of it is saved white with textured masking, and small accents of colour. These tiny areas of colour may be pale and few, but they create a powerful visual message in the eye of the beholder, forming shapes around the masking and leading to the visual conclusion of 'blossom'.

Artist insight: Painting blossom is the easy part. You need to paint very little, just small accents of colour. Masking fluid saves whites and allows you to place complex texture around the masked areas. The masking process also creates beautiful shapes and textures in its own right, opening up possibilities not available by other means. The landing stage was masked and painted after the water was finished.

COLOUR PALETTE

 cadmium lemon

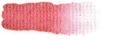 quinacridone magenta

 French ultramarine

 phthalo blue

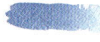 cobalt blue

 phthalo green

 Naples yellow

 burnt sienna

 burnt umber

Payne's gray

TEXTURED MASKING

Blossom texture can be reproduced by using an old brush thick with masking fluid as the applicator for the blossom masking. An untidy, haphazard means of application with plenty of interesting saved white shapes helps the blossom look convincing. As with all masking techniques you will need a hard-surface watercolour paper.

1 Mask the blossom with a brush thick with dried masking fluid; use a colour shaper to mask the trunk and some branches, and use a dip pen to mask some twigs. Masking fluid was used against a simple background. The trunk and some branches and twigs were also masked.

2 When dry, apply accents of a mix of Naples yellow and quinacridone magenta by dabbing with a scrunched up brush.

3 Without removing the masking, roughly dab on a violet shade of cobalt blue and quinacridone magenta with a scrunched up brush. Mix a dark from French ultramarine and burnt umber and roughly dab this on for the deep accents of shade straggled about.

4 Using the intense dark of French ultramarine and burnt umber, brush branches and twigs into the tree. Build up more intense rough tone in the central area, saving lights in addition to the masked blossom. Dab the brush vertically to get the multiplicity of tiny marks.

5 Remove the masking. This takes much of the colour with it, and it is not always a predictable process. Some of the masking will have to be reinstated, but this is very easy. The image changes a lot at this stage, but the blossom texture is well developed.

6 Replace some masking over the blossom and re-mask any branches that need protecting. Repaint the pink, and violet, and also the dark highlights, branches and twigs that had disappeared with the masking. Paint the trunk wet-in-wet with a mix of burnt sienna, cobalt blue and cadmium lemon. Add a dark of French ultramarine and burnt umber to the shadow. Drag streaks across. Remove the masking.

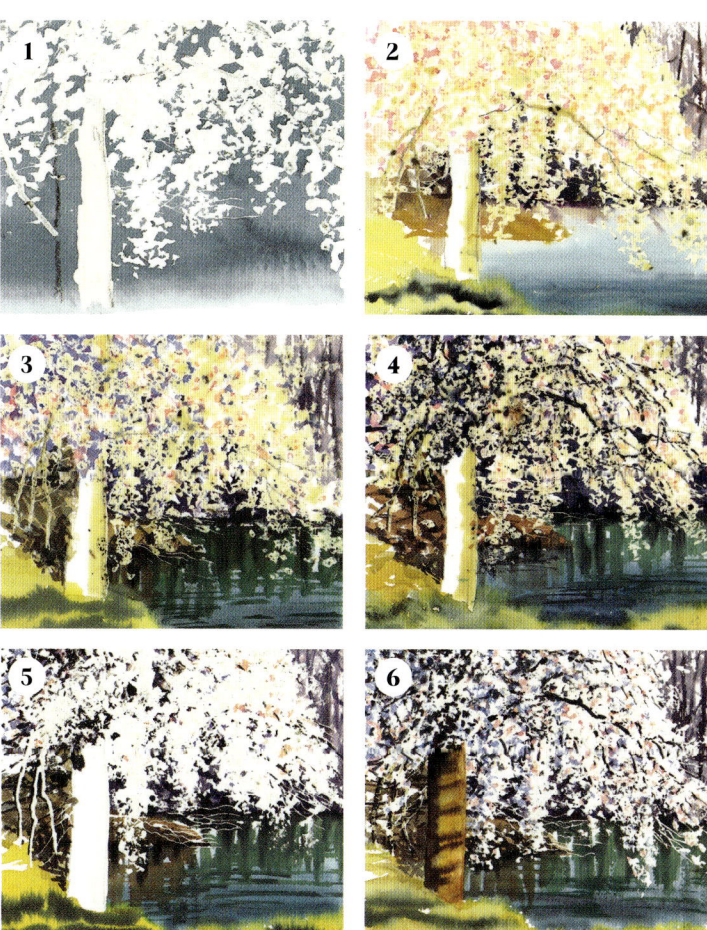

Techniques: *brush thick with dried masking fluid (scrunched up and messed up brushes), page 7; masking flowers, pages 28–29, 44–45; shaping tree trunks, masking trees, pages 42–43, 46–47; water, pages 66–67, 70–71, 78–81; water-edge grasses, pages 76–77; grassy ground, grasses, pages 30–31, 100–101; masking swans, pages 76–77; masking texture (similar method), pages 92–93, 104–105.*

Blossom colour

To get a subtle blossom colour use Naples yellow as a controlling medium, a soft pale yellow to mute, and pale mixes of quinacridone magenta and cobalt blue. Naples yellow with a little quinacridone magenta makes a pale peach colour. A little more quinacridone magenta gives a soft pink. Adding cobalt blue makes it violet. Cobalt blue with a little quinacridone magenta added is a deep blue violet.

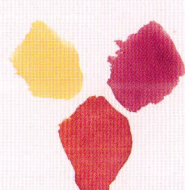

Naples yellow + quinacridone magenta

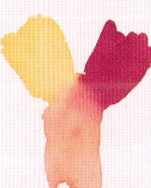

Naples yellow + quinacridone magenta

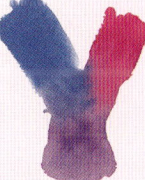

colbalt blue + quinacridone magenta

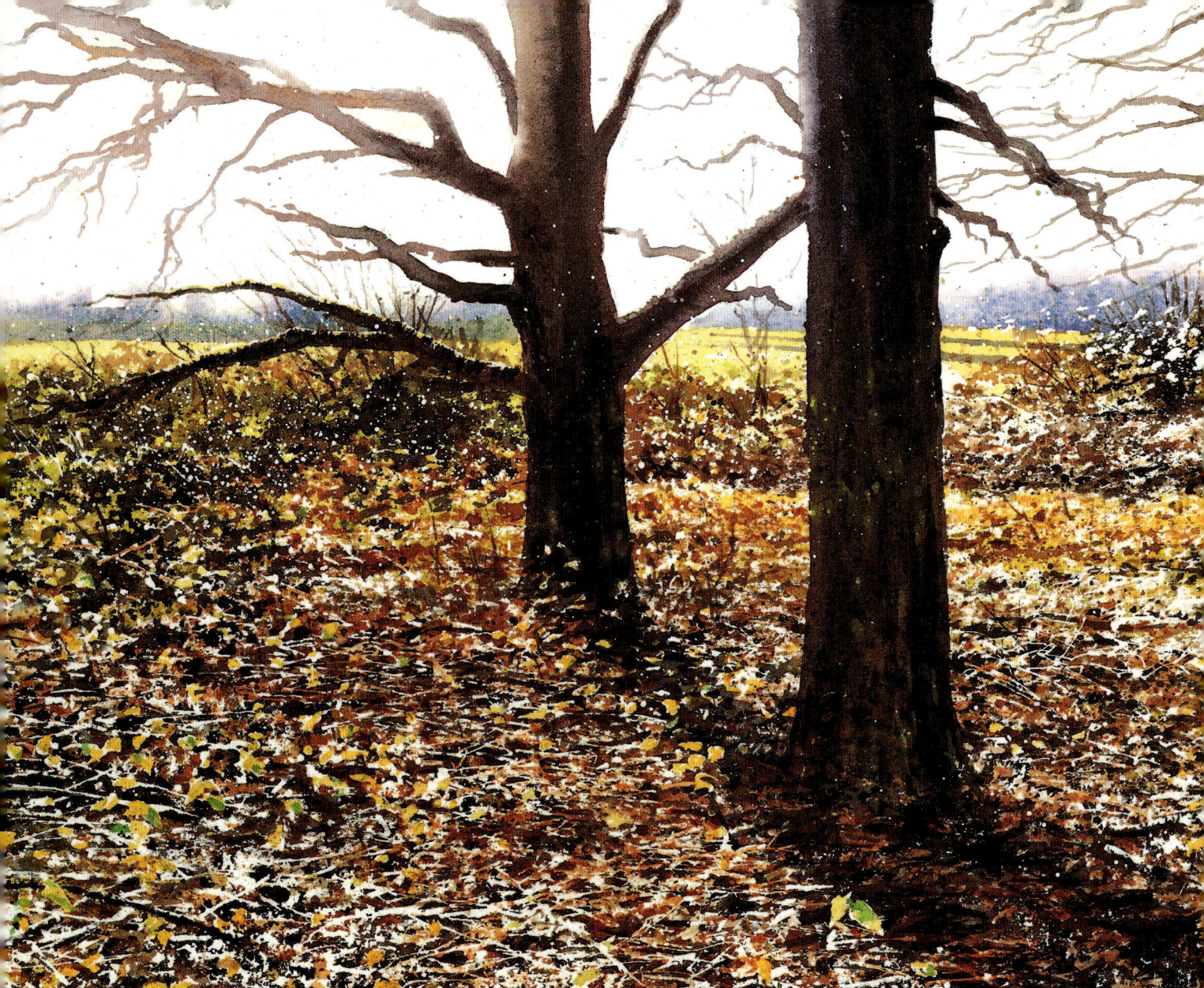

Undergrowth

A simple 'dryscape' of twigs can work well if you use convincing texture for the foreground and a radical tonal range from white to dark. The trees counterbalance the space to the left, the horizon is above the centre line to emphasize the foreground, and the shadow links to the foreground.

Artist insight: *The dried texture of a winter woodland floor appears to glint in low-angle light. When looking towards the sun, the light bounces off the twigs. Texture is often not just about the physical landscape, but the light in which it is viewed. For me this is often early or late in the day, looking towards the vicinity of the sun.*

Techniques: *composition, pages 10–11; mixing greys, page 23; spattering, pages 28–29, 98–99; trees, pages 42–43, 78–79; bright sun effect in trees, pages 42–43, 52–53, 62–63; masking ground detail, page 116–117.*

COLOUR PALETTE

new gamboge

quinacridone magenta

French ultramarine

cobalt blue

cerulean blue

phthalo green

burnt sienna

light red

burnt umber

Payne's gray

PAINTING UNDERGROWTH

1 Apply diagonal sticks and twigs with a colour shaper and dip pen nearby, flattening out further away. Apply toothbrush masking-fluid spatter. Gently apply masking fluid texture with the tip of a hog-hair brush. Dry it. Spatter burnt umber from bottom to top and brush a few marks.

2 Mask a few more sticks and twigs. Brush a darker colour mix of light red and Payne's gray for the fine tracery of shadows in the foliage. Spatter more of this colour to build the layers of twigs into the foreground. Add more layers of masking and colour as you wish.

3 Remove the masking fluid carefully and avoid smudging the dark colour. Notice here the way in which the rough pattern of twigs is laid according to the laws of perspective; although chaotic, the lines open out into the foreground.

4 Touch in the reserved whites with a little colour. At this stage also add detail texture to larger branches in your painting to give them form. Use a mix of new gamboge and a little green for the leaves, along with some light red.

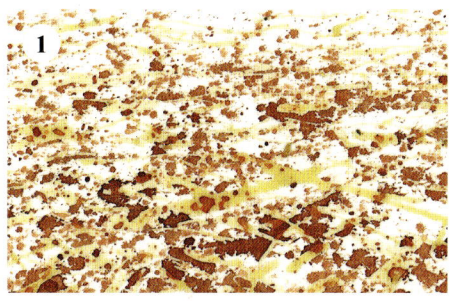

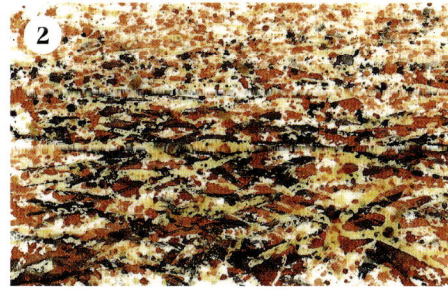

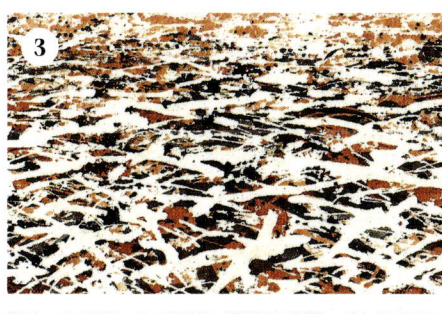

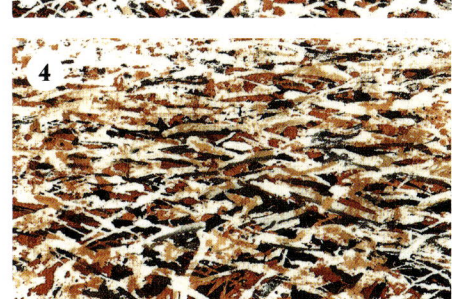

Creative brushmarks

Let the brush make the natural marks it is designed for, rather than trying to model realism for yourself. Experiment to find out the marks it can make and use them. A good-quality sable brush is a potent tool. Try using different types of brush for a variety of marks.

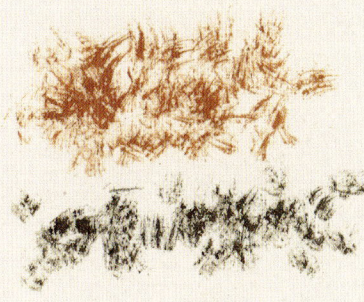

Hog-hair brushmarks.

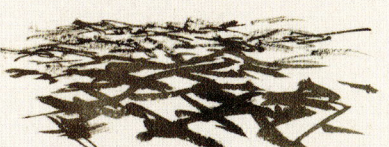

Marks made by point of sable brush.

SKY TREATMENT

Sky is not directly painted. The paper is left white. Here on the edge of a woodland it is so bright out in the open, that the light is off the scale of the painting's set of values. The sky does not need a wash of colour. Sky is implied by the treatment of the branches, the brilliance of light dazzling the eye and causing an optical effect which I refer to as halation. This is seen in Halated trees, page 52. Dazzle inside the eye causes a bleaching and warming of dark objects silhouetted against the brightness. This effect is inside the eye and conveys brightness.

Layered masking

Alternate layers of masking texture and colour combine to build real depth and more complex texture into a foreground.

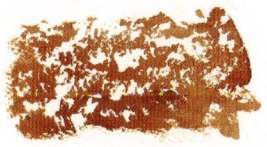

Masking with hog-hair brush messed up with dried fluid.

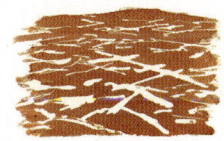

Masking pattern of sticks only, with masking removed to reveal shapes.

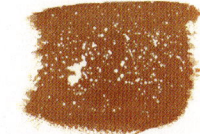

Spattered masking, by toothbrush.

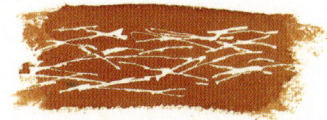

Twigs masked with Indian ink nib.

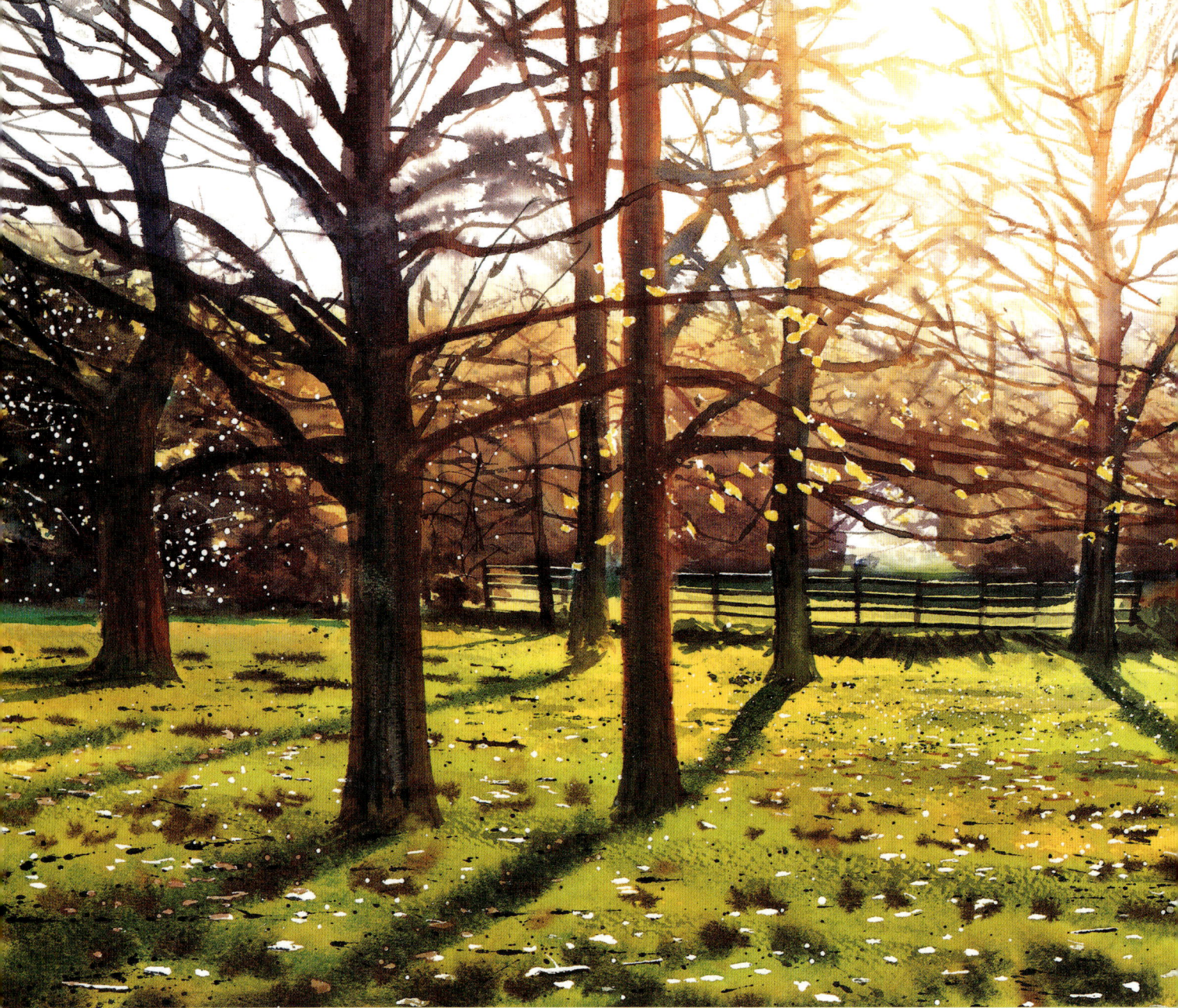

Halated trees

Instead of being silhouetted in front of bright light, here trees and objects are bleached out of existence, bent toward yellow. The colours move through orange and red to magenta, crimson and black – the halation rainbow – a partial spectrum caused by glare in the eye. With this treatment the whites can look brighter than the paper.

Artist insight: Fallen leaves glint like mirrors. They reflect bright low sun into the viewer's eye, seen only when looking toward the sun at the right angle. A view towards bright, low sun can appear full of glittering light from small objects.

COLOUR PALETTE

- cadmium lemon
- transparent yellow
- quinacridone magenta
- French ultramarine
- may green
- phthalo green
- Naples yellow
- burnt sienna
- Indian red

Techniques: *fallen leaves in perspective, page 17 (grid illustration); masking and tree texture, page 19; glazing, pages 20–21; meadows in evening light, pages 30–31; spatter, pages 30–31; landscape toward low sun, pages 38–39; branch dazzle, pages 30–31, 50–51, 58–59, 62–63; masked leaves, pages 44–45; winter trees, pages 46–47; leaf glints, pages 62–63.*

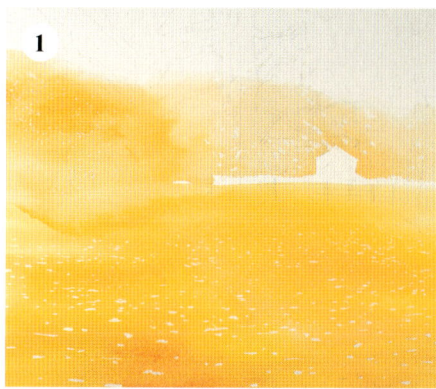

PAINTING THE SCENE

1 Sky is left as white paper. Mask the light on the fence, some backlit leaves, and some glinting fallen leaves. Add some toothbrush masking spatter. Allow to dry. Glaze Naples yellow and a little transparent yellow over the centre background, saving white for the house. Add more transparent yellow to the left. Glaze transparent yellow over the meadow and add burnt sienna in streaks, stronger in the foreground areas.

2 Work into the wet meadow by overglazing rough streaks into the grass area using may green. Brush in a little phthalo green in criss-cross fashion to start the pattern of shadows, leaving plenty of underglaze showing. Mix a dark green from phthalo green, French ultramarine and Indian red and brush in this colour for the shadows and dark clumps of grass.

3 Rewet the distant area, leaving 'flashes' of dry paper. Add colour, keeping the area below the sun lighter, using transparent yellow, then burnt sienna and next quinacridone magenta with a little phthalo green. On the left apply a mixed 'black' of quinacridone magenta and phthalo green. Brush colours for a few background branches. Stripe phthalo green along the field edge and paint the deep, far shadow. Leave spaces for the tree trunks. Spatter some dark into the field.

4 Build up branches. Nearest the sun they are pale, with Naples yellow and transparent yellow. Further away add burnt sienna. Then add quinacridone magenta in a continuously changing mix. Finally add phthalo green, progressively changing to 'black'. For the trunks, brush light colour in first, then add dark down the middle and let it spread out. The trees are darker further away from the sun.

5 Shade fallen masked leaves and twigs underneath with a mix of phthalo green, French ultramarine and Indian red. Remove the masking when dry. Touch in some of the now glinting leaves with a little burnt sienna. In the final painting, note that, although in shade, the house is backlit. There is a green cast where sunlit grass bounces the light onto the trunks near the ground.

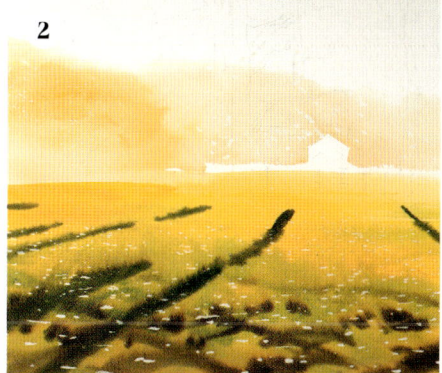

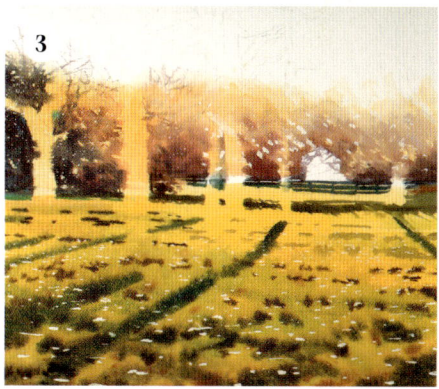

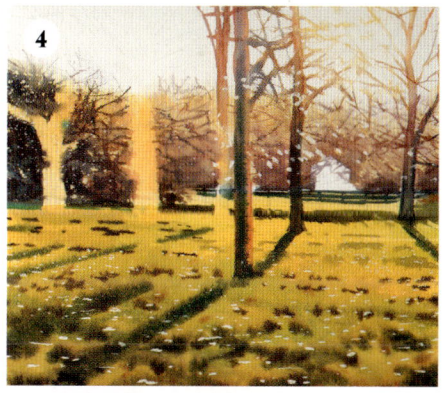

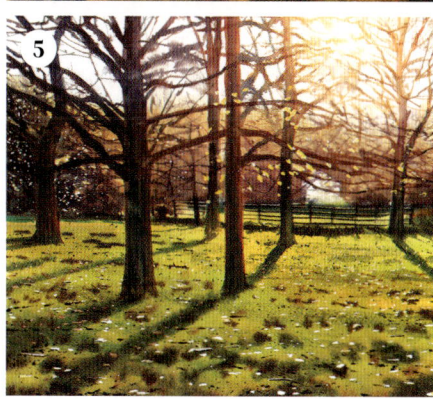

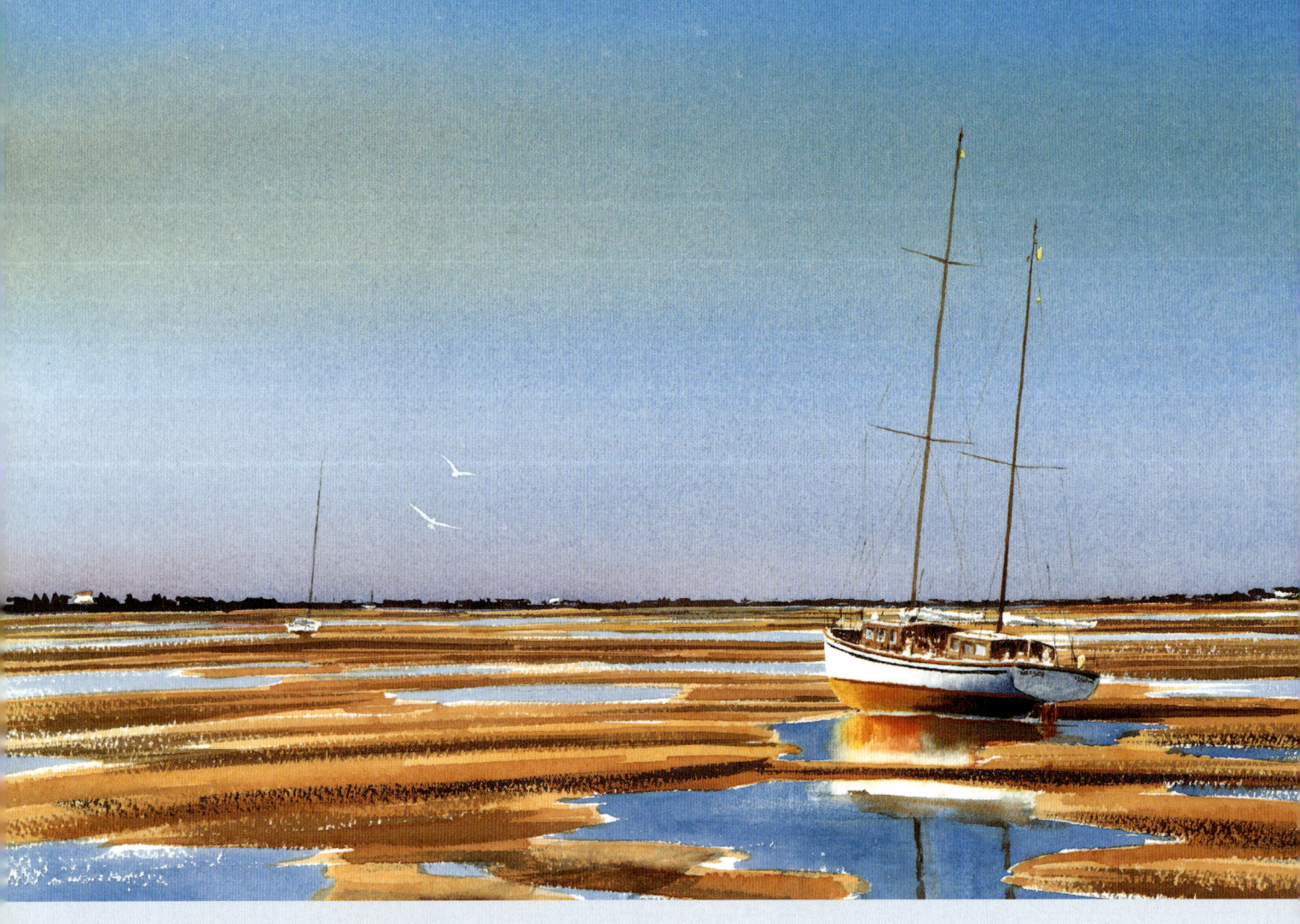

Fair weather

The sky here is a series of wet-in-wet glazes, giving control of the tonal effect and the colour distribution. It is painted from a corner opposite the sun where it is darkest, rather than the top down. Skies often darken imperceptibly at the horizon, and bringing this phenomenon out can give a scene more impact.

Artist insight: Primary colours red and yellow are present in blue skies, calling for a multi-layered approach. For a blue sky, this often means red low down, and warm brown or orange further up, transitioning to purer blue. This adds realism, and the resulting subtle, changing greys give depth.

Techniques: receding bands (perspective), page 17; wet-in-wet, wet-on-dry, and washes, pages 18–21; glazing, pages 20–21; beach, pages 72, 96–97; boats, pages 82–87, 92–95, 98–99; sea and distant horizon, pages 98–99; masking, pages 76–77, 104–105; reflections, pages 106–107, 112–113.

COLOUR PALETTE

- transparent yellow
- cadmium orange
- quinacridone red
- quinacridone magenta
- French ultramarine
- phthalo blue
- cobalt blue
- phthalo green
- yellow ochre
- burnt sienna
- light red
- white gouache

PAINTING THE SCENE

1 Place the horizon at about one-third up, with the boats away from the centre. Mask the complete boat hull up to the cabin roofs, but not the masts. Just mask a little masthead detail. Mask the distant boat hull too and a few distant lights on the horizon, as appropriate.

2 Wet the sky above the horizon. Brush quinacridone red along the horizon line so that it fades upwards into the white paper from halfway up. Brush in a broad band of cadmium orange wet-in-wet halfway up the sky, but not quite to the top.

3 With the sky wet, on the right of the painting brush in a pale wash of cobalt blue at the bottom of the sky and one of phthalo blue with a small amount of phthalo green at the top. Add a little French ultramarine along the horizon.

4 With the sky still wet, brush phthalo blue, over the sky more strongly, again from the top right-hand corner into the image, with less paint and more water on the brush as you work it down to the horizon. Many other colour options are possible for a blue sky.

5 Paint the sand with a basic wash of yellow ochre, wet-on-dry, adding a little light red to the foreground sand, and leaving lights for the pools. Sweep the colour across with the point of the brush in fine swathes, diminishing in width for the distant areas.

6 Brush in the dark streaks with a mix of burnt sienna and French ultramarine for a strong dark brown. Use the point of the brush and taper the strokes off, building the pattern of pools at low tide. The land stays lighter than the sky.

7 Brush the horizon with the burnt sienna and French ultramarine mix, and for stronger darks on the sand, dry-brushing some texture. Add a little gum arabic to the wet pool below the boat. Add a blue mix of phthalo blue, quinacridone magenta and burnt sienna to the pool, avoiding the boat reflection. Paint the other pools with the same colour wet-on-dry, leaving a few 'sparks' of light.

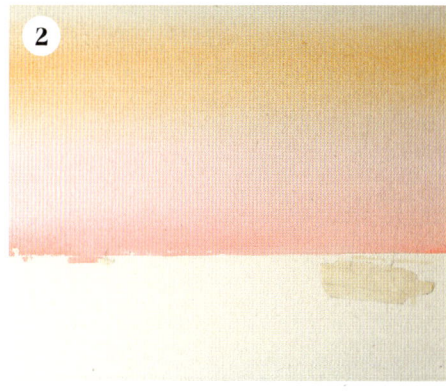
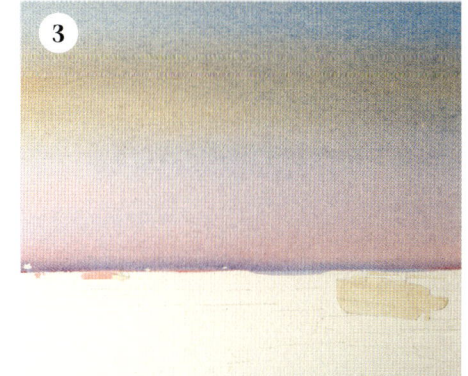
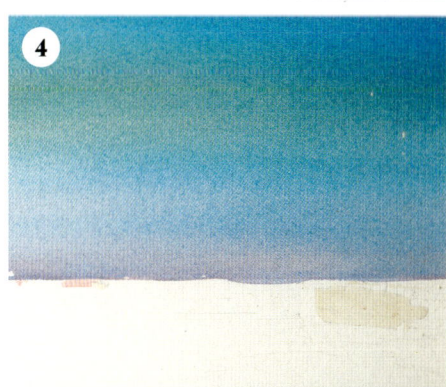
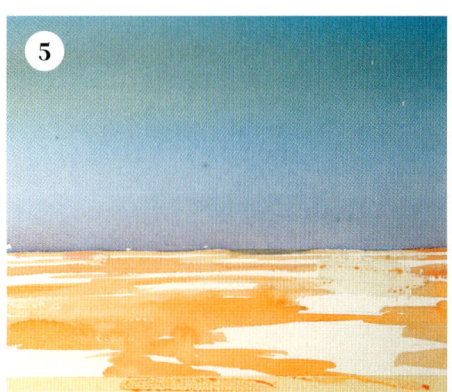
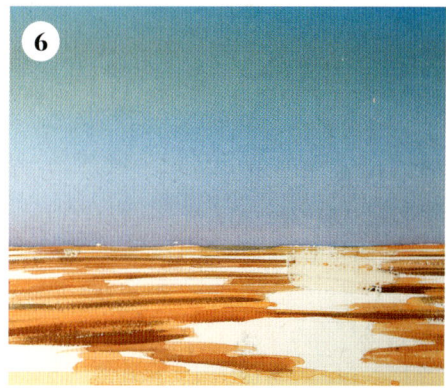

8 The masts and rigging were created with a size 2 sable brush. Cobalt blue with a little quinacridone magenta and burnt sienna is touched into the wet rear of the boat. When dry, the hull side is re-wet (but not the flat stern) and the previous colour added from the back of the side and allowed to fade forwards into the wet hull, defining the lighter stern. The lower part is painted wet-on-dry with transparent yellow and light red. The shadow area is emphasized with an intense dark underneath. Lines on the hull and cabin detail complete the painting. The birds were added with white gouache paint.

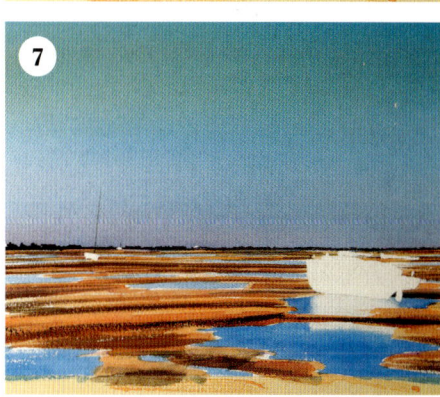
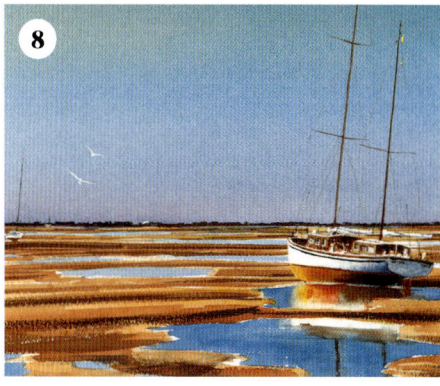

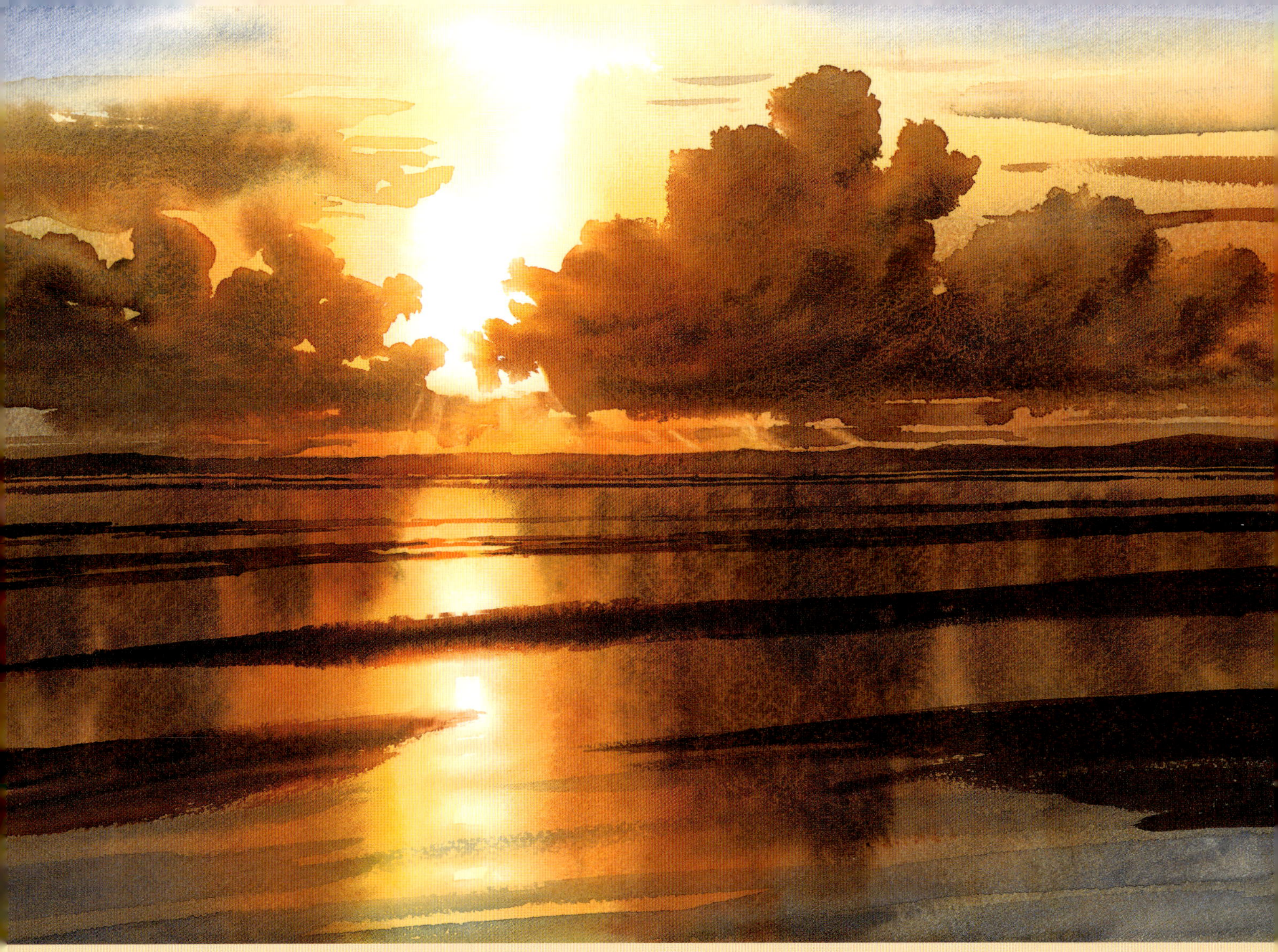

Dramatic sky

To freeze a moment of eternity on paper, it's what you do before you start that matters: mix plenty of paint beforehand, then run the colours straight onto the paper and leave them alone – this way you preserve vitality and expression in your skies.

Artist insight: To create the effect shown here, add cloud reflections to the water area while the paper is wet. When the first stage is dry, add the clouds, starting with the main large puffy ones; wet the paper in the cloud shapes, then drop in the colours, again working wet into wet; add streaks for long thin cloud. Wet the land and mud banks where they cross the sun's reflection. Brush colour along these wet areas, warmer and paler across the reflection. Finally lift a few shafts of light out above the land.

Techniques: wet-in-wet, pages 18–19; glazing, pages 20–21; skies, pages 54–55, 60–61, 64–65, 66–67, 70–71, 108–109, 120–121; sunset/sunrise skies, 38–39, 62–63, 68–69, 108; sunset clouds, 109; lifting, pages 93, 111; hard and soft edges (lost and found edges), pages 124–125.

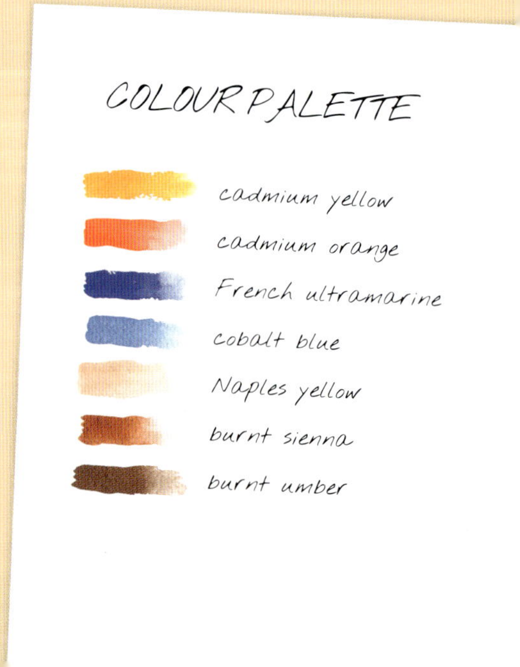

COLOUR PALETTE

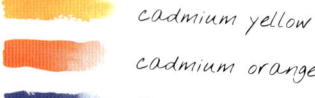
cadmium yellow

cadmium orange

French ultramarine

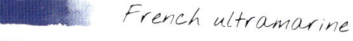
cobalt blue

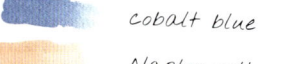
Naples yellow

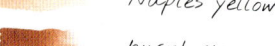
burnt sienna

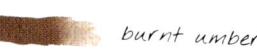
burnt umber

DABBING OUT

Create clouds by dabbing out colour from a wet wash, using a kitchen towel: a damp towel gives soft-edged marks, while a dry one produces harder edges (**A**). Another way is to lift out the colour with a damp clean brush, to create clouds and highlights.

CUMULUS CLOUDS

In this formation, lost and found edges form the masses of cloud. The top edges are hard and the lower ones are soft. The cloud base is straight edged on one level, as shown here (**B**).

HARD AND SOFT EDGES

Here, the cloud shapes were painted with clean water, and paint was applied into the wet area producing a sharp border at the edge of the wash, but a soft disappearing edge where it spread away from the hard edge into the cloud. Sample (**C**) is painted with a hard edge on the top, sample (**D**) with a hard edge on the bottom. Wait for each hard- and soft-edged wash to dry before painting the next. In sample (**C**), start with the top cloud wash and dry before proceeding with the next wash below. In sample (**D**) start with the lower wash, letting it dry before proceeding with the next wash above. The outer cloud edges of both where defined when the darker sky colour was applied.

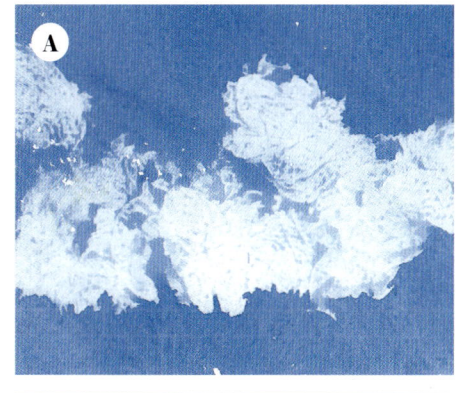

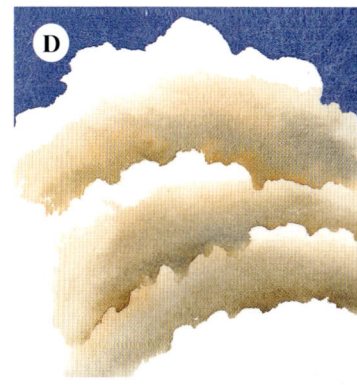

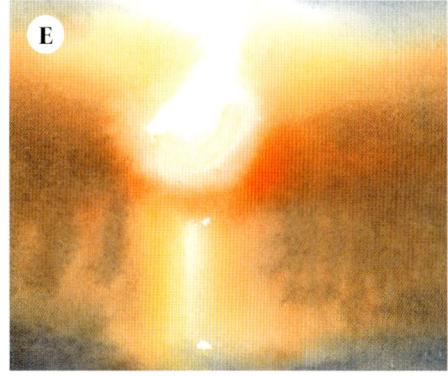

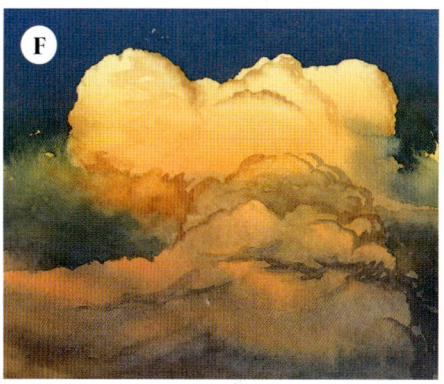

CAPTURING SUNSET

Keeping dry a large patch of light for the sun and a streak of light in the water, wet the paper. Working wet into wet, add the colours quickly, working from the lightest to the darkest and taking the colours to the sides of the paper. Rewet any hard edges and soften them. If the paint begins to dry, leave it to dry completely then rewet and begin again (**E**).

CLOUD FORMATION

A sense of the size of this mass of clouds is given by including the land just at the very bottom of the picture. The top of the cloud reflects the sun's light while the lower part is deep in shadow, further adding to the impression of size. The cloud colours for this painting were mixes of cobalt blue, yellow ochre and new gamboge (**F**).

Clouds – warm to cool

This sequence demonstrates how adding first warmer and then cooler colours to a basic yellow wash can produce different effects in similar shapes. Remember that colours tend to be warmer near a light source and cooler further away.

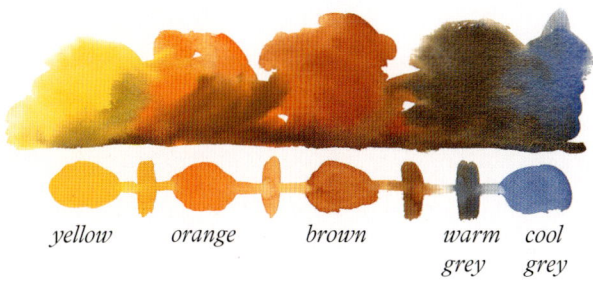

yellow   orange   brown   warm grey   cool grey

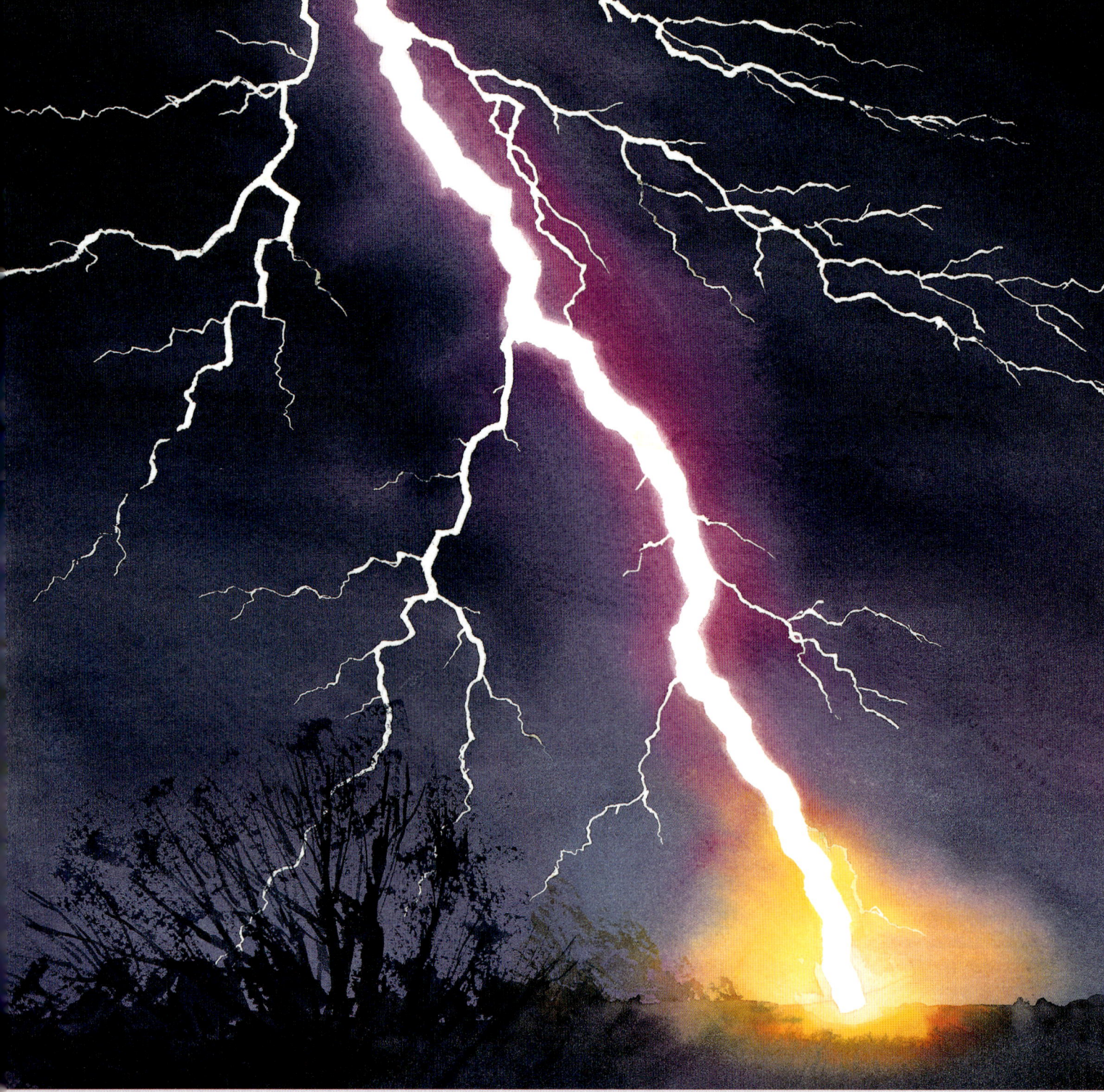

Lightning storm

Here is how to put the 'zap' into lightning. Lightning travels in a series of straight lines, each in a different direction as it follows the path of least resistance. Often a main central bolt has branches spreading off horizontally near its root in the sky, splaying to almost vertically downwards – exactly like an upside-down tree.

Artist insight: *In this scene, thick masking achieves energy, and heat stems from the deep violet-red. Lightening the colour along the track of the bolt creates glare; softening the edges energizes it further. Use this techniques for any intense light source. Colour round the base of the lightning bolt is paler and warmer – refer to halation. Dry-brushing achieved the tree effect.*

COLOUR PALETTE

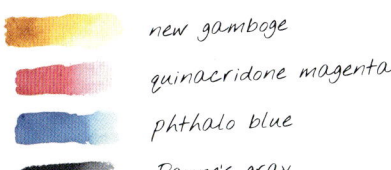

- new gamboge
- quinacridone magenta
- phthalo blue
- Payne's gray

Techniques: *lifting, pages 60–63; dazzle, pages 62–63; scratching out, page 83; masking, pages 46–47, 50–51, 110–111; sky (daytime), pages 54–55; sky (evening), page 109; sky (night), pages 110–111.*

PAINTING A LIGHTNING STRIKE

1 Mask the lightning using a narrow piece of card dipped in masking fluid. Add branches with a colour shaper. Make thinner branches with a pen nib, or scratch them out later. When dry, wet the paper and apply quinacridone magenta down the track wet-in-wet.

2 While still wet apply a dark blackish blue colour over the Image, avoiding the track of the bolt. Then let some of the dark colour spread across the bolt. Use a soft brush or a fan blender to blend the colour across a little. Let it dry.

3 Gently 'scrub' the edges of the lightning, working away from the masking fluid. The masking protects the white of the lightning bolt from any incursion of colour, but the scrubbing produces the shimmer. Remove the masking to reveal the bolt. Let it dry.

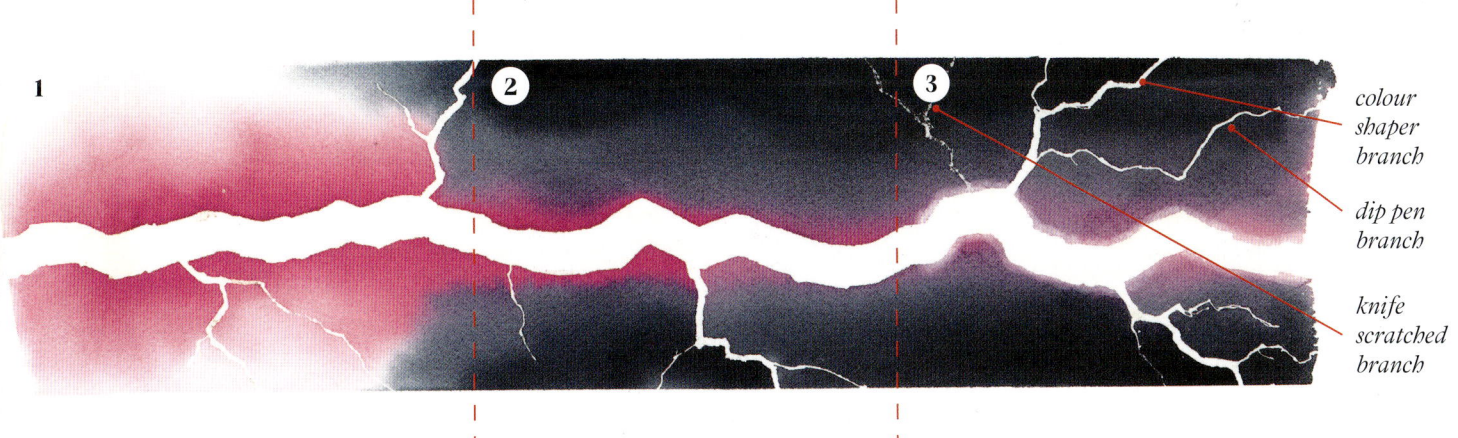

colour shaper branch

dip pen branch

knife scratched branch

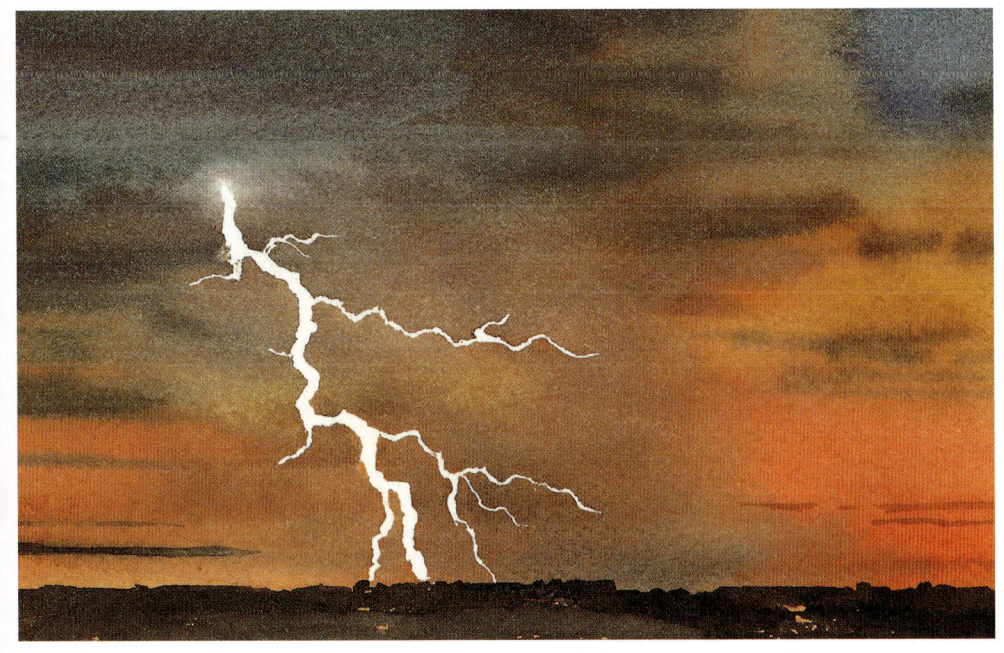

Lightning in the landscape

Here, the lightning is masked using a colour shaper, and left to dry thoroughly. The branches are masked with a pen nib. For this distant view the glaring effect of the shimmer is not applied, and the lightning is simply left as sharp focus. The intense dark in the cloud, the strong colour in the sky and the dark of the land all combine to contrast with the lightning. – if you want lightning to look bright you need the contrasts of dark tone.

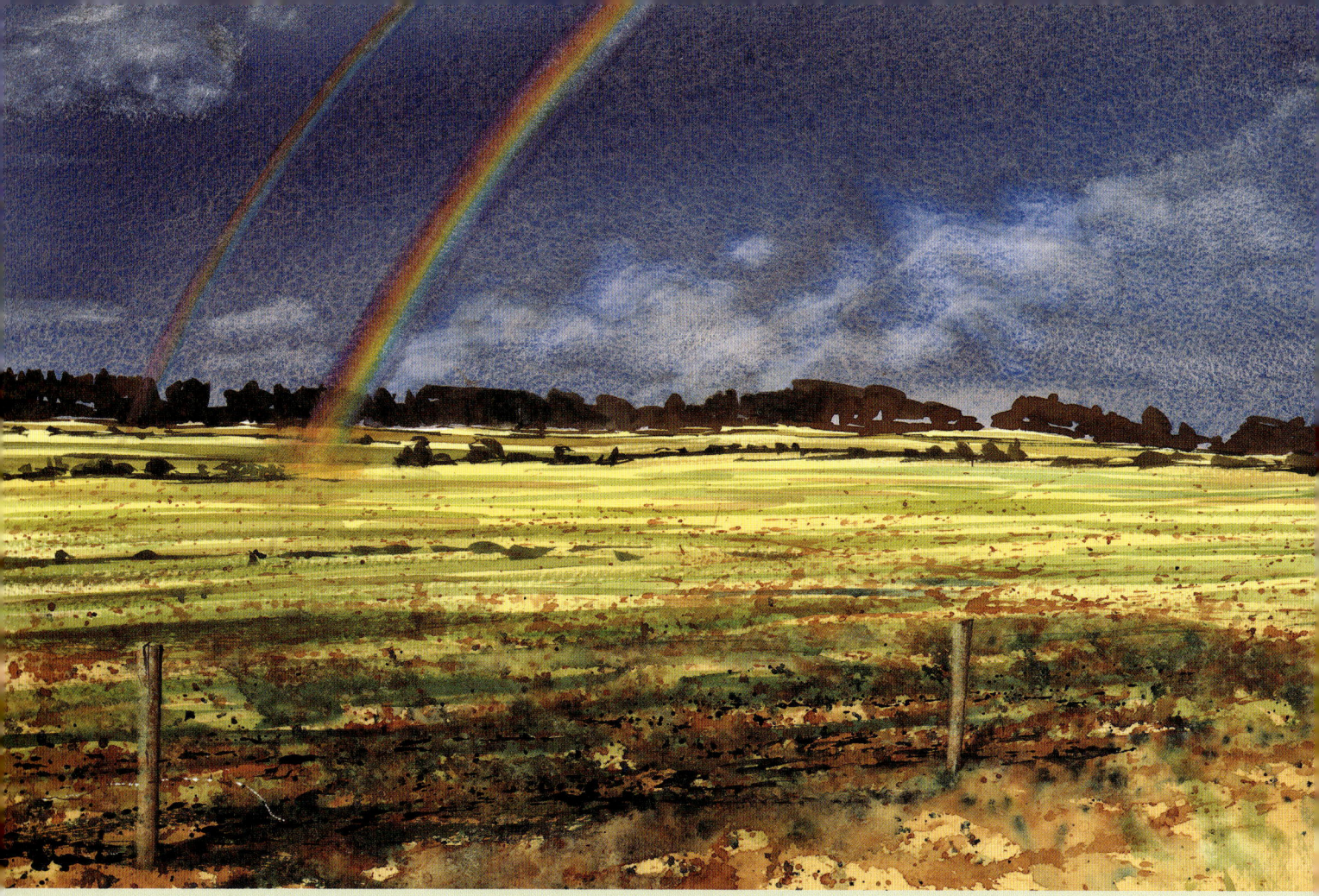

Rainbow

Rainbows usually appear with a backdrop of grey sky, from a passing rainstorm, very dark and violet. The land below the rainbow will often be alight with intense clear sunshine after the rain, so paint the land lighter than the sky. Here the rainbow shape is lifted from the grey-violet sky after the painting is virtually complete.

Artist insight: *If you are looking dead on at a complete rainbow, the sun is exactly behind. If you observe the right half of a rainbow the sun is over your right shoulder, and the left half, over your left shoulder. Any shadows and lights need to take account of this.*

Techniques: *skies, pages 54–55; wet-in-wet, page 18–19, washes, pages 18–21; mixing colour, page 22; mixing greys, page 23; fields, pages 30–31; landscape, pages 34–35; lifting out, pages 62–63, 66, 70, 93, 111; clouds, pages 56–57.*

COLOUR PALETTE

- cadmium lemon
- transparent yellow
- translucent orange
- quinacridone magenta
- ultramarine violet
- French ultramarine
- cobalt blue
- cobalt turquoise light
- green gold
- yellow ochre
- burnt sienna
- burnt umber
- indigo

PAINTING THE SCENE

1 There should be no pencil lines in the sky, so make the drawing on tracing paper and overlay it to get the rough position of the rainbow. You will still make some changes, or they will creep in.

2 Wet the sky. Paint a strong wash of 'lifting' colours: French ultramarine, quinacridone magenta and burnt sienna. Brush on ox gall for swirling cloud. Paint the land with transparent yellow. Overlay yellow ochre and burnt sienna in the foreground, and a little green gold wet-in-wet.

3 Paint the distant hilltop tree line with a 'dark' of French ultramarine and burnt umber. Spatter burnt sienna into the foreground horizontally from the side, working the brush up the image so the spatters are smaller in the distance. Spatter water over the still-wet foreground spattered paint, to make the area look more textured.

4 When dry, mix green gold, burnt sienna and yellow ochre. Paint in green lines on the field and spatter over the foreground, followed by dark spatters of indigo. Spray this with a short burst from a large water sprayer held about 50cm (20in) away. Just before it dries, drop in some large-grain salt crystals.

5 Using a soft, damp brush, lift the shapes of the rainbows by gently scrubbing the sky and down into the land in the distance. Remove the colour with a piece of kitchen towel, carefully keeping the two arcs synchronized. You can use your original tracing as a reference by laying it over the painting.

6 Place the colours in the rainbow – five is enough, or even three. Include a tertiary colour, such as cobalt turquoise light, to get across the feeling of the colours blending into one another, and the iridescence. The colours used here are ultramarine violet, cobalt turquoise light, cadmium lemon, translucent orange and quinacridone magenta.

7 Finally, the second rainbow is completed, and is pale and ephemeral. At the base of the main rainbow is a pool of orange light on the field, painted by wetting the field and running in translucent orange. The cloud is spread right across the sky using the lifting technique.

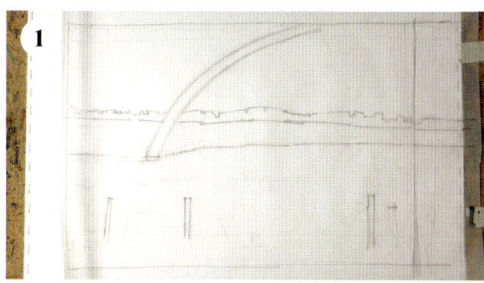

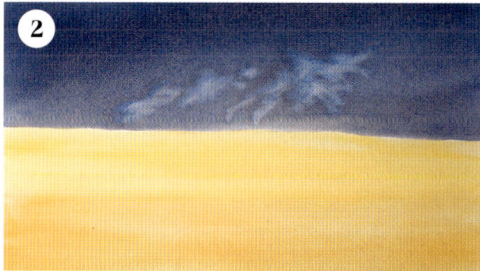

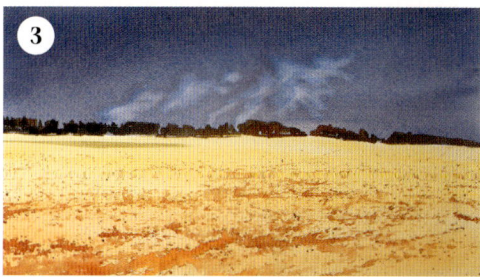

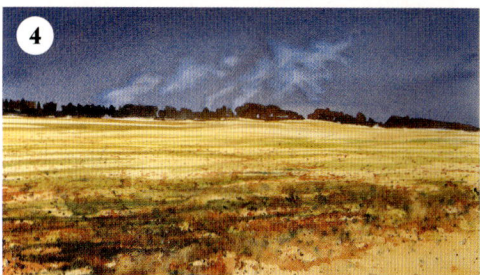

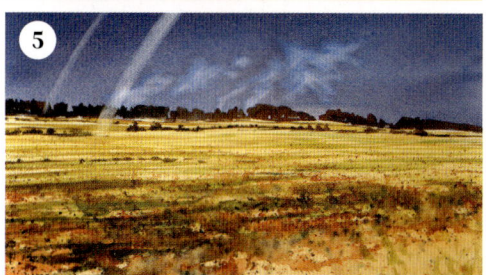

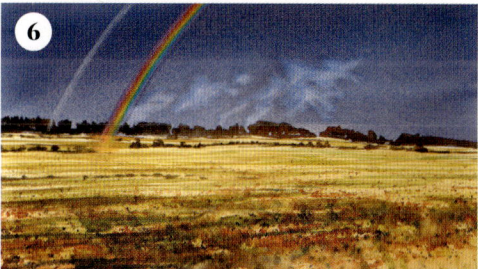

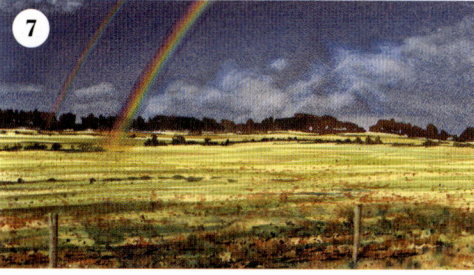

Colouring a rainbow

The rainbow is said to have seven colours; science tells us six primary and secondary colours. Most of us only perceive four or five. It's difficult to fit more than five colours across this space and keep them pure and stable. What is really needed? An elusive quality – iridescence. How do you get it? Not with great accuracy – just four or five vivid colours can give the needed iridescence.

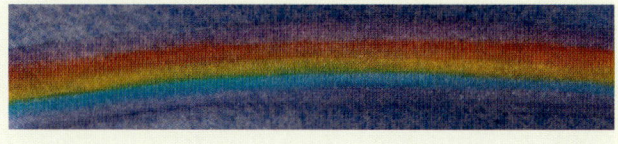

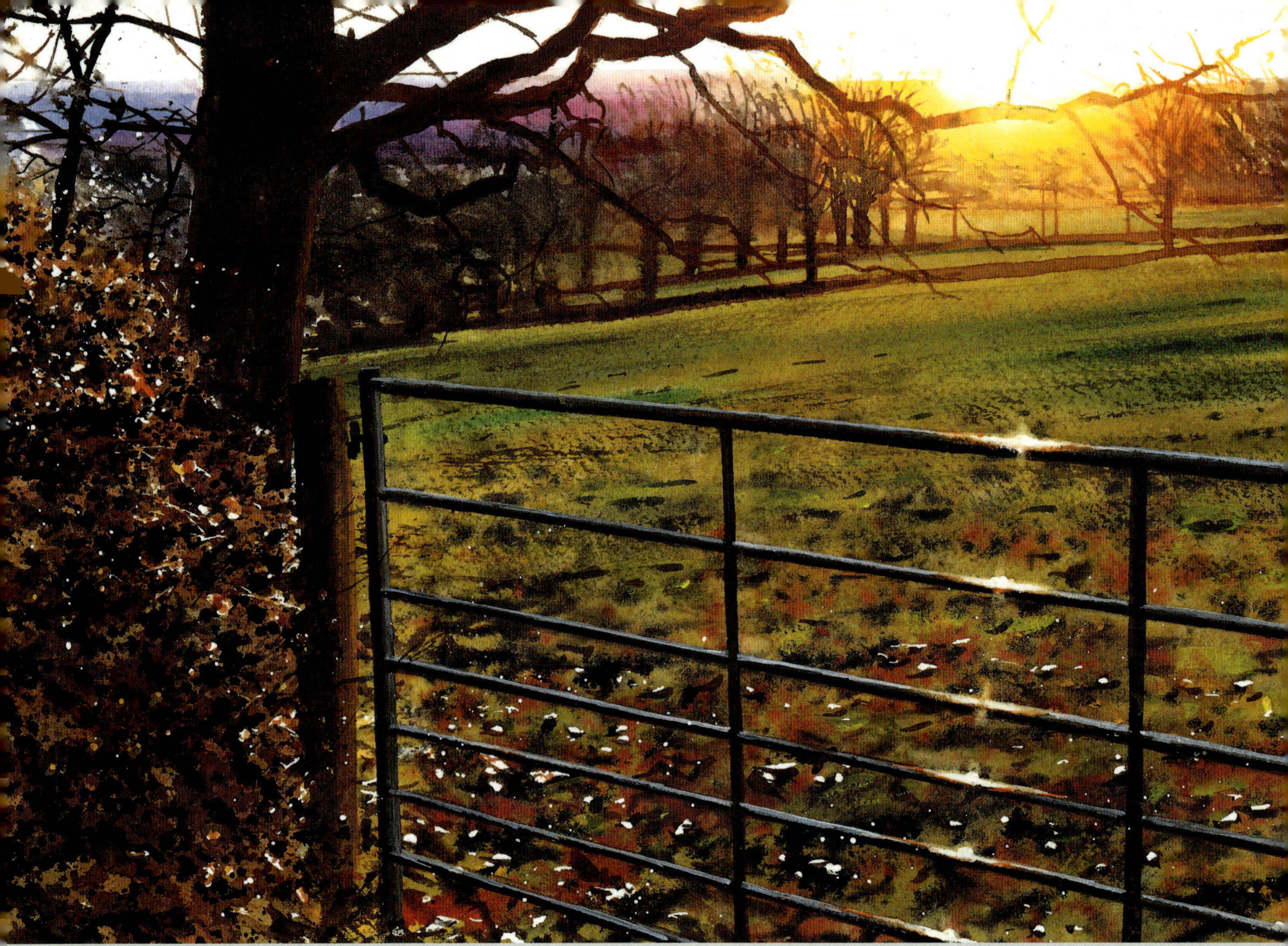

Sunset

For glittering lights and a blazing setting sun, carefully save the white, leaving a larger area for the sun than you think is necessary. The colour radiating out of the light source moves from warm to cool, and the effect contrasts bright colour with intense dark.

Artist insight: In this vivid autumn scene, strong tones balance bright colours, sometimes applied unmixed. I like to paint a scene looking through layers. There is the gate, then layers of field-edge trees, and an unfocused distance — the scene seems to go forever. The blurred glare provides a focal point, but not a point of focus, so the mind assumes the detail. Sun glints in the bushes and on fallen leaves in the field were masked. Twigs were masked with dip pen, and colour darkened with spattered Payne's gray.

Techniques: water feathering, pages 19, 74–75; low sunlight on meadow, pages 30–31; painting toward bright sun, pages 42–43, 50, 56–57; sunrise/sunset, glinting fallen leaves, pages 52–53 (refer to step 1); into sun, pages 38–39, 52–53, 56–57, 108–109; warm evening light, pages 82–83, 106–107; masking, pages 30–31; lifting (light glints), pages 30, 31; lifting, pages 92–93; warm to cool, toward the sun, page 57; field at sunset, pages 30–31; trees, pages 42–43, 52–53, 78–79.

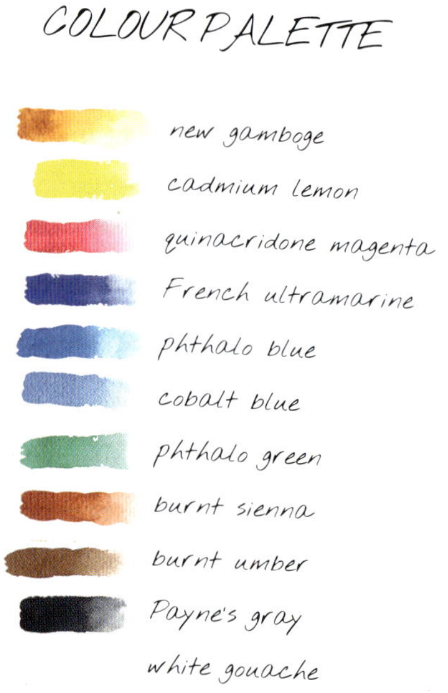

COLOUR PALETTE

 new gamboge

 cadmium lemon

 quinacridone magenta

 French ultramarine

 phthalo blue

 cobalt blue

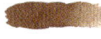 phthalo green

 burnt sienna

burnt umber

Payne's gray

white gouache

PAINTING THE SETTING SUN

Paint only the effect the sun has on colour – objects near the sun are almost invisible, pale yellow or orange like the branch in this painting. The colour sequence is white, yellow, orange and red, with darks to the edge.

1 Wet the land area, keeping the sun glare-area dry, and add a wash of new gamboge wet-in-wet. Keep the colour away from the sun area. This is the key stage to building in glare, the hottest of a sequence of colours radiating out from the central white zone, and the underlying heat in subsequent glazes of burnt sienna and quinacridone magenta

2 Paint darker colour on the field. Wet a halo around the sun and add new gamboge to the outside of it, keeping the inside soft focus. Add burnt sienna on the left, and further out quinacridone magenta. On the right, add burnt sienna. Run in a distant blue horizon of phthalo blue, keeping this to the left, merging with the quinacridone magenta.

3 In the sunset area brush the hedges in with burnt sienna, making them paler as they approach the sun. Add water into the edges of the sunset with dry-brush and brush the tree colour into this in thin strokes, letting the colour spread (water feathering). Darken the edges of the browns further away from the sun with burnt umber and a little Payne's gray.

4 Drag darker green across the field for a dry-brush, textured effect. Paint the big tree branches that lie across the sun in a pale yellow, using new gamboge. Adding burnt sienna a little further way, then progress to a more intense orange with strong mix of burnt sienna and a little quinacridone magenta. Finally add a dark mixed from burnt umber and Payne's gray.

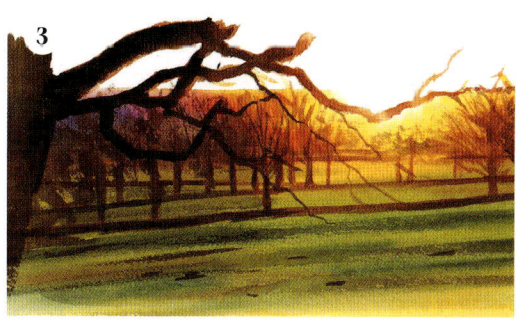

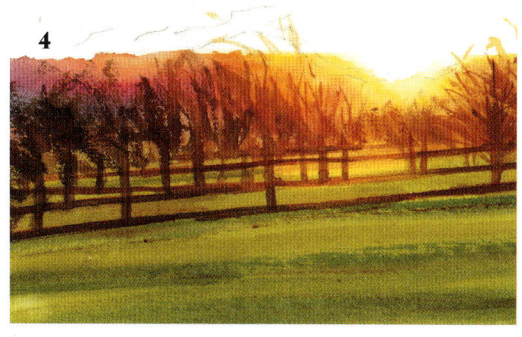

Painting glints

Where the sun is reflected in glints on the bars, gently scrub across them with a small, damp stiff-bristled or 'bright' brush to lift a ray of light then dab with kitchen towel. Remove the masked highlights. Touch in their edges with burnt sienna. Retouch the top of the bars using cobalt blue mixed with white gouache.

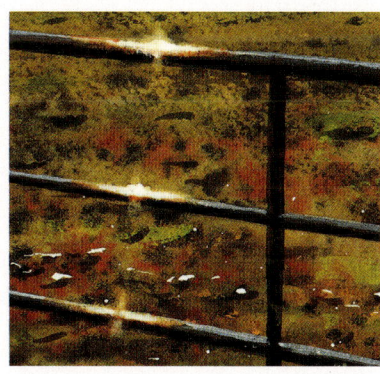

WATER FEATHERING AND ADDING WHITE GOUACHE

Brush water gently on the surface, so it just touches the bumps of the paper, glancing along them and leaving the dimples dry. Brush the paint from the point of a brush and it will take on a semi-diffuse look for tree branches spreading into twigs. Add white to colour for an opaque body colour to cover small areas of underlying dark.

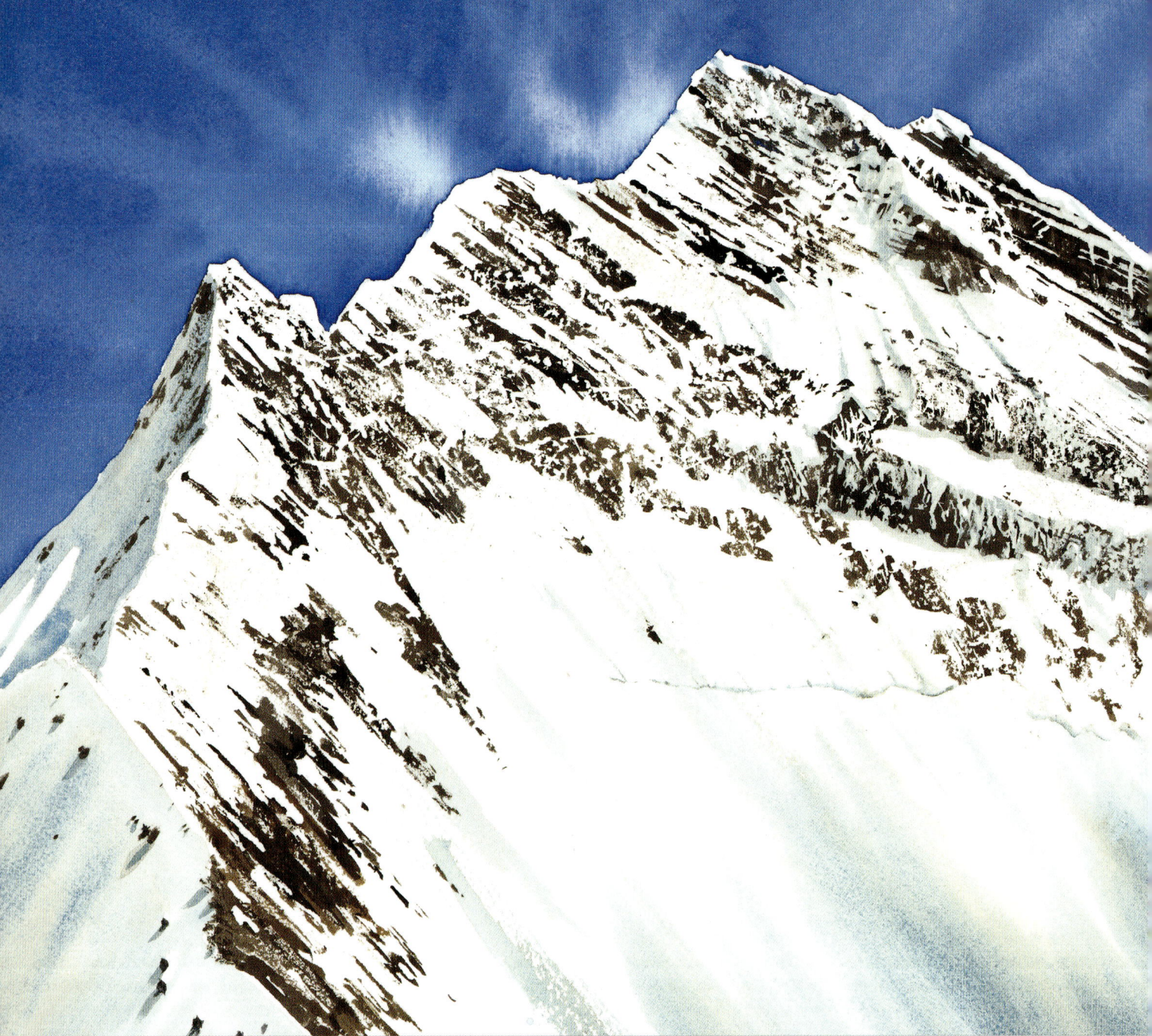

Snowcapped mountains

A mountain is a complex pattern of fissures and cracks, snow and bare rock, light tones and shadows, highlights and textures; chaotic, and yet logical – randomness within order. Painting positive space with colour over negative masked space achieves complexity; combined, they make texture. Brushmarks without masking, saved whites and dry-brush will all render mountains effectively.

Artist insight: *In the main painting, the sky was wet, but not to the mountain ridge. Colour stayed workable for long enough to take it up to the mountain edge in a smooth wash. The 'crown' of ice-crystal cloud was produced by a 'dropping' technique. Ox gall was 'dropped in' from the point of a sable brush touched onto the surface while it was still wet. The lower slopes are a mix of cerulean blue and burnt umber. Fine white marks were masked with a dip pen.*

COLOUR PALETTE

French ultramarine

phthalo blue

cerulean blue

burnt umber

neutral tint

Techniques: *lost edges, pages 56–57; mountains in snow, pages 66–67, 70–71; misty mountains, pages 68–69; mountainsides with trees, pages 40–41, 74–75; rocks, crags and cliffs, pages 36–37, 72–73, 88–89, 96–97, 100–101; wax candle texture, pages 37, 45; wet-in-wet, page 19; lifting out, page 111; snow, pages 114–115, 116–117; skies, pages 54–55.*

PAINTING A MOUNTAIN

1 After lightly sketching the mountain, wet it and paint the lower half with a mix of French ultramarine and a little added neutral tint. Lose the edge of this wash in the wet upper mountain – a lost edge. Deepen the colour at the base of the wash.

2 Paint the sky wet-in-wet, defining the mountain top. Mask untidy marks on the upper mountain with an old brush. The marks run horizontally here, with narrowing columns of lines going down the mountain before disappearing.

3 Dry-brush neutral tint, leaving more whites. Streak dark brush strokes for bare rock. Paint across the upper areas where they are masked, but leave the underlying colour unpainted further down.

4 Remove the masking. Notice that the mountainside running down to the right-hand corner was masked in streaks. The masking removes some of the underlying colour, which produces lighter tones that enhance the effect of snowy texture. Masking and colour interact to create realism.

1

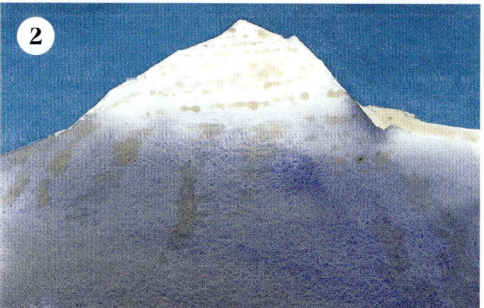

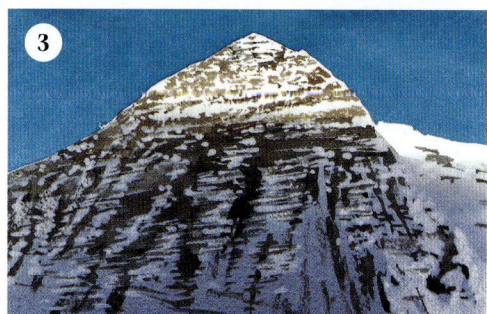

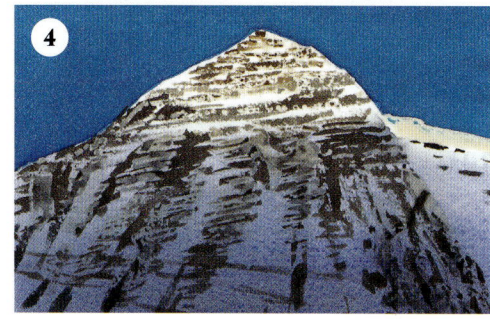

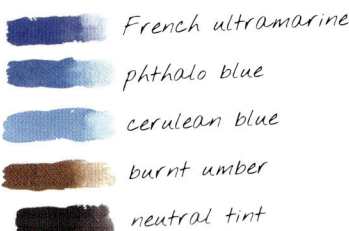

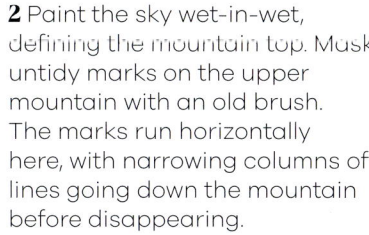

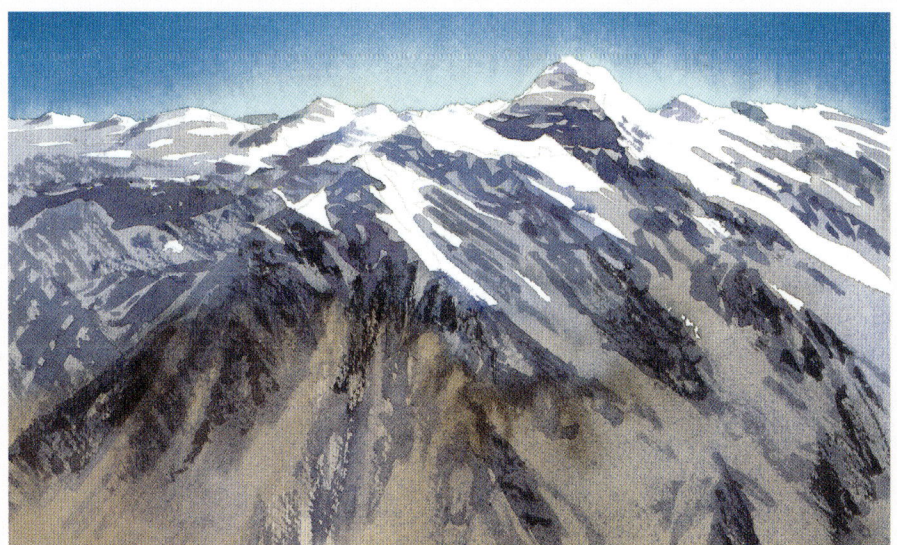

High altitude

Paint the sky and leave the mountains white. In this example (left), fine strokes of a light wash produce distant peaks and broader strokes linking to a single wash produce the near ones. Finish with darker washes.

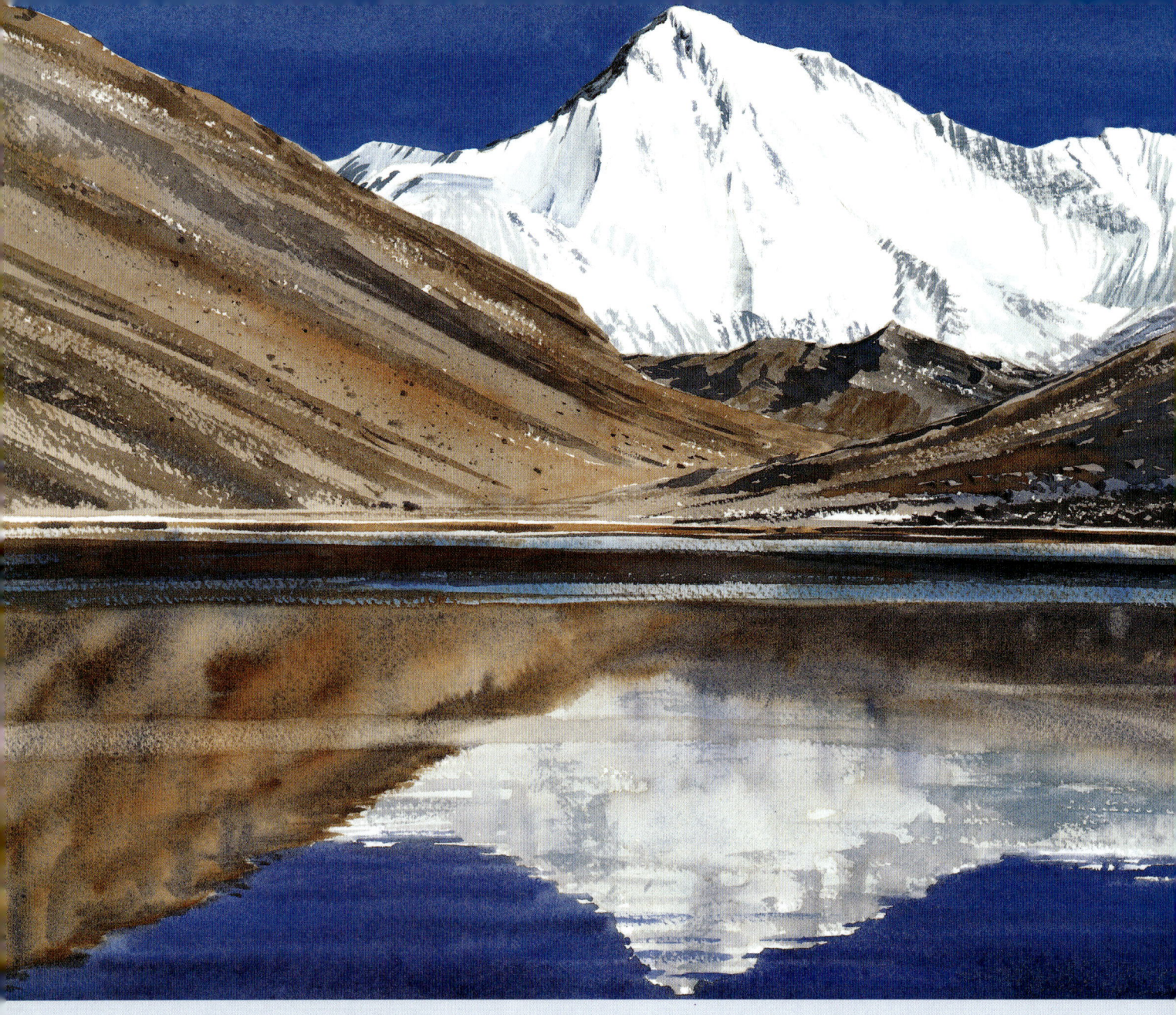

Mountain lake

High altitude mountains are fundamentally different from almost all other landscapes. The atmosphere is thin, affecting the way the light behaves. Some conditions give piercing light and severe blues, where the lack of haze makes a mockery of long distances. You can simply paint around the mountain with dense colour, yet it will have mass and bulk.

Artist insight: Here, the sky over Cho Oyu is a mix of phthalo blue and French ultramarine. Shadow on the snow is a mix of cerulean blue and light red, with darks of French ultramarine and light red. Foreground slopes of French ultramarine and light red reflect wet-in-wet, allowing vertical strokes to blend. The light mountain reflection and upper streaks are saved whites touched in with dry-brush work. Nearby streaks were lifted. Soft snow reflections are made by brushing blue into dry-brushed water, or water feathering. The light mountain reflection and upper streaks are saved whites touched in with dry-brush work. Nearby streaks were lifted.

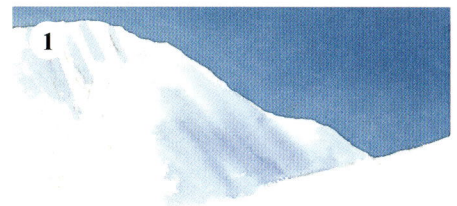

quinacridone red

French ultramarine

phthalo blue

cobalt blue

cerulean blue

raw sienna

burnt sienna

light red

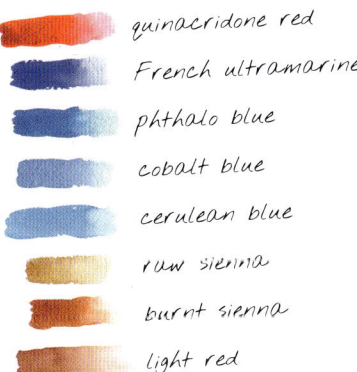

Techniques: *rocks and crags, pages 36–37; snowcapped mountains, pages 64–65; reflections, pages 70–71, 78–87; reflections (mass zone/ break zone), pages 78–79 (step 6), 87 (under 'Reflections and ripples').*

PAINTING A MOUNTAIN LAKE

The steps here suggest one way in which you could render the type of mountain lake scene shown here. Notice the reflection has a mass zone and a break zone. The mass zone is wet-in-wet. For the break zone, ripples are dragged off wet-on-dry. Colour is worked vertically in the mass zone and looks blurred. If texture is blurred and vertical it will look wet.

1 Paint the sky and lake with quinacridone red and phthalo blue wet-in-wet. Add a strong mix of this with burnt sienna to the foreground in a graduated wash. Paint the mountain shadows with a cobalt blue and burnt sienna mix. Mask some snow.

2 Streak the mountain with raw sienna with a little light red in places, saving the whites and lights of the previous wash. Drag some colour for additional texture. Brush some streaks of phthalo blue on the water foreground.

3 Brush a warm brown of quinacridone red, burnt sienna and French ultramarine on the mountain. Dry it and brush on a dark blue version of this mix. Run mountain colours into the reflection wet-in-wet and drag out ripples onto the dry paper below.

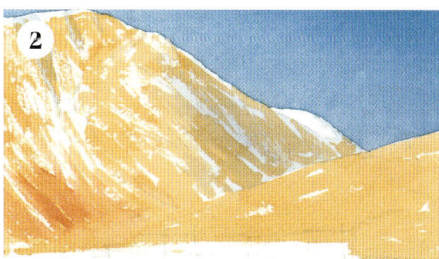

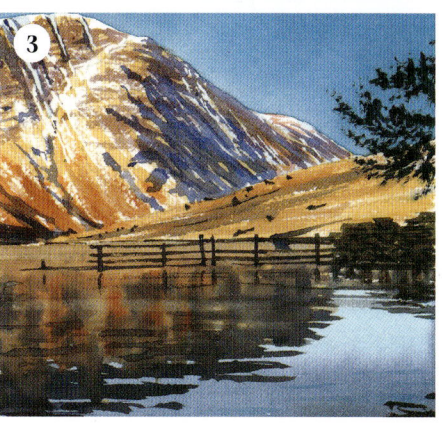

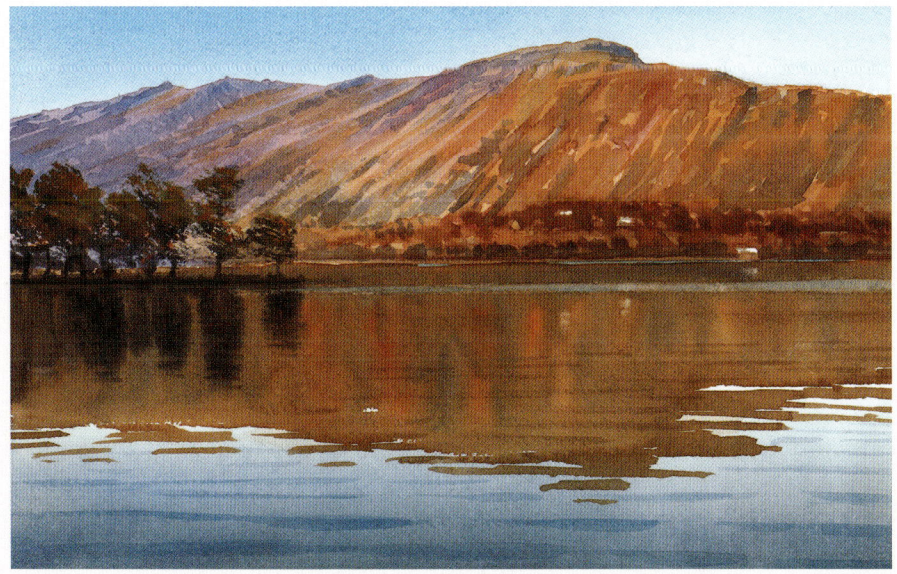

Flat reflections

To create the effect shown here (left) paint a lake with a wash of phthalo blue, quinacridone magenta and burnt sienna, fading in the distance. When dry, streak the mountain reflection vertically wet-in-wet. Add a little gum arabic to the paper, to 'stiffen' the mix, allowing colours to sit soft focus, yet separate – a very wet effect. Drag out the wet reflection area in ripples on dry paper. Brush on blue ripples.

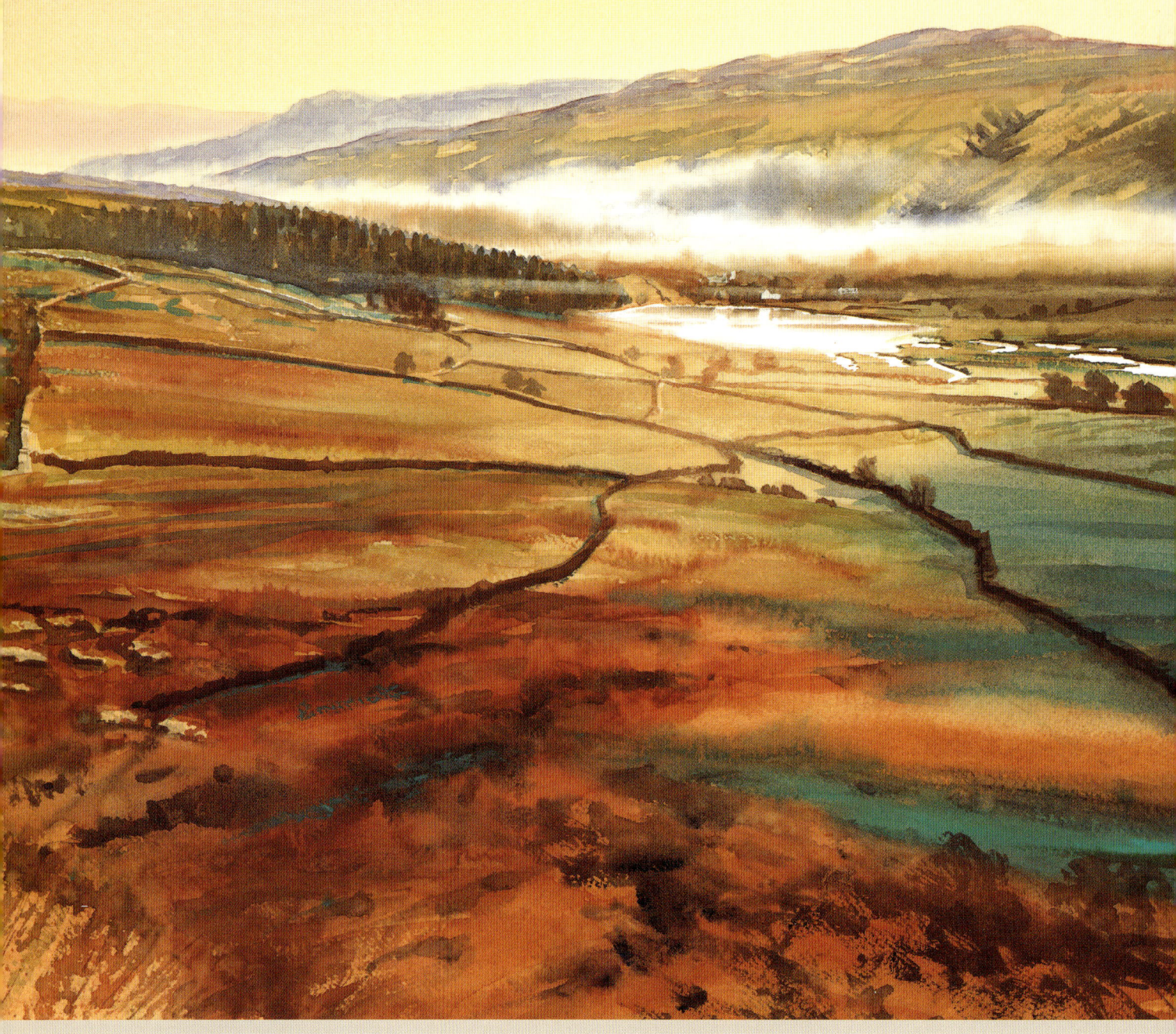

Misty mountains

To paint mist, save whites by wetting the paper and adding colour around them in soft-edged washes. Some mist has pale tone saved in subsequent washes; some retains its whiteness. Paint wet-in-wet to create the diffused edges of mist. Sparingly add brushstrokes of gum arabic to these areas for improved control.

Artist insight: After removing the masking fluid, final touches to this scene include painting distant mountains to the left, warm reflection greys in the water, dry-brush texture, and darks. A single mix of raw sienna and Naples yellow provides unity at the start. The ridges are a series of wet-in-wet washes, with hard edges above, and soft below. Violets and pinks are made with quinacridone magenta and French ultramarine, combining with previous layers or mixed with other colours. Variegated washes with spaces are painted for the distant rugged texture.

COLOUR PALETTE

- cadmium lemon
- quinacridone magenta
- French ultramarine
- cobalt blue
- Hooker's green
- Naples yellow
- raw sienna
- burnt sienna
- light red
- Indian red
- burnt umber

DEFINING AREAS OF MIST

1 Mask the water and houses. Apply a mix of raw sienna, Naples yellow and cobalt blue wet-in-wet to the whole image including the foreground, saving whites for mist. This image is unfinished and shows the process of applying colour from top to bottom. Allow to dry.

2 Apply mixes of cobalt blue and burnt sienna wet-in-wet for the ridges and land, leaving an additional area above the previously saved white mist area for a cream-coloured mist. Mask other light areas and features, such as here for the light edges of the field walls, to be saved.

3 Apply a mix of French ultramarine, Indian red and Hooker's green to the forest in the mid distance. Add cadmium lemon to the mix and touch this in here and there to help shape the trees. Brush French ultramarine and quinacridone magenta onto the distant hills.

4 Wet the mist. Apply a cobalt blue and burnt sienna mix wet-in-wet, saving some white. Brush onto the fields, adding Hooker's green in places. Add light red to the foreground. Paint dark detail and the shadowed parts of the walls, opposite the masked sides. Lift the mist band.

RISING MIST

The mist and mountain were both painted wet. The mist was painted yellow for light reflected from sunlit meadows, and the mountain was painted grey-violet The mountain dried first. The water from the mist invaded the drying wash, causing an accidental back run – an additional mist effect (**A**).

PAINTING MIST WITH WHITE

Although it is easier to paint mist by adding white, as shown in sample (**B**), it is better to use the technique sparingly. This method can lack the beauty of true watercolour, where saved whites look natural and transparent layers of tone are vibrant.

Techniques: *evening or dawn, pages 38–39; skies, pages 54–55; hard and soft edges, pages 56–57; sunset clouds, pages 56–57, 109; mountains with trees, pages 70–71, 74–75; mountains in snow, pages 64–65, 70–71; mist and fog, page 120; wet-in-wet, pages 18–19; lifting out, pages 93, 111.*

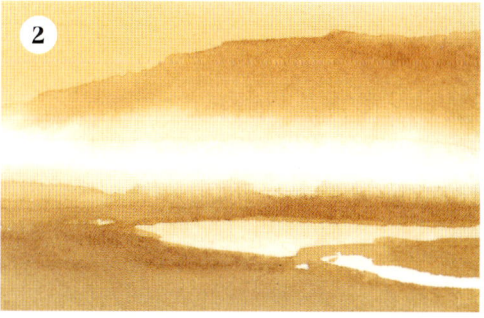

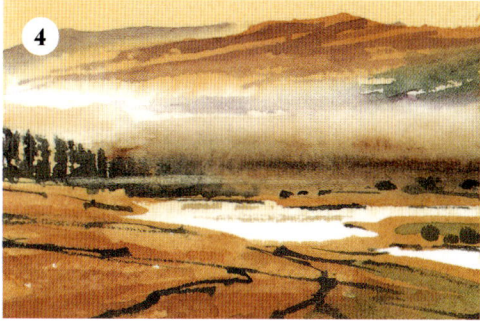

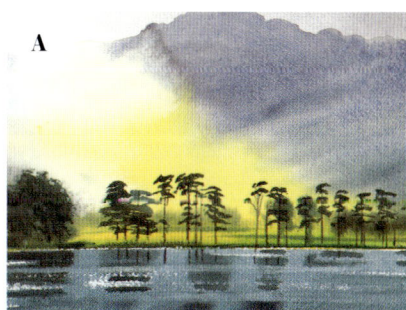

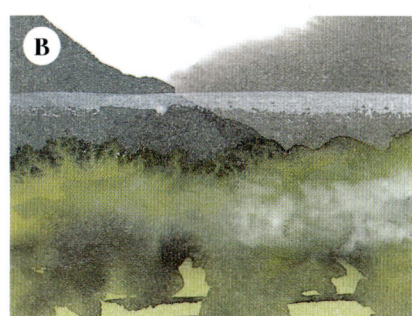

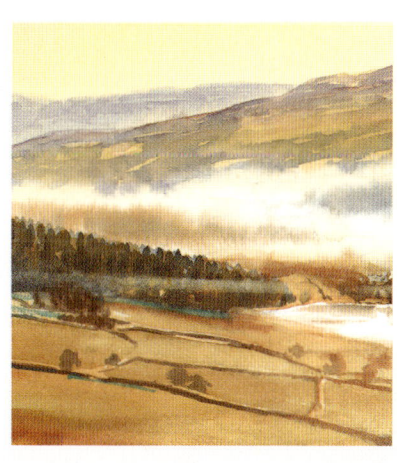

Misty mountains in cloud

Allow each layer of the painting to dry before proceeding to the next. Brush on water and 'let in' the colour for the subtle washes; these are contrasted with strong colour painted wet-on-dry. The forest is a series of brushmarks. Overpaint glazes of colour with brushstrokes of other colours to produce texture. Most of the mist can be left out or 'saved' in overlying washes, but lift the thin band.

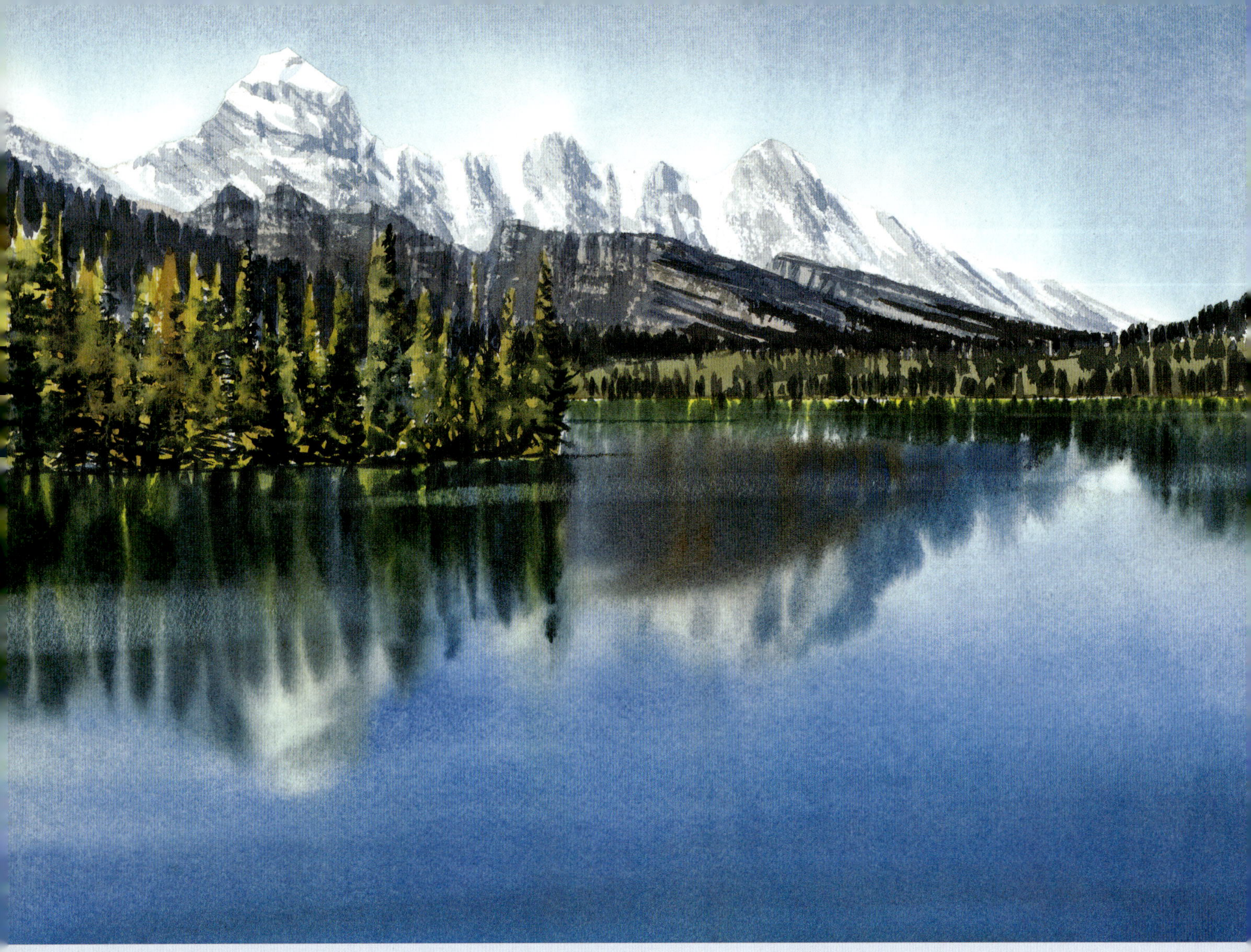

Tree-covered mountains

The lightest of touches achieves the massiveness of a distant range. If an object is pale and large the viewer visually reads it as being vast. A layered approach, with the lightest tones furthest away and the darkest nearest, gives the feeling of distance. Tone puts the visual message across more than colour.

Artist insight: Lifting scuffs of wind from the water in step 7 puts the surface on the wetness, giving it perspective. It is a useful technique for painting convincing water, and can even make water look wet when used as a single technique. Notice also a couple of dark lines on the surface; these are simplified — a shadow, a wildfowl trail, and a scuff of wind on the water.

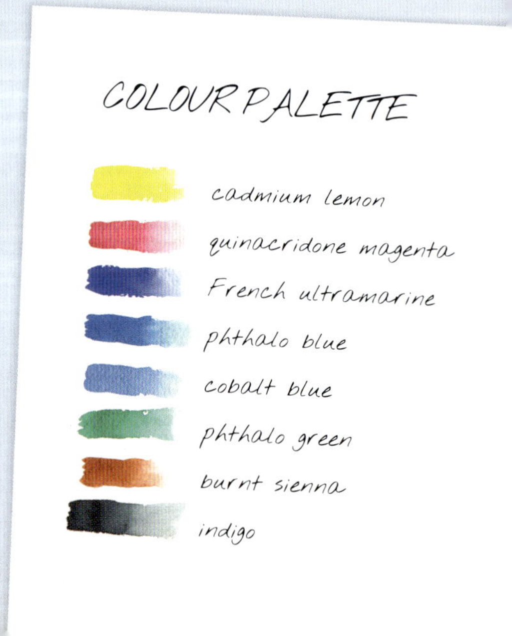

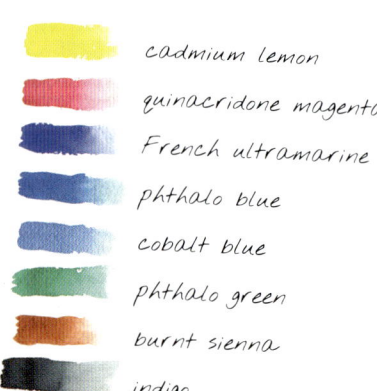

COLOUR PALETTE

cadmium lemon

quinacridone magenta

French ultramarine

phthalo blue

cobalt blue

phthalo green

burnt sienna

indigo

PAINTING THE SCENE

1 Make a simple drawing on tracing paper, retrace it in reverse and then retrace it through to watercolour paper, leaving a faint but precise outline. Wet the sky, but completely avoid all the mountain masses. Brush on a blue mix of phthalo blue, phthalo green and quinacridone magenta.

2 Dry-brush a pale grey-blue colour mixed from cobalt blue, quinacridone magenta and burnt sienna on the mountains. Make sure plenty of whites are saved on the mountains. Using the grey-blue mountain mix, brush a wash of this colour onto the nearer, lower mountain range, building the background tone for a nearer, stronger layer in the middle distance.

3 Mix French ultramarine, quinacridone magenta and burnt sienna, and dry-brush over the distant mountains and range below. Paint the trees and hills with various greens (see 'Mixes for tree greens'). Paint the nearest range with a darker mix of the mountain colour just used, defining the tops of the trees.

4 Use a wet-on-dry criss-cross approach, wet in some places and dry in others, by brushing water back and forth; then apply darks in roughly diagonal strokes for tree foliage. Brush in more darks in the lower mountains. Wet the lake and paint a little gum arabic around the mountain reflection areas. Paint from the bottom up with phthalo blue, burnt sienna and quinacridone magenta, avoiding reflection areas.

5 Brush a light yellowish wash onto the lake below the trees. While still wet, brush the mountain range colours into the water. Use vertical strokes of dark tone for the further tree reflections.

6 For the near tree reflections, brush in indigo, phthalo green and cadmium lemon wet-in-wet in vertical strokes, mixing the colours a little and also letting them mix on the paper. Brush in the darks wet-in-wet too. Some hard-edged lights contributed to the tree reflections. The blurred soft-focus vertical shapes give the impression of wetness.

7 When dry, use a damp brush to lift some scuffs of wind off the surface – a broad one nearby, a narrow band further away, and a fine one in the far distance.

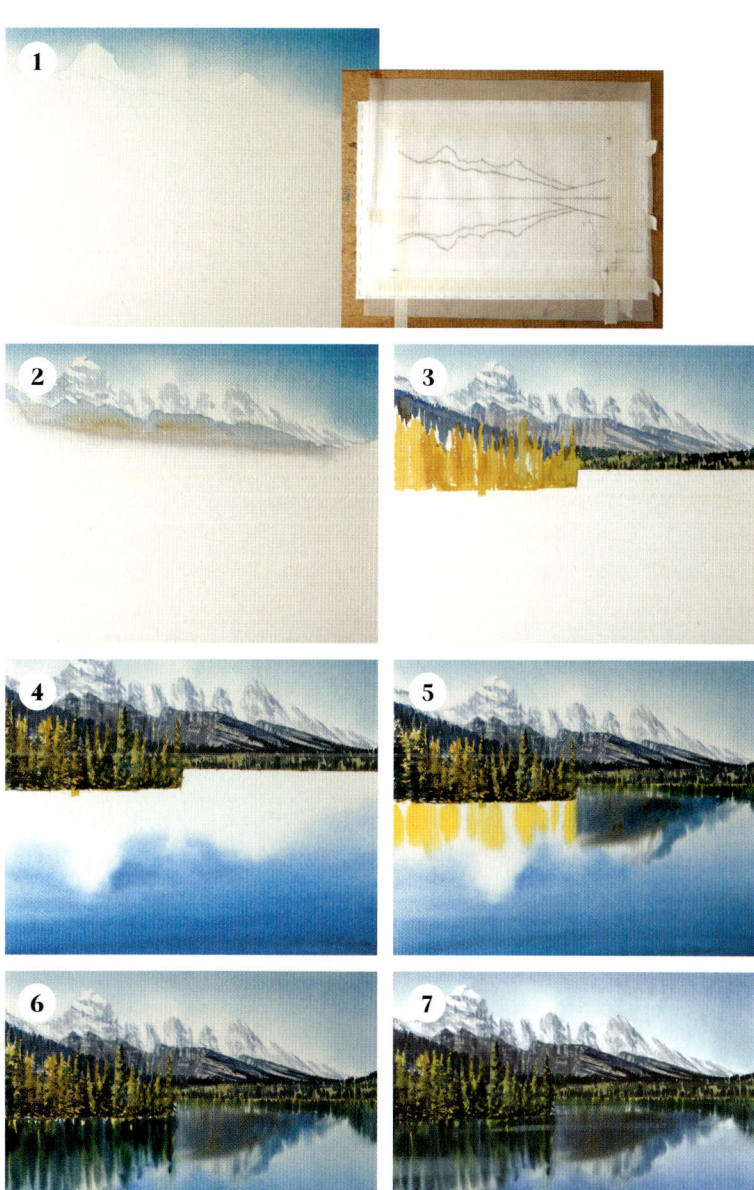

Techniques: wet-in-wet and wet-on-dry, page 19; dry-brush, pages 27, 65, 72–73; dry-brush/dragging, pages 37, 66–69; mountains (with trees), pages 40–41, 68–69, 74–75; mountains (with lakes), pages 66–67; mountains in snow, pages 64–67; reflections/soft focus, page 82, 106–107; reflections/ripples hard focus, pages 78–79, 86–87.

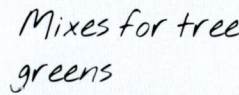

Mixes for tree greens

Lighter greens: cadmium lemon/a little phthalo green/burnt sienna.
Darker greens: cadmium lemon/indigo/phthalo green or cadmium lemon/ultramarine blue/burnt sienna.
Greys and greens: phthalo green/quinacridone magenta (add burnt sienna for pine/fir tree green).

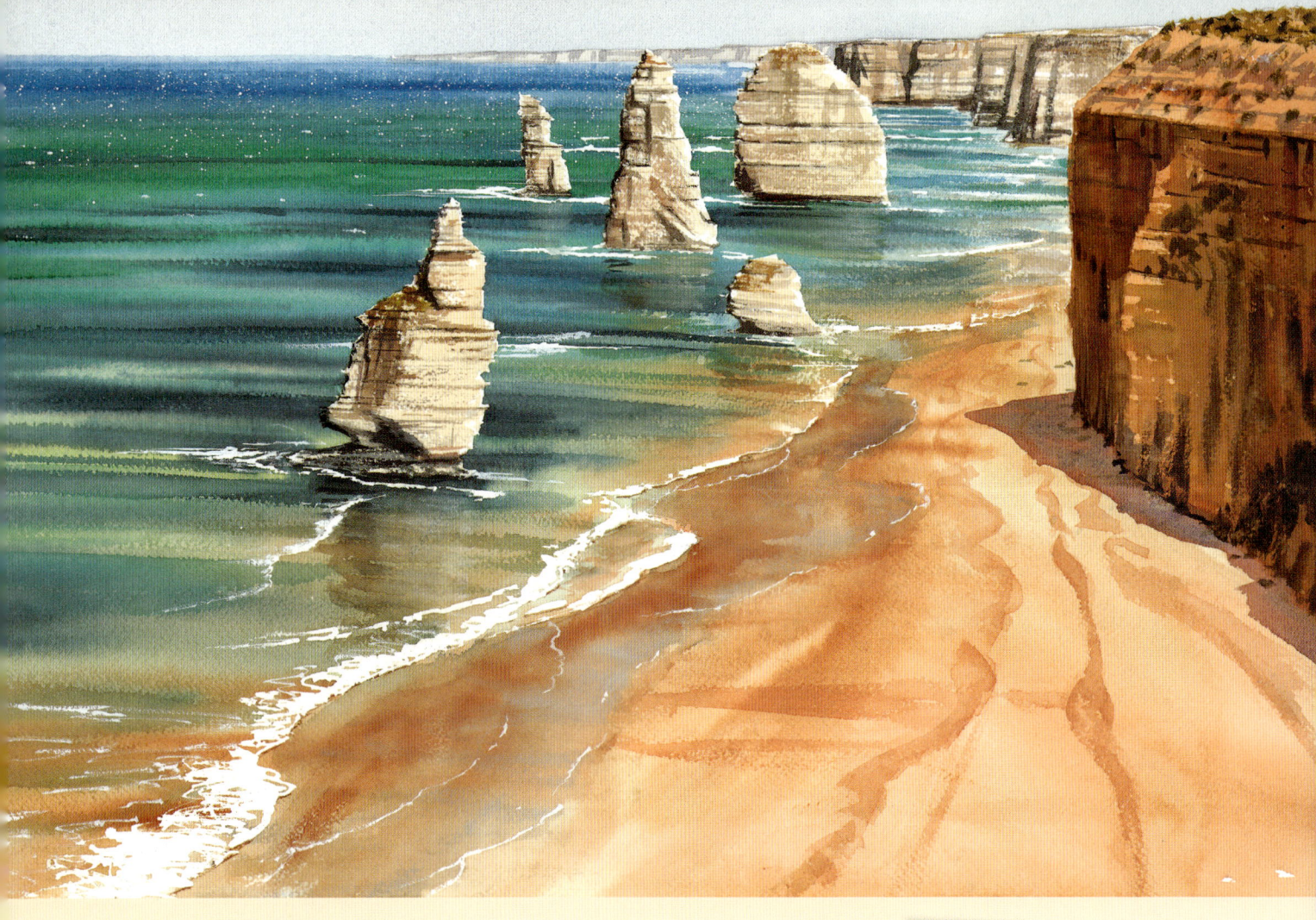

Rocky outcrops

With a vast ocean dragging acres of foam through shoaling reefs and past several freestanding rocks, masking fluid provides a solution to painting the sea and the rocks separately. Four light washes of colour are dragged across the rocks in succession to give the texture, with very little detail being modelled. Keep it simple.

Artist insight: In this scene, masking fluid was spattered from a toothbrush and brushed in streaks into the sea. The sea colours were worked wet-in-wet, including the darks of Indian red and French ultramarine. The foam trails were masked; at the end a little white paint was added on these, on some of the foam patterns and the fine breakers on the sand. Streaks on the sand were brushed with light red, and some cobalt blue with added white.

Techniques: *glazing, pages 20–21; dry-brush/dragging, pages 27, 37, 65, 66–69; rocks and crags, pages 36–37, 65, 67; rock face, pages 88–89; sea sparkle, pages 92–93; sea and beach, pages 96–97; cliffs, pages 96–97, 100–101; sky and sea, pages 98–101; saving lights in blue sea, pages 118–119.*

COLOUR PALETTE

- translucent yellow
- transparent orange
- cadmium red
- cobalt violet
- French ultramarine
- phthalo blue
- cobalt blue
- cobalt turquoise light
- phthalo green
- viridian
- green gold
- Naples yellow
- yellow ochre
- light red
- Indian red
- burnt sienna
- white gouache

Changing colours

The foreground cliff in shade had taken on a deep underlying tone that I rendered with yellow ochre and translucent orange. I 'calmed' this colour slightly with a grey of burnt sienna and cobalt blue. For shadow on the cliff face the colour was altered by adding cobalt violet in a transparent wash, leaving a few highlights. I carried this shadow onto the beach.

Painting rock strata

Paint the rocks with light washes, drying them each time. Washes are pale and transparent. Dry-brush the rocky texture. For a final touch, paint the cracks and fissures with the point of a brush in dark and very dark layers to build convincing rock strata.

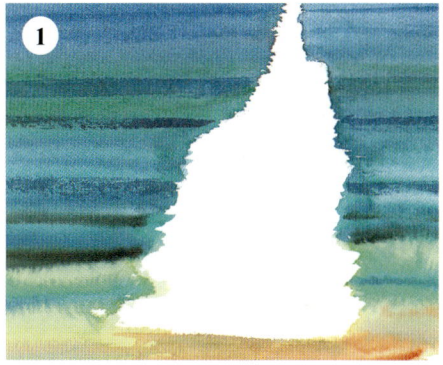

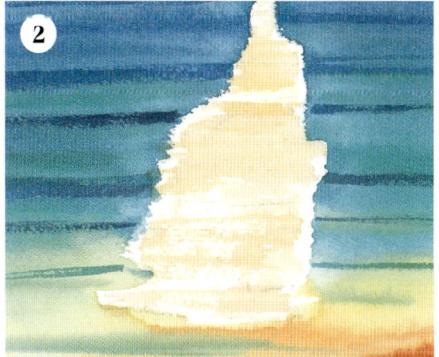

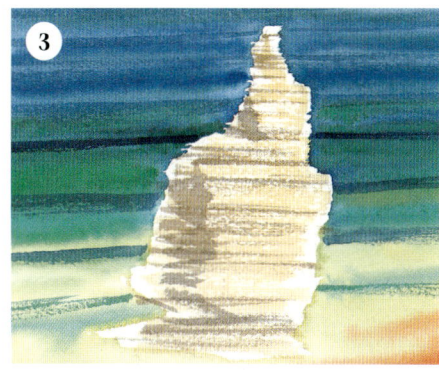

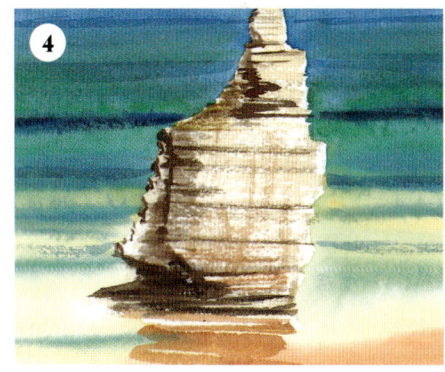

TWO TECHNIQUES

Masking these rocks allows you to paint the sea past them as though they are not there, giving a three-dimensional illusion. Alternatively, you can wet the sea area around the rocks, save their approximate shapes as dry paper and add colour to the sea. Draw the paint up to their edges. Edges can be modelled more finely with this method than with masking.

1 The rock is saved white here, but masked in the main painting shown, where the sky was painted in cobalt blue and cadmium red. A sequence of colours runs down, with phthalo blue, cobalt turquoise light, viridian, transparent yellow, Naples yellow with streaks of Indian red and French ultramarine, then Naples yellow and light red on the beach.

2 Brush the rocks with a pale wash of mixed burnt sienna and cobalt blue, leaving flecks of white. This provides the base colour of the rocks and is applied with a dry-brush technique, 'glancing' the belly of the brush along the surface. Leave the painting to dry thoroughly. Repeat the technique with subsequent washes.

3 Dry-brush a stronger wash of cobalt blue and burnt sienna, saving some more whites and underlying lights. Consider the directional strata. Here it runs across horizontally, with the brush being used in the same direction, linking all the rocks together. Try to follow the direction of the strata with your brush.

4 A medium dark wash is followed by intense dark accents. Endeavour to paint these with natural sweeps of the brush. First, dry-brush a wash of French ultramarine and burnt sienna. There are also accents of green gold and light red for plant life growing on the shoulder of this monolith. When dry, add intense darks with French ultramarine and Indian red.

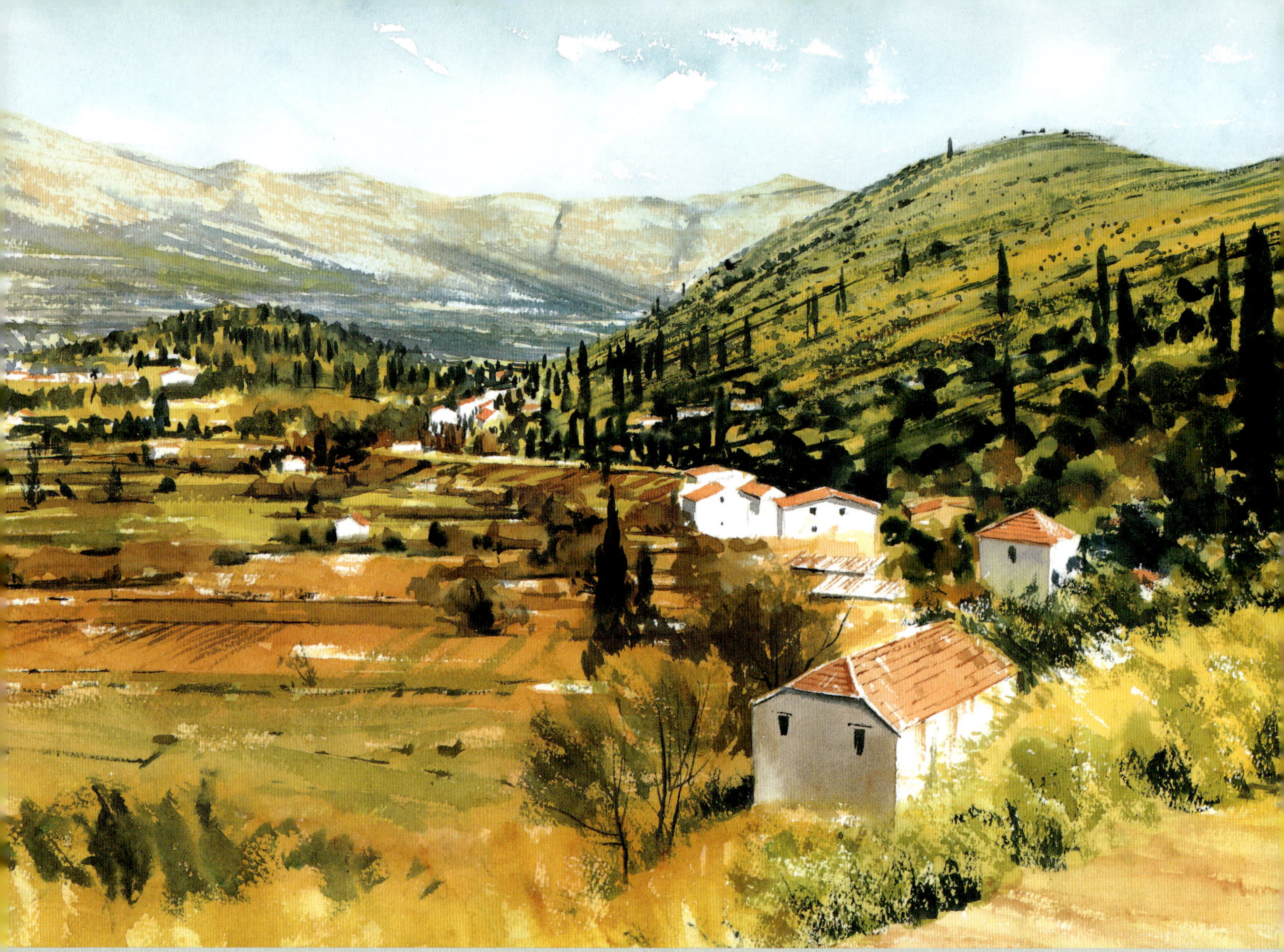

Mediterranean mountains

Fading blue-greys in the distance create a feeling of recession, enhanced by warm foreground colour. Do not work every area, but leave space and allow the mind to wander. Here detail emerges from successive loosely treated layers, but the tone runs the full range from dark to light and gives the painting strength, with many different greens giving variety.

Artist insight: Minimal foreground detail allows the eye to follow the houses and road into the landscape. The sky is painted like a veil dropping into the mountains. These are rendered with pale colour, and aerial perspective is applied by using warm foreground colours and cool distant ones.

Techniques: wet-in-wet and wet-on-dry, page 19; tree clad mountains, pages 40–41, 68–71; landscape, pages 26, 34–35; buildings, pages 26–27, 40–41, 114–115; aerial perspective and distance, pages 17, 26; skies, pages 54–55; dry-brush, page 27; water feathering, pages 62–63.

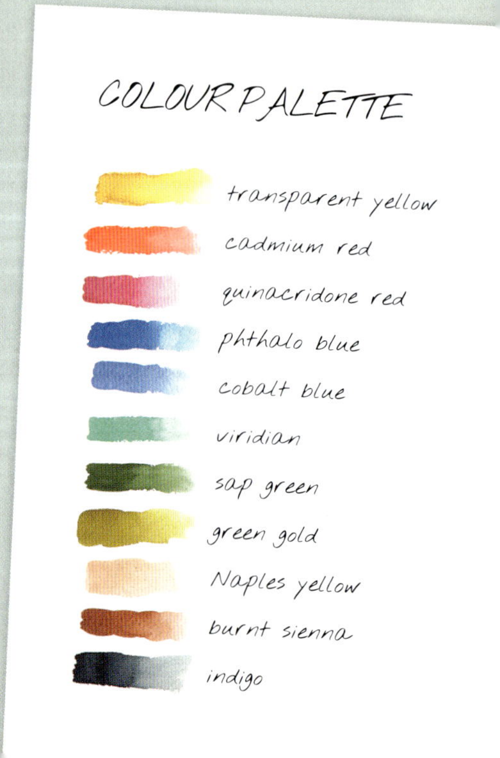

COLOUR PALETTE

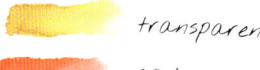

transparent yellow

cadmium red

quinacridone red

phthalo blue

cobalt blue

viridian

sap green

green gold

Naples yellow

burnt sienna

indigo

PAINTING THE SCENE

1 Create a blue-grey mix of cadmium red and phthalo blue, using a lot of water. Apply a rapid wash of this colour to the sky wet-on-dry, leaving flecks of white. Add some phthalo blue to the top of the wash to darken it.

2 Paint the distant mountains using a pale wash of cobalt blue, Naples yellow and viridian. When dry, use a water feathering technique – drag a damp brush across, leaving flecks of dry paper, and apply a mix of phthalo blue, viridian and quinacridone red for the shadowed gullies and streaks.

3 Build up the undertone of the land using transparent yellow for the mid distance, mixing it with burnt sienna. Use Naples yellow in the foreground. Leave white spaces in the distance and nearby white building shapes, and vary the tone and colour.

4 Apply more colour and add various shades of sap green and green gold, dragging them wet-in-wet and wet-on-dry across the distant and middle-distant fields in places. Drag warm colour of burnt sienna across the paper in the foreground.

5 Brush green gold on the slopes. Add streaks of mixed cobalt blue, viridian and quinacridone red, and marks of indigo wet-in-wet, but wet-on-dry for the cypress trees. Brush burnt sienna on the fields again.

6 Apply more field colour, and finish the edge details with darks. Dry-brush the foreground with green gold, burnt sienna and indigo mixes. Paint the roofs Naples yellow and quinacridone red. Paint shaded walls with cobalt blue and burnt sienna.

7 Brush in the windows with a strong mix of indigo. Keep the tops of the windows straight, but leave them a little unfinished at the bottom. Dry-brush the dark texture in the foreground with green gold, burnt sienna and a little indigo. When dry, dry-brush more indigo on top for the darkest tones. Use burnt sienna to start some of the roof detail.

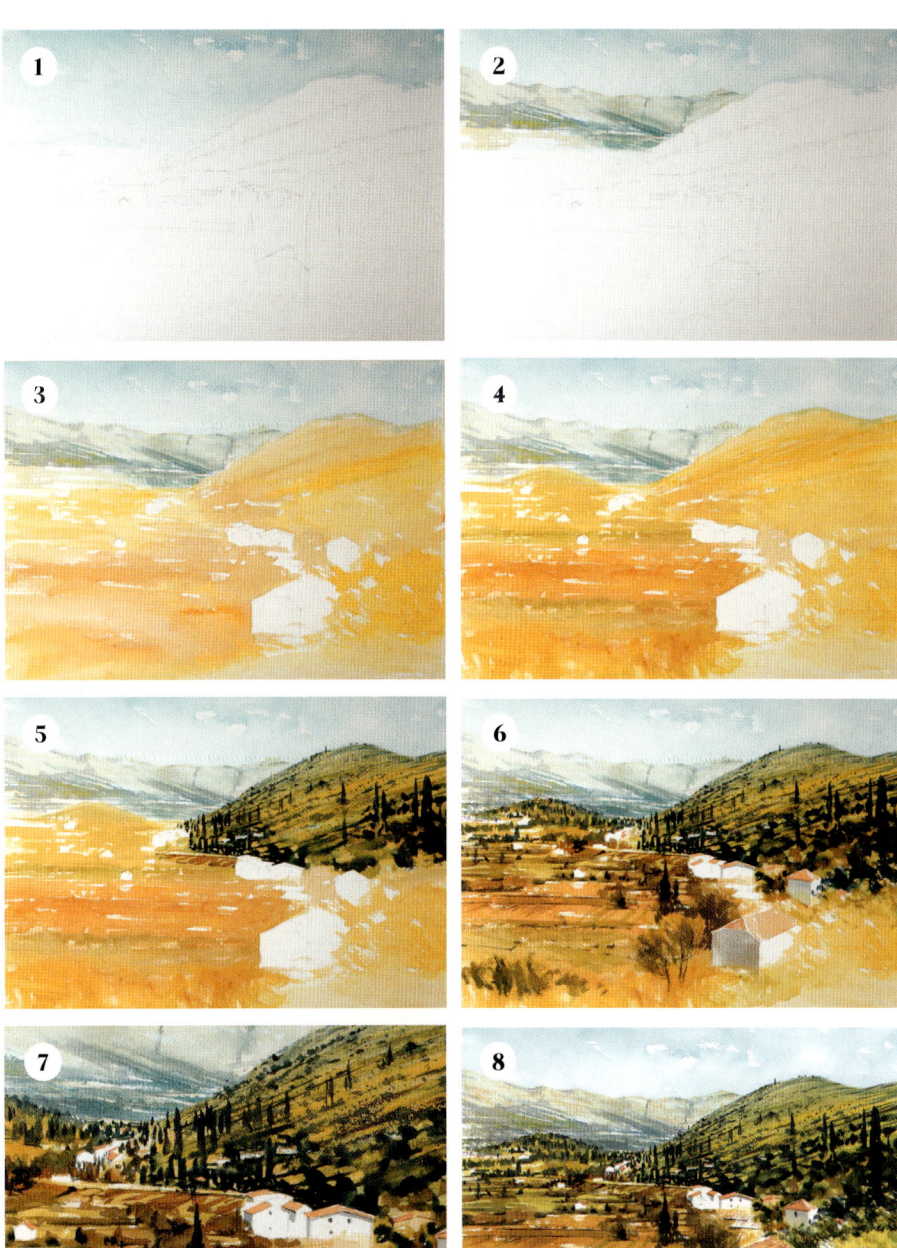

8 For the final stage of this landscape, the right-hand foreground was rewet with a dragged brush, and burnt sienna dragged across to place a surface. White spaces are left throughout the scene; masking fluid was not necessary. Extreme darks contrast with white paper. The painting was built up with successive glazes and many colours. This quick method is especially suited to working on site.

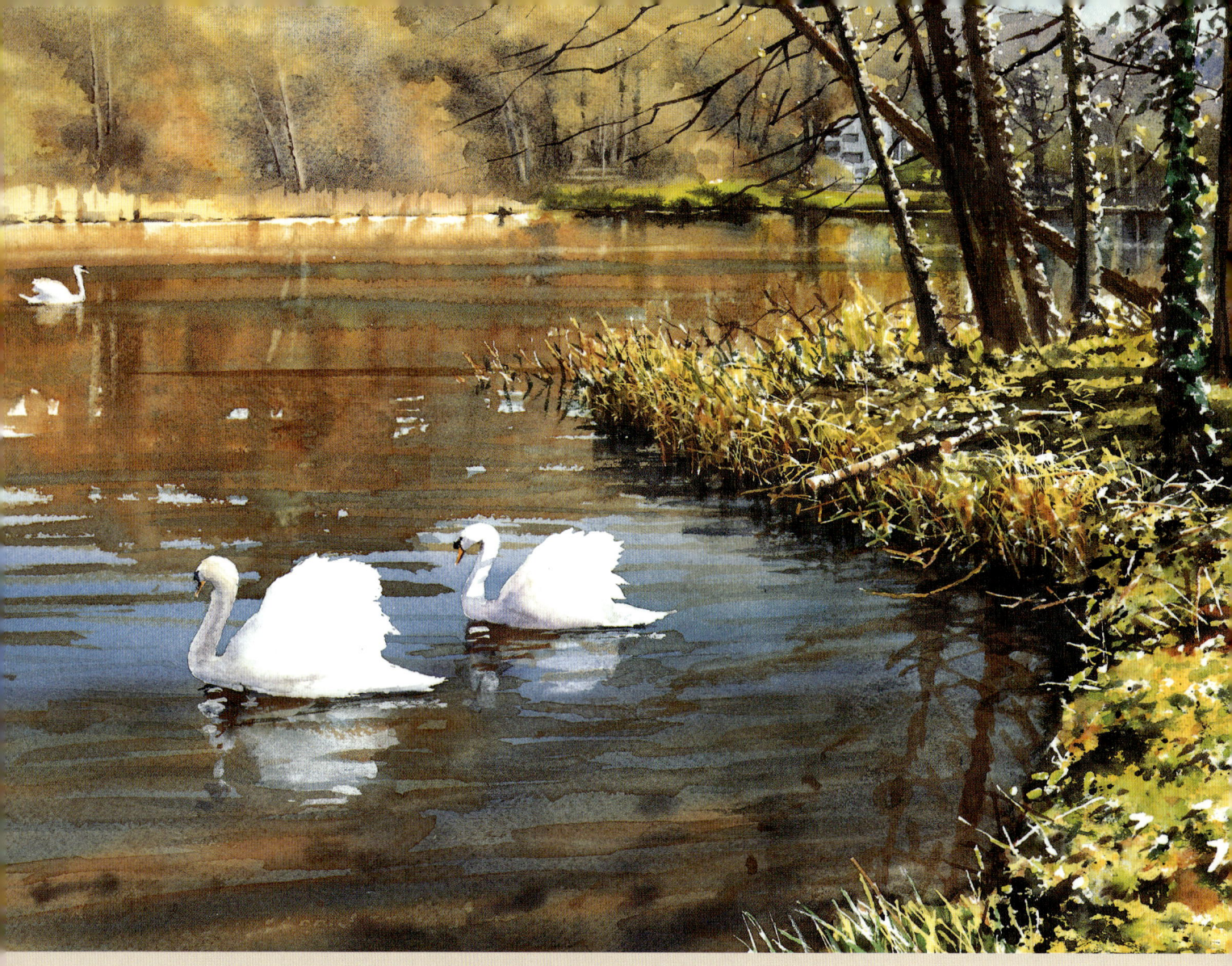

Lake with swans

The swans are not painted, but are masked at the beginning with a colour shaper and forgotten about, only to be unmasked near the end of the painting with just a little work to finish them. Masking allows you to brush colours across the silhouettes, so textures and washes create a naturalistic three-dimensional illusion.

Artist insight: In this painting, white gouache was applied sparingly in the swan reflections wet-on-dry. This is an example of using 'body colour' opaque white on its own or with colour to cover darker tone. Add blue-grey shadow colour to the white. Other colours were spattered, brushed or applied in flat washes. Cerulean blue was used in the distant areas to create a misty granulation, mixed in places with raw sienna, burnt sienna, French ultramarine, cadmium lemon and light red. Many colours were applied wet-in-wet, then left alone.

Techniques: masking objects, pages 30–31, 84–85; masking texture for nature, pages 26–29, 48–51, 116–117; lifted streaks/wind scuffs, pages 66–67; lake (mountain reflection), pages 66–67; reflection ripples, pages 42–43, 78–87, 94, 116–117, 122–123; trees, pages 42–43, 52–53, 78–79; grass, pages 97, 100–101.

COLOUR PALETTE

- new gamboge
- cadmium lemon
- quinacridone magenta
- French ultramarine
- phthalo blue
- cobalt blue
- cerulean blue
- phthalo green
- raw sienna
- burnt sienna
- light red
- indigo
- white gouache

PAINTING SWANS

Painting light over dark is less successful in watercolour than other mediums. Light objects that would otherwise require careful avoidance can simply be covered with a removable resist of liquid masking fluid, which dries hard. The process gives a beauty all its own. Use a colour shaper or small well-pointing synthetic brush to apply the masking fluid on the swan bodies and a pen for detail.

1 Mask the swans with a colour shaper. When the masking fluid is dry, apply the water wet-in-wet. In the main painting, the shallow foreground water is brushed with burnt sienna and darks are let in while still wet.

2 Brush the background reflection and swan reflections wet-on-dry. Add colour to the background reflection wet-in-wet. Though the swan is white, the reflection is dark because at the waterline the swan is silhouetted against the sky.

3 Remove the masking fluid. Apply a pale blue to violet-grey mix of cobalt blue, quinacridone magenta and burnt sienna to the shadow areas, and touch in stronger colour underneath. Touch in the bills with orange and accents of black, and the swan reflection with white gouache.

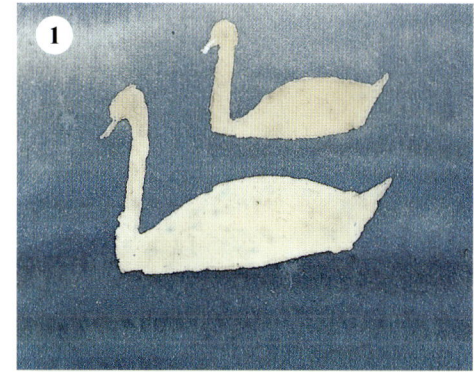

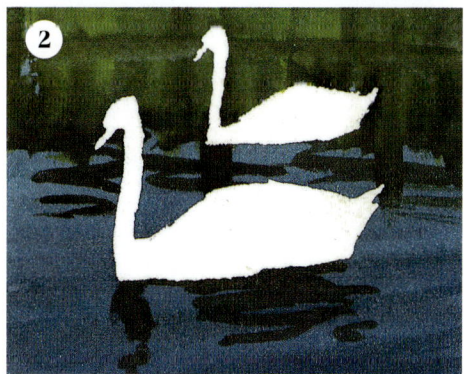

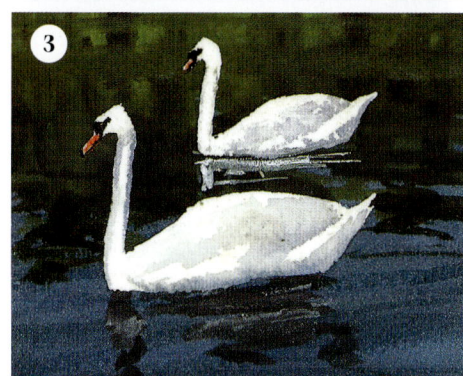

PAINTING WATER-EDGE GRASSES

Multi-layered masking has many uses. Apply the masking and paint in alternating layers, drying each stage before proceeding to the next. Use a pen to mask individual blades, only a few at each stage. They soon become a countless mass.

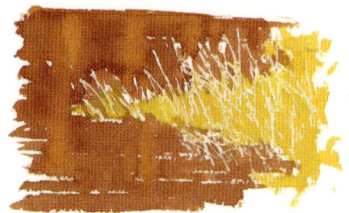

1a Mask the reeds with a dip pen. Drag a yellow green of cadmium lemon, burnt sienna and phthalo green; leave flecks of white paper. Brush the surrounding colour, leaving the ragged edge round the reeds.

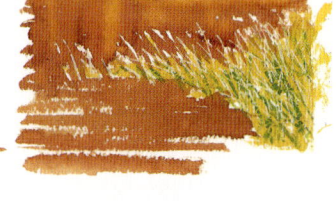

1b Apply a greener mix, dragging it again in a dry-brush fashion, and leaving underlying lights showing through. Mask more blades with a dip pen.

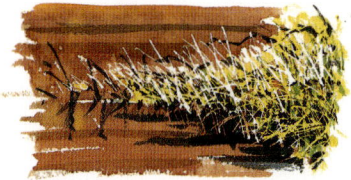

1c Roughly brush a darker and greener mix over the reeds. Mask more blades when the colour has dried.

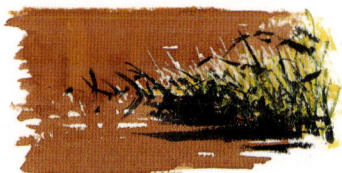

1d Brush untidy marks of dark indigo and phthalo green mixed. Use this for reflection ripples. Remove all the masking fluid. Touch colour into some of the saved whites.

Painting gentle ripples

To paint the water, begin with phthalo blue, quinacridone magenta and burnt sienna – blue and paler in the distance, darker nearer and with more burnt sienna in the foreground. Add dark marks to the foreground for underwater debris; blurred accents of partially seen objects. When dry, use the water mix to brush transparent strokes over the foreground water, and place the tree trunk reflections. Lift a few scuffs of wind on the surface and brush on other elongated accents. Lift some vertical trunk reflections with a damp brush and a piece of kitchen paper.

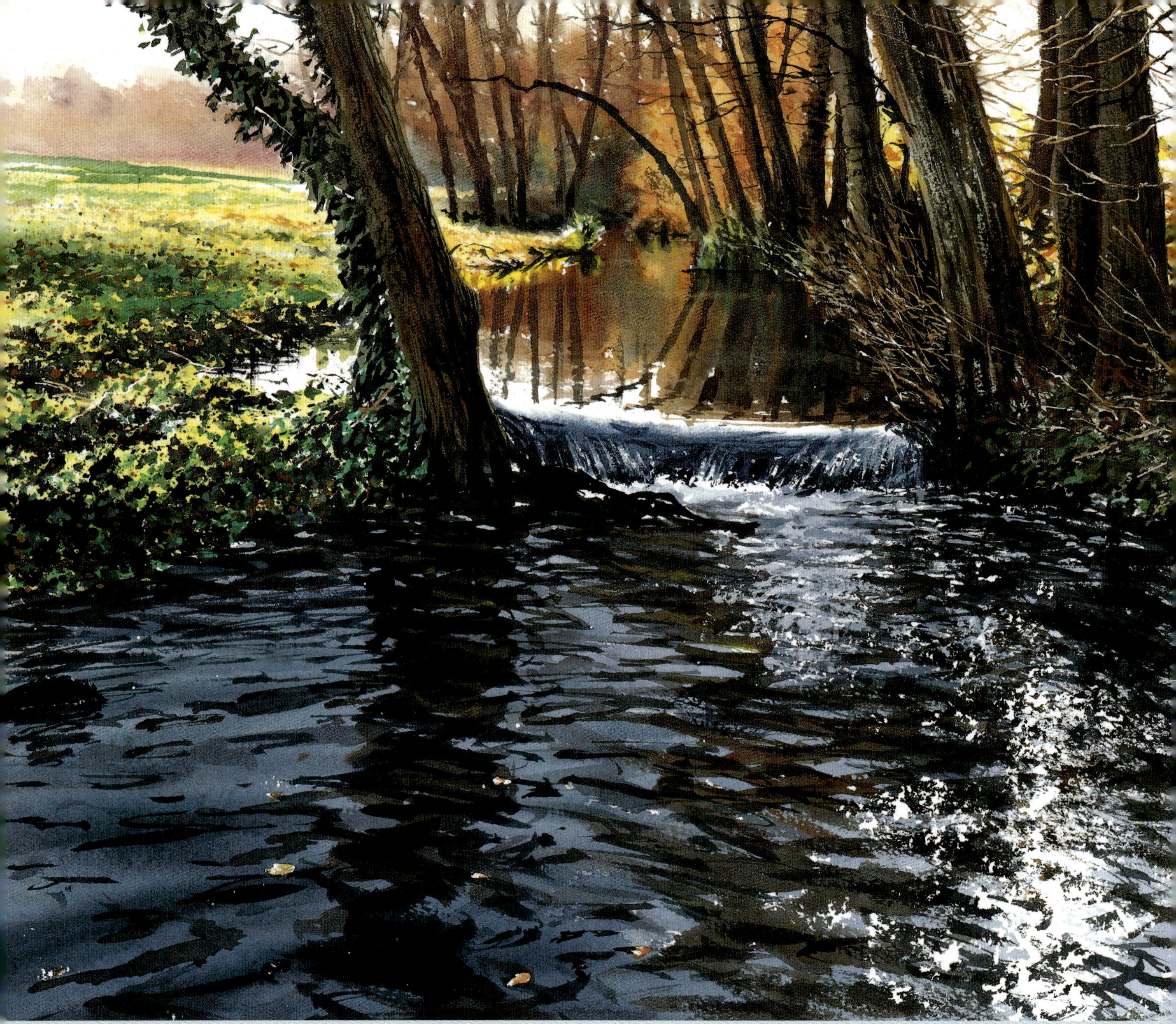

Flowing stream

This scene may seem complex, but you can make it much easier to paint by breaking it down into sections and working it one piece at a time. When you have finished one section, look away from it, then stand back; seeing the painting from a distance will often reward you with confidence.

Artist insight: *When painting moving water, keep the water washes separate. Work loose but be disciplined about saving the whites. Control the 'lost and found' waterfall edge and the white above it.*

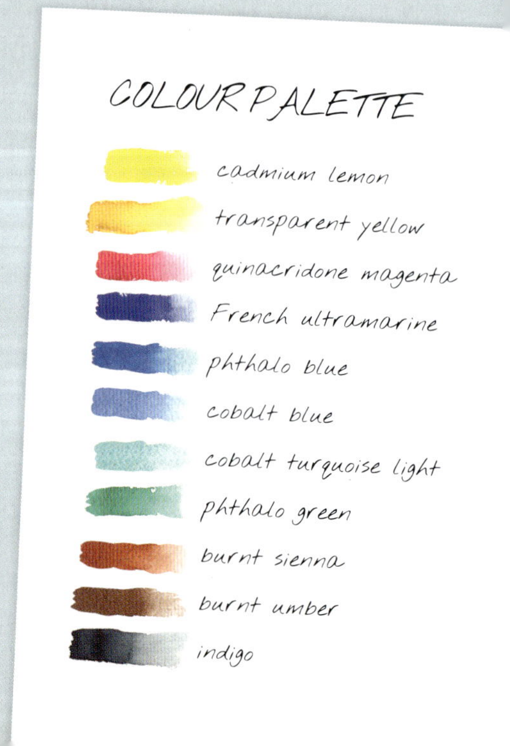

COLOUR PALETTE

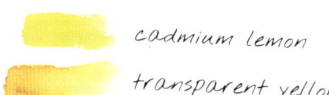

cadmium lemon

transparent yellow

quinacridone magenta

French ultramarine

phthalo blue

cobalt blue

cobalt turquoise light

phthalo green

burnt sienna

burnt umber

indigo

PAINTING THE SCENE

1 Mask branches and ivy, lights on the falls and floating leaves. Spatter toothbrush masking for woodland sky holes. Mask sparkles with hog-hair brush bristle tips. Spatter cadmium lemon on the grass. Brush transparent yellow on distant grass; burnt umber and French ultramarine mixes on trees; and quinacridone magenta, cobalt blue, burnt sienna, and transparent yellow on the distant hill.

2 Brush on a mix of burnt umber and French ultramarine for the trees. Spatter water over the damp trees to spread colour. Spatter water and then a green of phthalo green, cadmium lemon and indigo on the grass, brushing wet-on-dry in the distance. Spatter darks of indigo and phthalo green into the river bank, building this up and completing it in step 3.

3 Finish the trees. Apply a blue mix of phthalo blue, quinacridone magenta and burnt sienna below the fall, dry-brushing across the sparkles. Wet the top half of the reflection above the fall. Brush a little gum arabic. Apply dark vertical streaks of cadmium lemon and burnt sienna.

4 Working above the waterfall, with the paper dry, brush the trunk reflections wet-on-dry over the distant soft focus reflection. Add the blue mix to the fall from the base, wet-in-wet, letting it spread up into a lost edge. When dry, apply dark strokes for ripples in falls drop off. Scratch whites into the fall; brush darks into the ivy and bark.

5 Brush the ripples with the sky reflection mix. Dry it and brush more ripples with dark colour. Brush the roots below the fall and dry-brush ripples near the masked sparkles for texture.

6 Add more ripples, remove the masking, then touch in excess whites, some sparkles, and floating leaves. The 'reflection mass zone' is soft focus. Colour ripples off below this in a 'break zone' of hard-edged texture. For wet effects, apply mass zone colour blurred in vertical strokes. Above the water, transparent yellow gives warmth; difficult to use in smooth washes, it sinks into the paper. The base colour for the distant reflection area is cadmium lemon, which is easy to control and has covering power. Adding cobalt turquoise light to the distant trees gives recession.

Techniques: water feathering (trees), page 19; lost and found edges (hard and soft edges), page 57; ripples and reflections, pages 80–87, 94, 116–117, 122–123; sparkles, pages 42–43, 90–94, 108; water spattered foliage, pages 80–81; waterfall, pages 90–91; brush strokes, pages 20–21; trees, pages 42–43, 52–53, 84–85, 112–113; distant reflection area (mass zone), page 87.

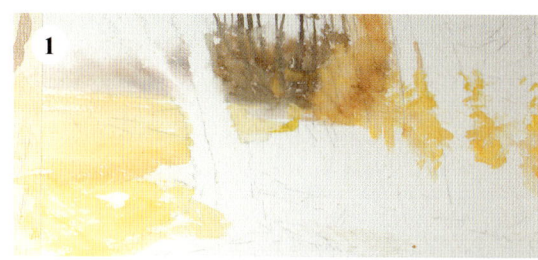

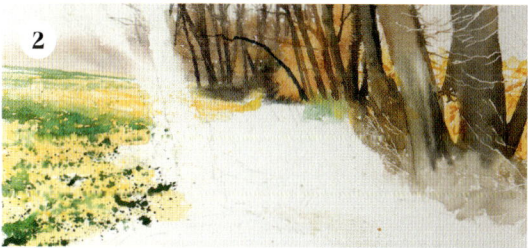

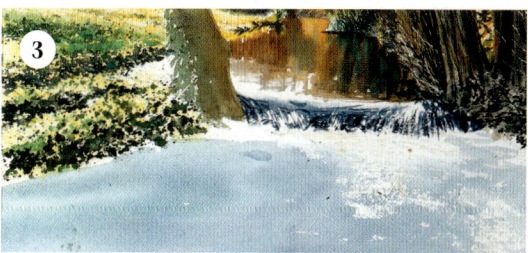

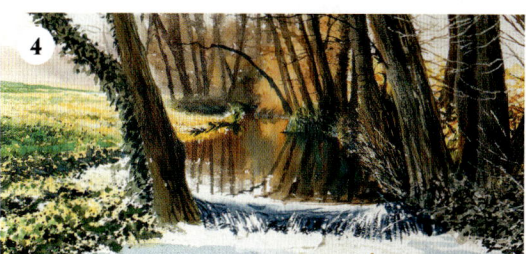

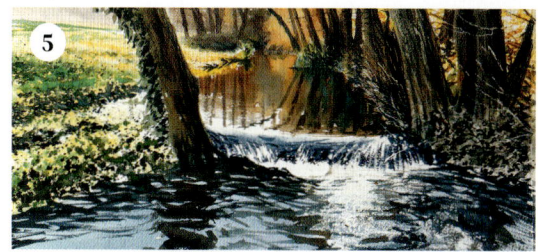

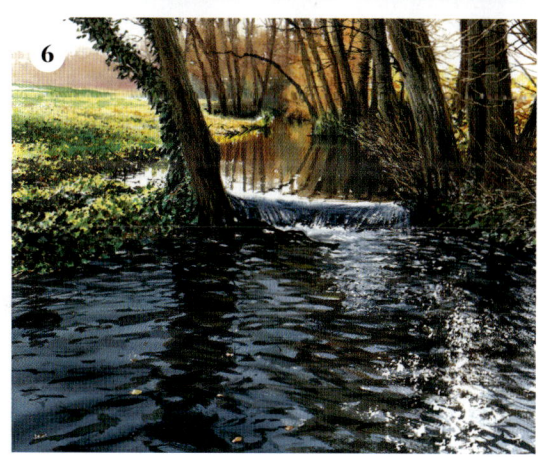

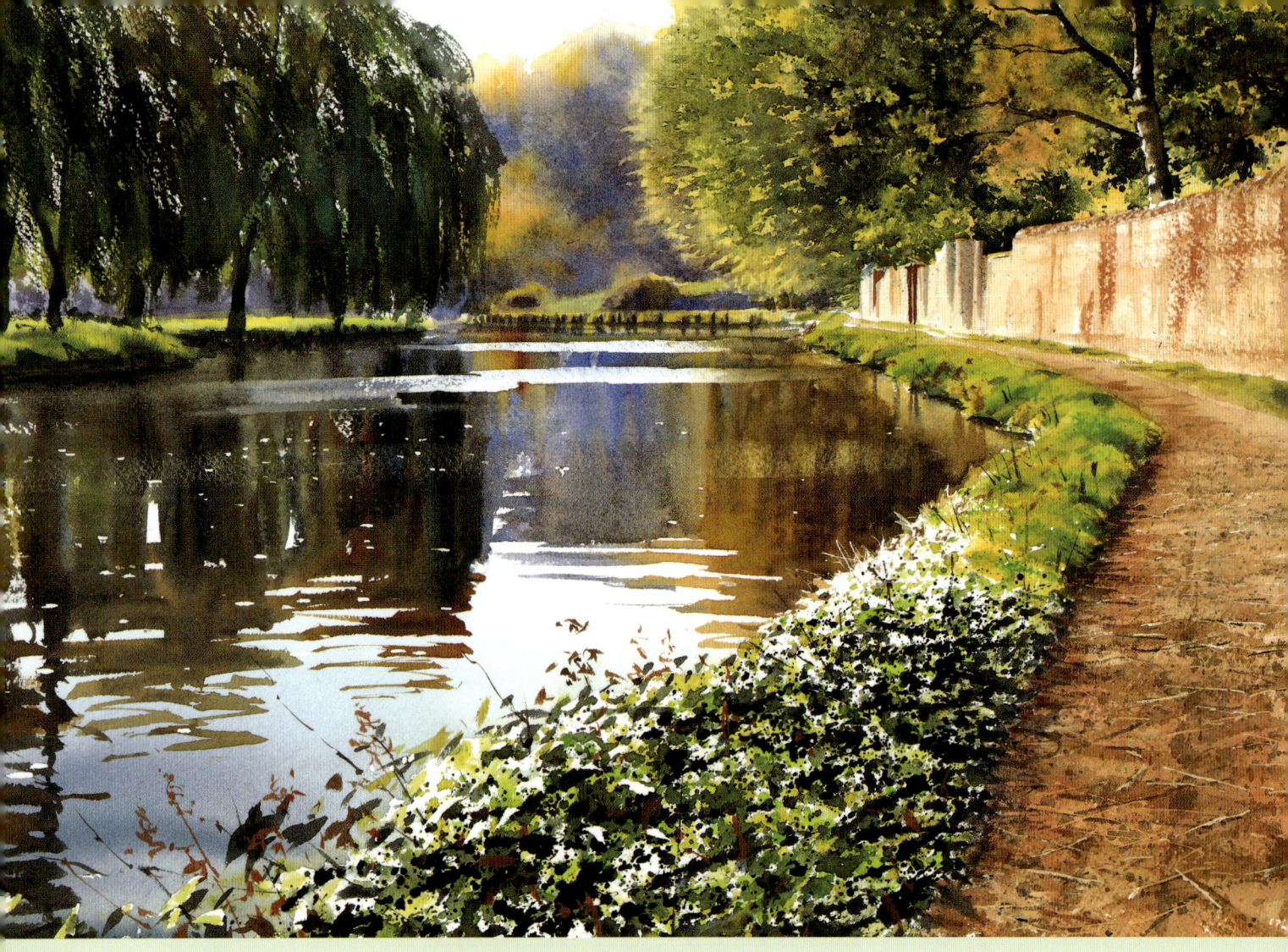

Deep-water river

The setting is important when painting a scene that features a deep-water river. In this picture the close and angled foreground visually pushes the river even further back into the distance and makes it seem broad. I seek out a riverscape that creates reflections in the water and enhances the wet look.

Artist insight: Burnt sienna and cadmium lemon added to the reflection colours gave a deep brown, and a sable brush point produced ripple reflections on dry paper below the wet-in-wet reflections. Manganese violet and French ultramarine painted over dry transparent yellow gave the distant masses. The mid-distant river bank is may green, and right-hand trees are green gold. Dark reflections are indigo, and the sky reflection is a mix of quinacridone magenta, phthalo blue and burnt sienna. The wind scuffs were masked whites, retouched with colour. For the tree canopy, overpaint light green with darker green leaving many loosely placed directional gaps and spaces. Underlying colour will show through these gaps as leaves catching the light.

COLOUR PALETTE

- cadmium lemon
- transparent yellow
- quinacridone magenta
- manganese violet
- French ultramarine
- phthalo blue
- cobalt turquoise light
- phthalo green
- may green
- green gold
- burnt sienna
- light red
- indigo

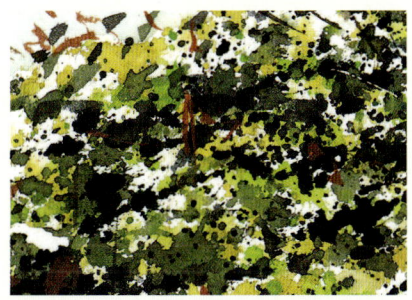

Summer greens

Add a little phthalo green to cadmium lemon for spectrum green. Add burnt sienna to make the green mature. Add indigo for a darker green. Mix indigo or Payne's gray and phthalo green for an intense dark. Try other greens, yellows, browns and oranges in three-way mixes. Split green into a light, yellowy, sunlit mix and a cool, dark, shade mix.

WATER-SPATTERED FOLIAGE

Colour spattered into spattered water gives convincing foliage. Dry it between each layer. Combine it with masking for a realistic river bank.

1 Mask some foreground foliage leaves, and grass blades further away. Spatter a little masking fluid with a toothbrush. Spatter water on the foliage, then spatter a mix of cadmium lemon, burnt sienna and a tiny amount of phthalo green over this.

2 Add indigo to the mix and spatter into water spatter, banging the brush handle down on the palm so paint flies off the tip. Work from bottom to top for diminishing droplet size. Align the brush diagonally in the foreground, flattening with distance for perspective.

3 Model the river colour around the foliage. Into the foliage, spatter intense darks and other colours such as cobalt turquoise light. Several layers of colour can be applied before finishing, as you wish. Note the masked twigs on the path.

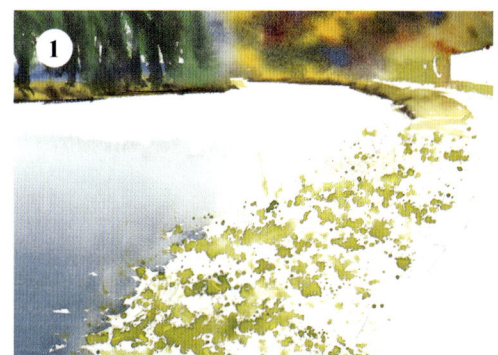

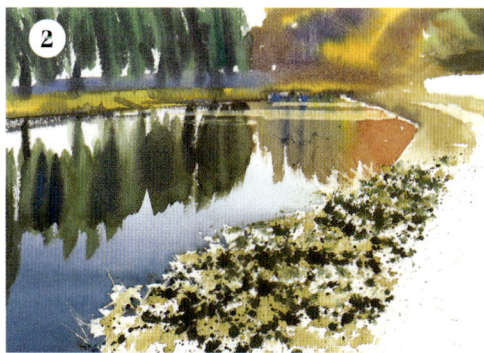

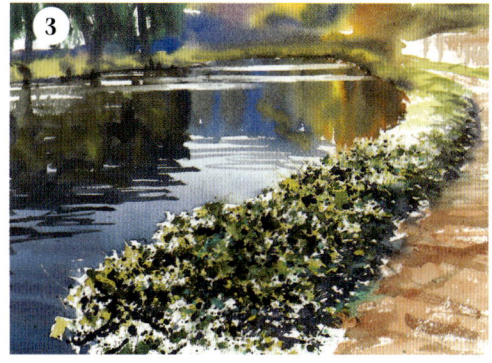

MASKING AND SPATTERING

Save the whites between spattered layers, leaving previous marks showing through each layer. Mask some leaves. With the masking removed, stalks appear to weave under leaves. Paint dark leaves above the river and touch in masked ones with pale colour. Spatter light red and cobalt turquoise light as separate colours for a finishing flourish.

RIVER PERSPECTIVE

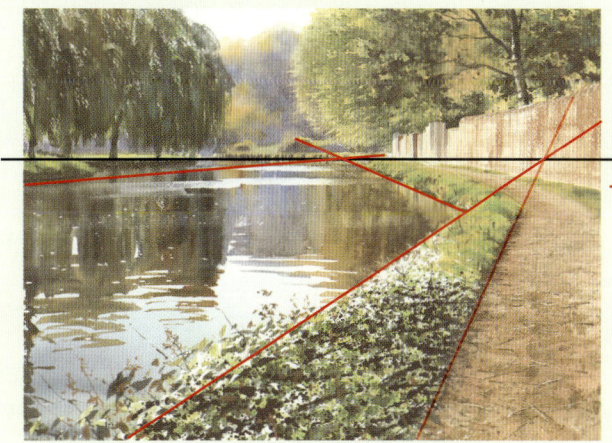

multiple vanishing points project from an invisible horizon

theoretical horizon
perspective lines

Notice that the perspective line for the opposite river bank is very close to the horizontal.

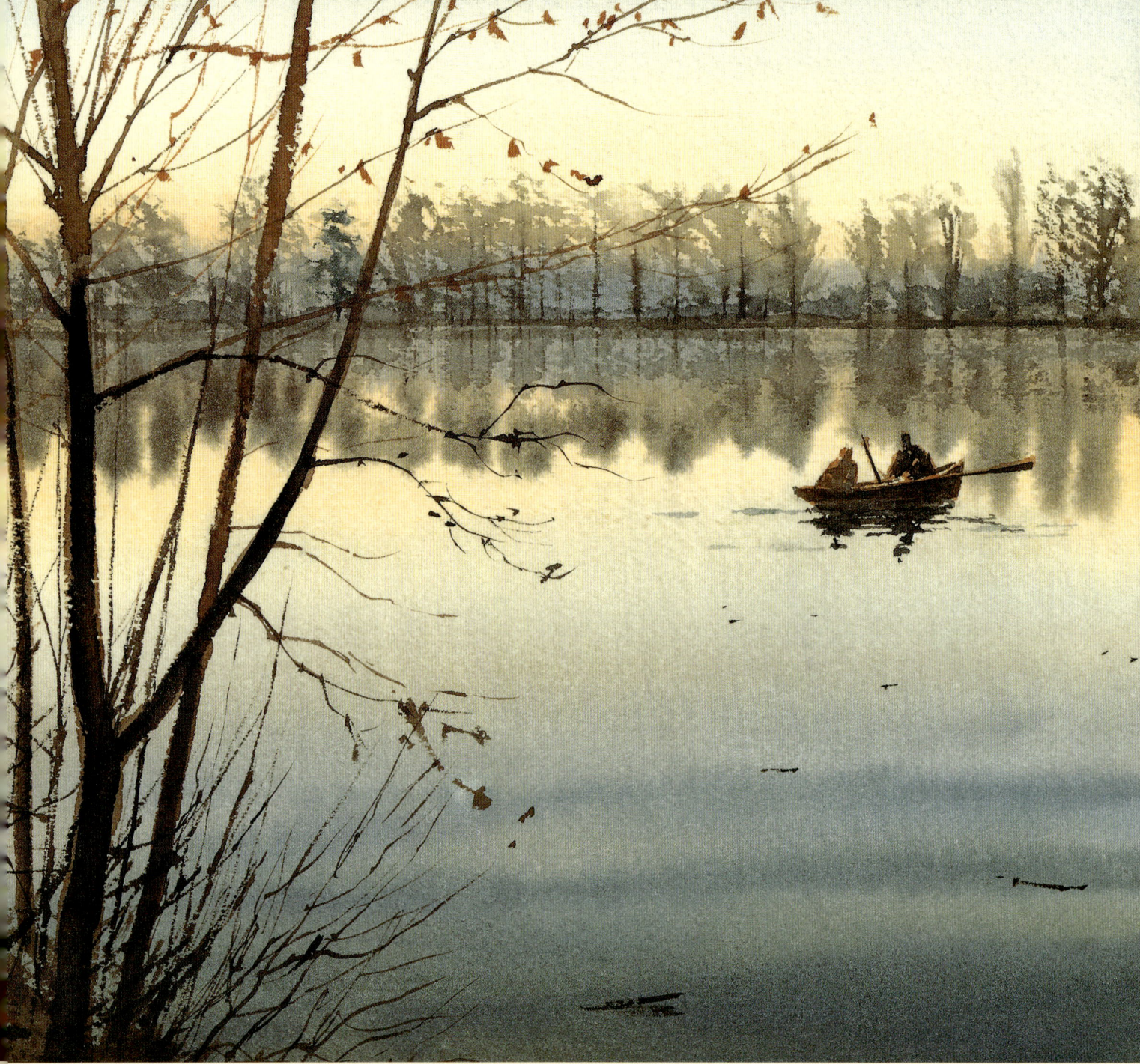

Rowing boat on a lake

Paint a rowing boat with people in it as an entity, mapping out the overall shape of the people, boat and reflection first. A rowing boat sits at an angle and the people sit in it crooked; caught in movement, they tend to lean in the opposite direction to the tilt of the boat.

Artist insight: *Cobalt blue, burnt sienna, Naples yellow, and raw sienna were applied to sky and water. Neutral tint darkened the water. Background trees were painted with cobalt blue, burnt sienna and indigo. Foreground trees were painted with indigo and burnt sienna using a sword liner, and woodcock feather for fine lines. A well-pointing round brush and a rigger can be used instead.*

COLOUR PALETTE

- cadmium red
- phthalo blue
- cobalt blue
- Naples yellow
- raw sienna
- burnt sienna
- neutral tint

Techniques: canal barges, pages 84–85; boats in harbour, pages 86–87; yachts, pages 92–95; beach boat, pages 98–99; scratching out, pages 58–59; lakes, pages 66–67, 70–71, 76–77; washes and warm wash colours, pages 38–39, 68–69; trees, pages 52–53, 78–79.

PAINTING BOATS

People in boats are not always relaxed. They are tense, and counteracting all sorts of forces, often crouched low to keep the precarious centre of gravity down, or swaying in mid movement. It is useful to capture these positions on camera; a photograph eloquently tells the whole brief process of the rowing action. Keep the heads of the figures in boats very small indeed.

1 Paint the water with a mix of burnt sienna and cobalt blue, applying the colour around the shape of the boat, figure and reflection.

2 Apply water colour, leaving areas of undertone for the reflection and ripples. Paint inside the boat, its stripe and shadow areas of the figure.

3 Paint a few darker streaks on the water, and add darker ripples. Complete the boat and figure. Touch in the oars underneath.

Rowing action

These colour sketches show oar strokes with rowing action caught at different stages.

A The oars have just been dipped and pulled a little way into the stroke. The boat reflection is creamy Naples yellow.

B The oars are back, approaching the beginning of the stroke. Dripping water is made by knife scratches. The water is phthalo blue and neutral tint.

C The oars are lifting at the end of the stroke. Water dripping off the oars is created by knife scratches. Colours used are cobalt blue, burnt sienna and quinacridone magenta.

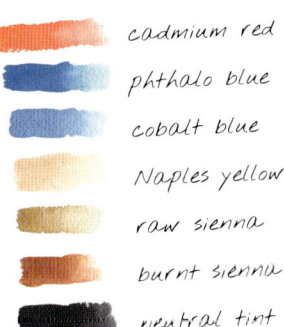

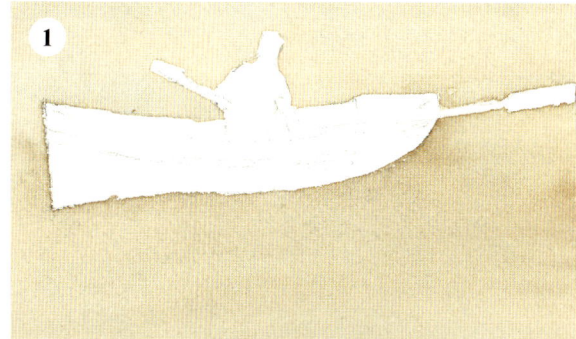

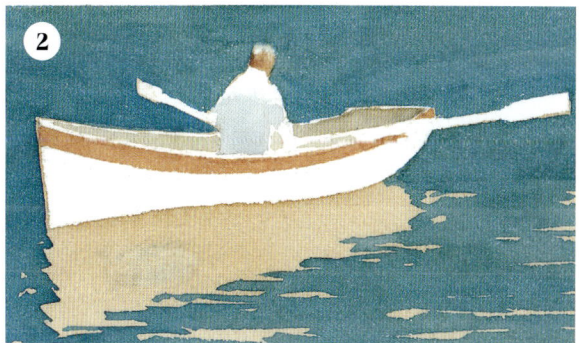

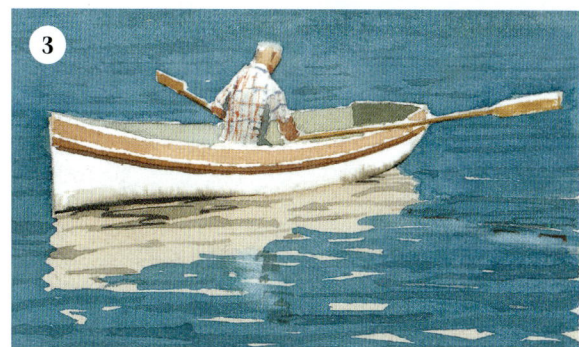

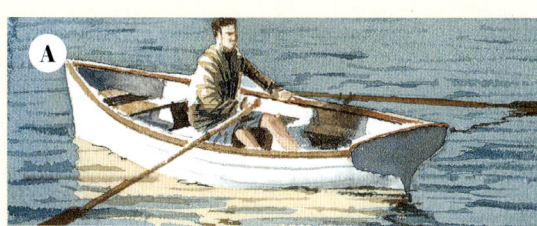

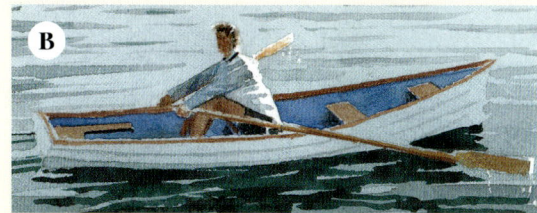

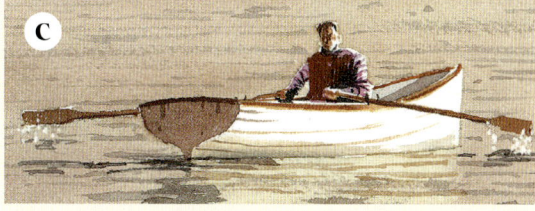

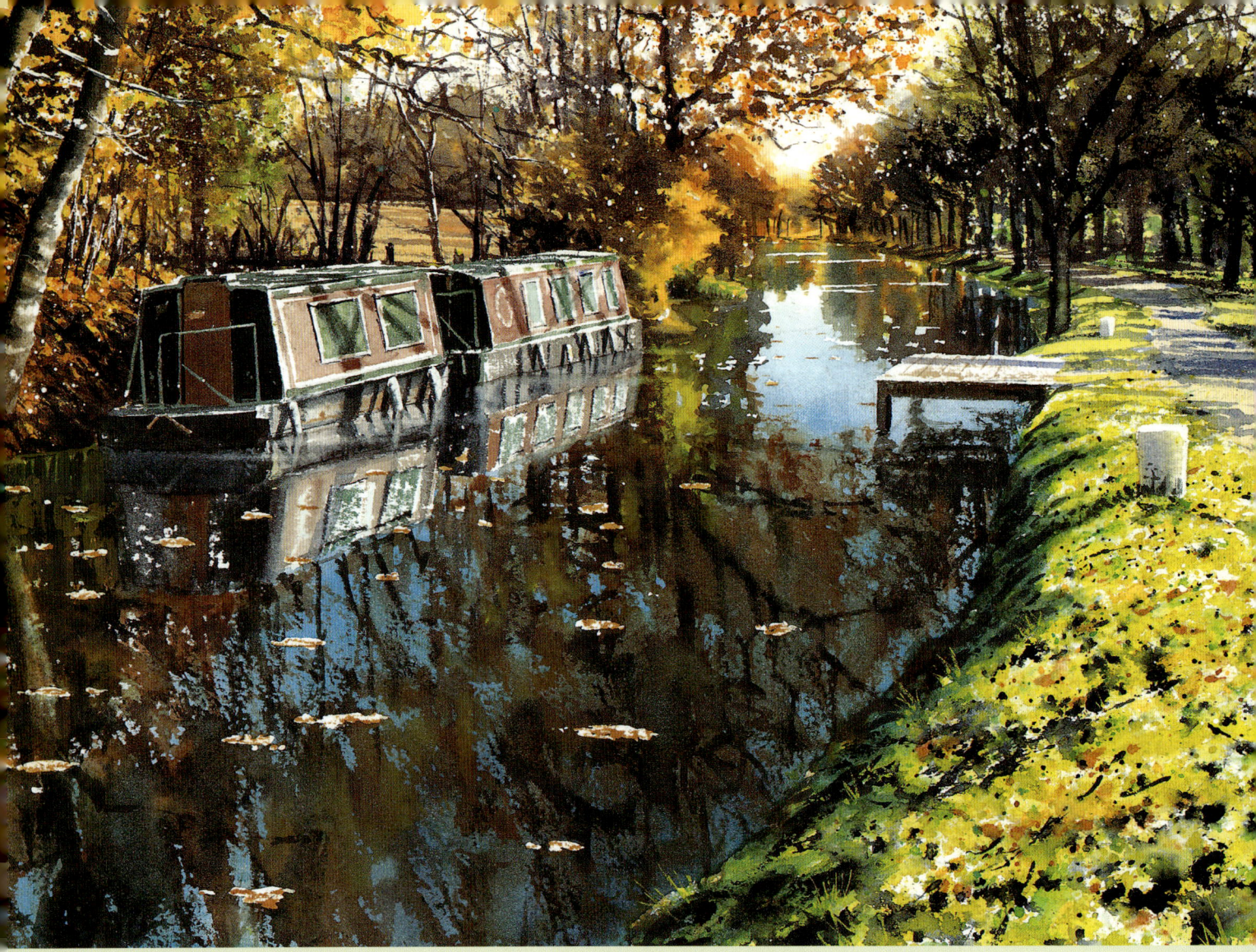

Barges on a canal

Straight man-made barges contrast with ragged passages of nature. Vibrant transparent lights of burnt sienna and new gamboge are offset with strong darks. Masking is both problem solving and creative, and the combination of accurate and loose reflections is achieved with a water feathering technique. Many intense colours are built up loosely in this canal scene.

Artist insight: Three kinds of spatter rendered the foreground: wet-on-dry, wet spatter into wet spatter, and wet spatter on wet paper. Mixes of new gamboge, cadmium yellow, phthalo green and burnt sienna, were overworked with darks and cobalt turquoise light. Toothbrush masking spatter in the trees was spattered over with new gamboge, burnt sienna and quinacridone magenta leaf colour. Darker colours made by adding French ultramarine and burnt umber or Indian red was spattered over these in places. Bollards, barges, jetty and streaks in the water were masked. The spattered mixes were worked from bottom to top to create a 'texture gradient', the droplet size diminishing as the load on the brush reduced. Grass blades were painted with white added to the mix for opaque 'body colour'.

COLOUR PALETTE

- new gamboge
- cadmium yellow
- quinacridone red
- quinacridone magenta
- French ultramarine
- phthalo blue
- cobalt blue
- cobalt turquoise light
- phthalo green
- raw sienna
- burnt sienna
- light red
- Indian red

PAINTING BARGES

1 Mask the barge rooftops, rails, rope, and fenders, the tree trunks and branches on the left, and floating leaves. Paint a raw sienna backdrop. Paint the water wet-in-wet using phthalo blue, and raw sienna on the left. Save the whites. Spatter and brush the backdrop with burnt sienna, a burnt sienna and cobalt mix and darks with a mix of Indian red and French ultramarine.

2 Paint the cabin backs with a dark of phthalo green, Indian red and French ultramarine, and the hulls with light grey from cobalt blue and burnt sienna. Stripe the shadows wet-in-wet with Indian red and French ultramarine. Wet the water area, leaving speckles of dry paper. Brush in palette darks and cadmium yellow, phthalo green and burnt sienna.

3 Darken the barge backs again, leaving the door. Paint the door light red. Paint the reds with quinacridone red and burnt sienna, the greens with phthalo green, cadmium yellow and burnt sienna, and save any whites. Wet the barge reflections, leaving speckles of dry paper. Apply the barge colours wet-in-wet. Remove all masking. Touch in the roofs, fenders, ropes and rails and then dry-brush burnt sienna on the leaves.

Techniques: masking detail, pages 32–33, 76–77, 94–95, 116–117, 120–121; reflections, pages 76–81; distant tree texture, pages 19, 112–113; tree trunks, pages 46–47, 78–79; water feathering, pages 19, 62–63; foreground spattering, pages 28–31; foreground foliage, pages 80–81; river perspective, page 81; foreground grass masking, pages 76–77; foreground grass painting, pages 100–101; boats, pages 82–83; 86–87, 92–95.

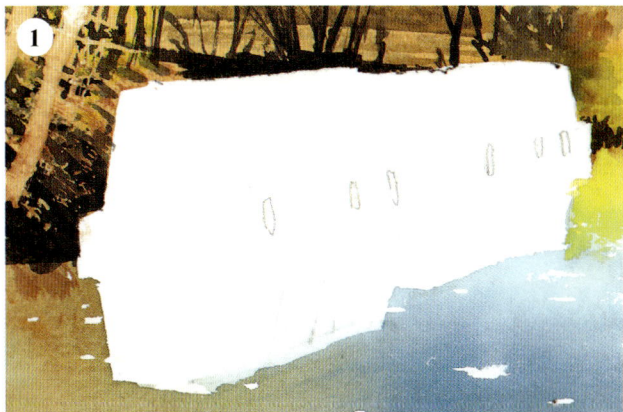

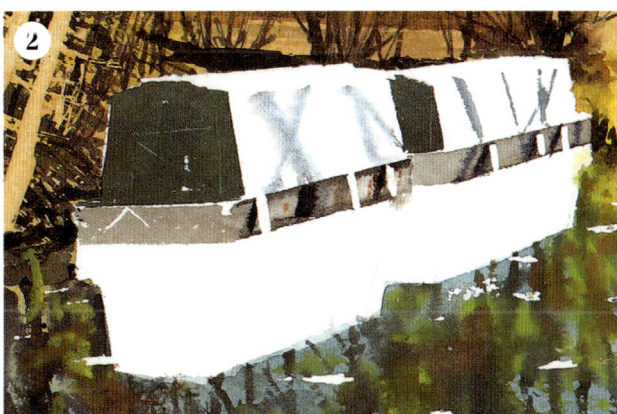

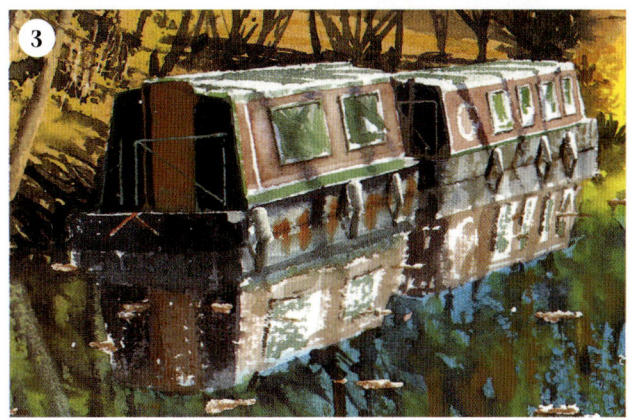

Deep water effects

Dark vertical texture implies depth, and soft focus implies wetness. To achieve this, dry-brush water across the canal, and run the tree reflections straight down through this while wet. This is water feathering and it produces soft and hard focus marks. Horizontally masked bunches of floating leaves, elongated with the foreshortening effect of perspective, enhance the depth and place a surface on the water. Other colours are added wet-in-wet.

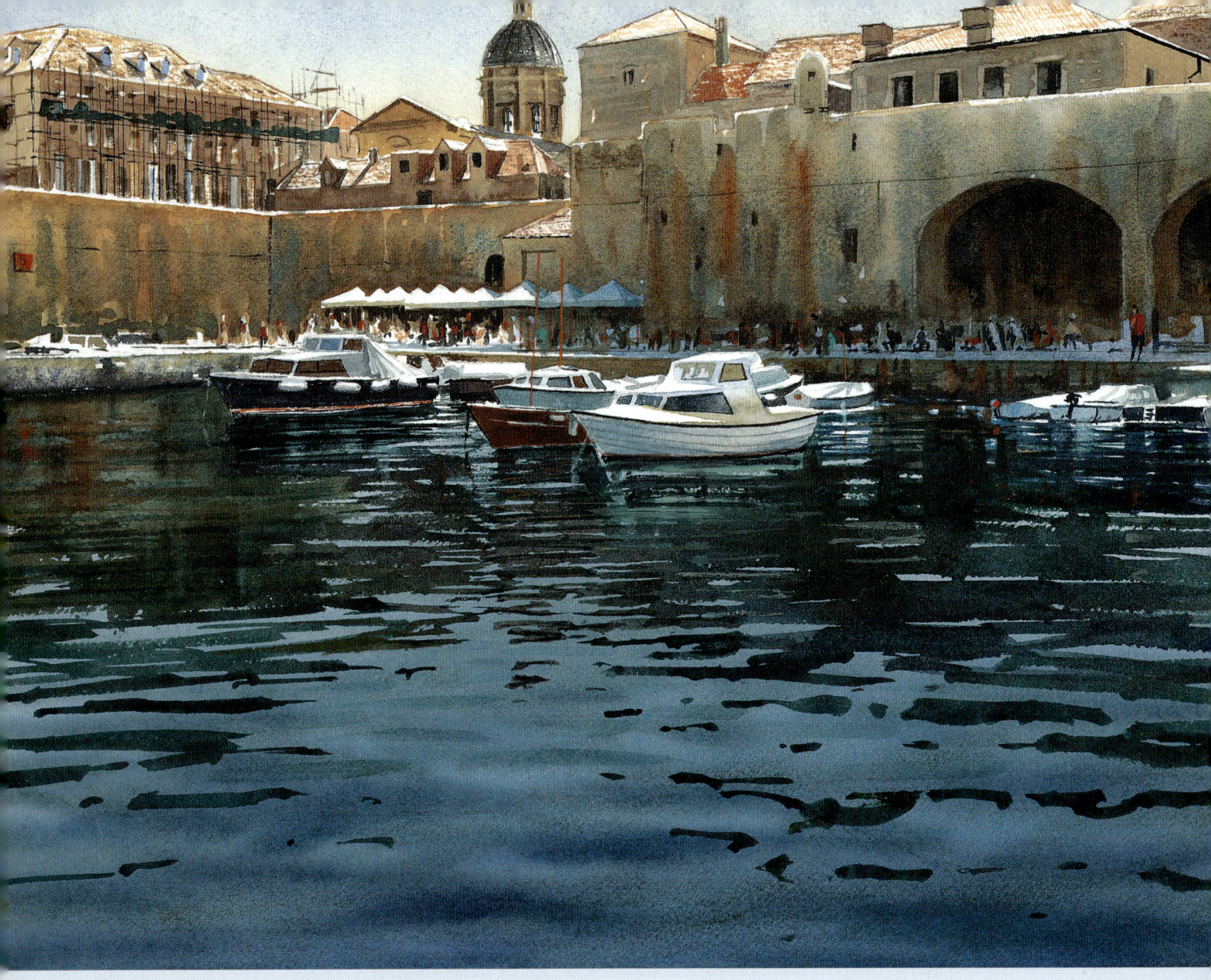

Reflections

Watercolour is the ideal medium for painting water – it behaves so similarly on paper to water in much greater quantities. Use strong colours wet-in-wet and let them mix. Mix large quantities of colour and have plenty of clean water. Work fast and loose, and let the ripples flow off the brush.

Artist insight: There are many small touches of bright colour and some are dabbed into the water. Tertiary colour is used, particularly turquoise, to give impact. The water is unusually dark in this old harbour, and achieved with a deep blackish blue. Try to find people who are engaged in an activity that is defined by the posture; note the figure in red on the right is curved as he uses a mobile phone.

Techniques: wet-in-wet, page 19; tertiary colours, page 22; mixing greys, page 23; skies, pages 54–55; reflections, pages 76–85, 122–123; buildings, pages 40–41, 122–123; boats, pages 82–85, 92–95, 98–99; same harbour from above, pages 118–119.

COLOUR PALETTE

- cadmium orange
- cadmium red
- French ultramarine
- phthalo blue
- cobalt blue
- Naples yellow
- raw sienna
- yellow ochre
- burnt sienna
- light red
- Indian red
- neutral tint

HARBOUR REFLECTIONS

Use plenty of water and colour. Keep detail within the mass reflection blurred. Paint the ripples off the bottom of the mass reflection with rapid sharp-focus brushstrokes.

1 Paint the harbour wall and quayside with loose marks of raw sienna, cobalt blue, light red and Naples yellow. Brush streaks and some mixed darks. Wet the water area and paint an upside-down sky with phthalo blue and raw sienna mixed.

2 Complete the boats and dark detail above the water. Mix Indian red and French ultramarine, and add phthalo blue and raw sienna, and loosely brush this for dark ripples across the harbour with a nicely pointed sable brush of about size 6 to 8.

3 While the wash is still wet, add other colours and allow them to run. Let the wash dry and lift a few vertical highlights by pressing and dragging a damp brush down and dabbing the paper with kitchen roll. A few pale ripples were added to the painting using the point of a brush.

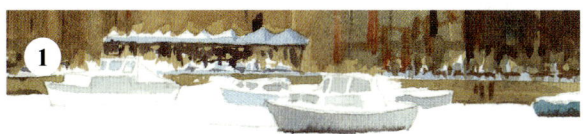

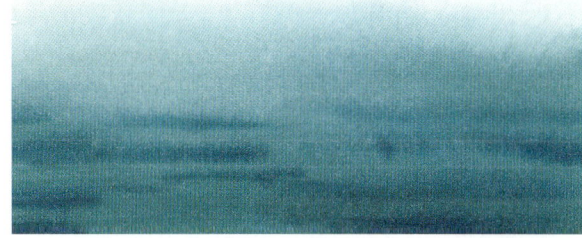

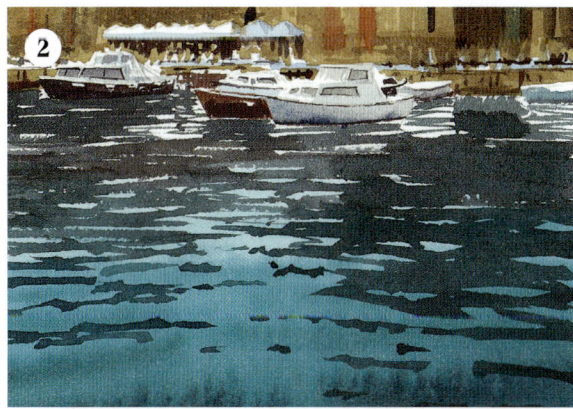

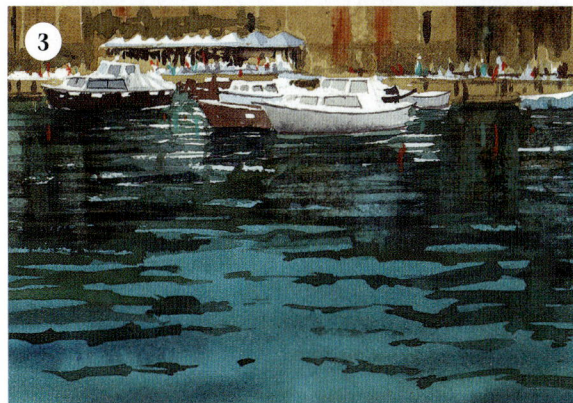

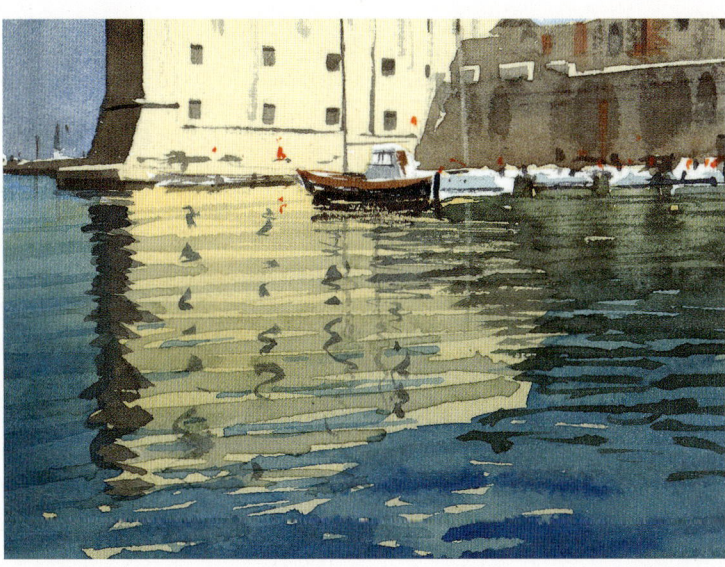

Light on dark

The wall tone and its reflection of yellow ochre mixed with a grey of cobalt blue and burnt sienna is the background glaze for the whole painting, and is left out when surrounding colour is brushed in a single wash of French ultramarine sky and phthalo blue water. Save whites for boats. Apply the wall reflection wash twice to strengthen it. The wall reflection ripples are a darker mix of wall colour.

Reflections and ripples

Reflections can fall into two zones – mass zone and break zone. Mass zone is wet colour, break zone strokes of colour break off the mass zone, wet-on-dry. Add colour to the mass zone in vertical strokes, wet-in-wet. Apply horizontal strokes to the break zone wet-on-dry in a diminishing sequence ending with a few marks and lines.

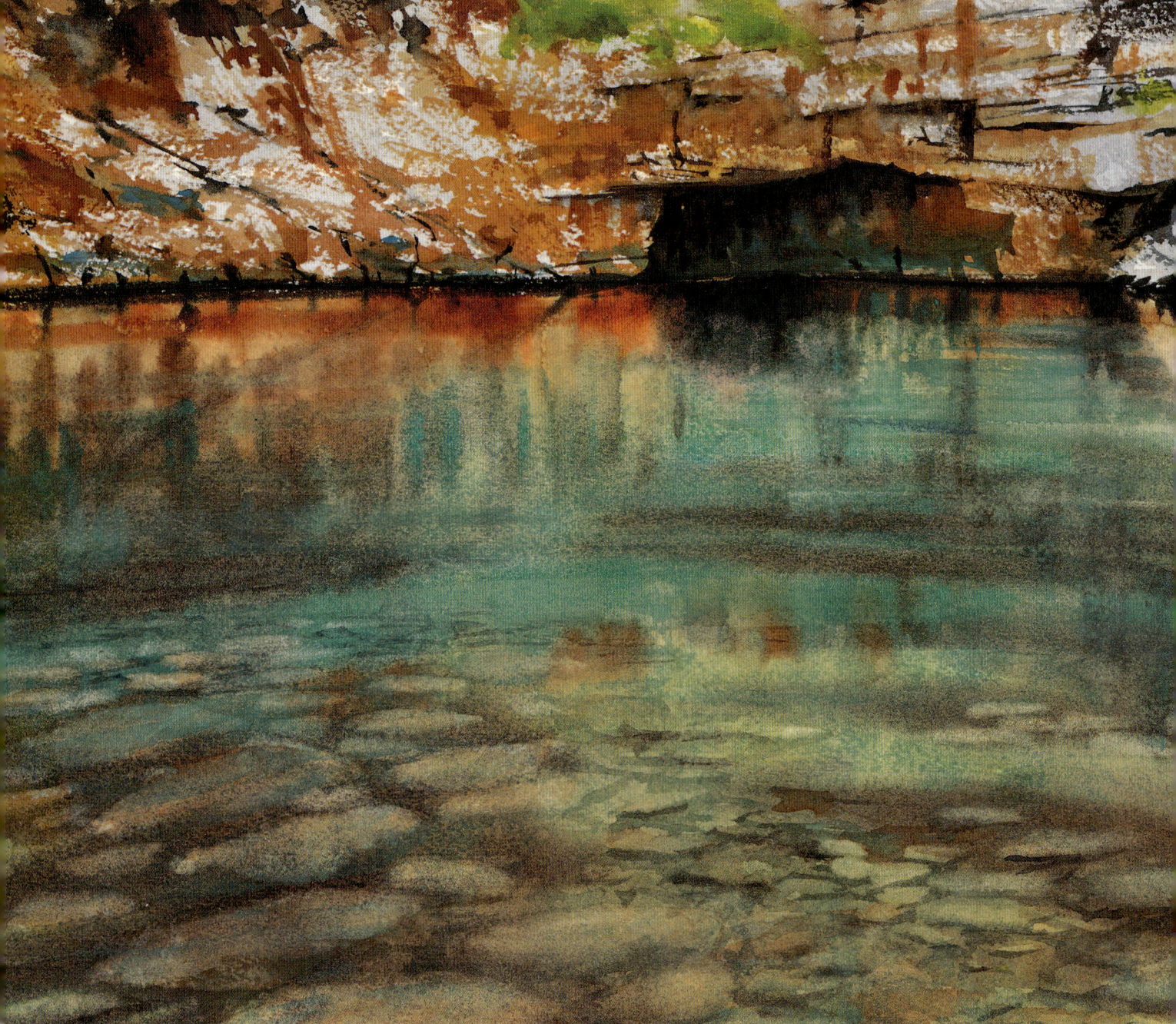

Shallow water over rocks

A rocky turquoise pool can be visually stunning, but the lack of features could deter some painters from having a go. Keep the water's edge and cave away from the centre. Create many abstract patterns and textures. Apply colour mostly wet-in-wet for the water and wet-on-dry for the rock face.

Artist insight: *Painting water needs a large amount of colour, mixed on the flat, ceramic household plates that I use as palettes. I mix plenty of strong, flowing tube colour, with paint tubes to hand. Spare paint is squeezed out to the palette edges.*

COLOUR PALETTE

- translucent orange
- French ultramarine
- cobalt blue
- cobalt turquoise light
- Naples yellow
- burnt sienna
- Indian red

Techniques: wet-in-wet, pages 18–19; warm colours, page 23 (under 'Greys and darks'); feathering, pages 19, 62–63, 112; water, pages 78–81, 84–85; rocks, rock-formations and cliffs, pages 36–37, 65, 67, 72–73, 100–101; mixing intense darks, page 73 (step 4).

Underwater effects

- Underwater objects appear elongated due to refraction – the bending of light.

- Lift rocks for a softened look, as though blurred by water.

- Touch in the lifted rocks with burnt sienna to 'put them under water'.

PAINTING THE SCENE

1 Plan the position of the pool's edge and the cave on tracing paper (**1a**). Draw on the reverse of the tracing, place it over the image and trace through. Brush the rocky grotto wall with a light wash of burnt sienna and cobalt blue (**1b**).

2 Use water feathering to produce a dark fissured texture of cracks. Pick out the pattern of fissures with the point of a brush (**2a**). Repeat the water feathering for warmer colours in the rock, letting this spread into the cave mouth and leaving some lights inside the cave reflected from the water (**2b**).

3 Wet the pool. Add Naples yellow and burnt sienna to the base of the wash, letting this spread upwards.

4 Rewet the pool. Add burnt sienna below the rock face. Run in dark reflections. Brush in vertical strokes of cobalt turquoise light in the mid area.

5 Brush in washes on the water left and right. When dry, lift out oval rock shapes using a damp brush. Dab with kitchen towel to remove the colour.

6 To finish, build dark shadows between the rocks, using the point of a brush wet-on-dry. Build up a 'pavement' of these shadows in the area between the two dark masses. When dry, lift a few more underwater rocks from this area. Notice some underwater rocks are in sharp focus, while some are soft.

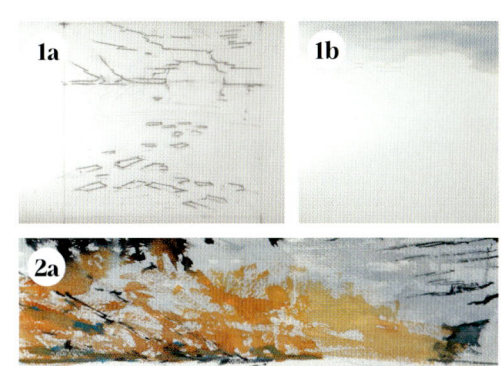

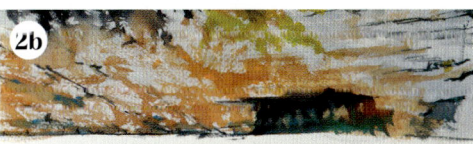

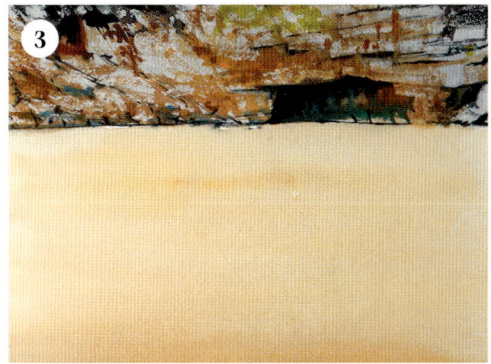

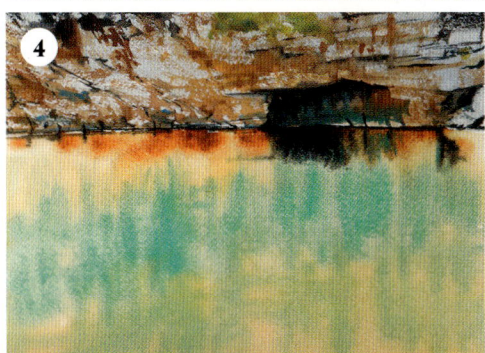

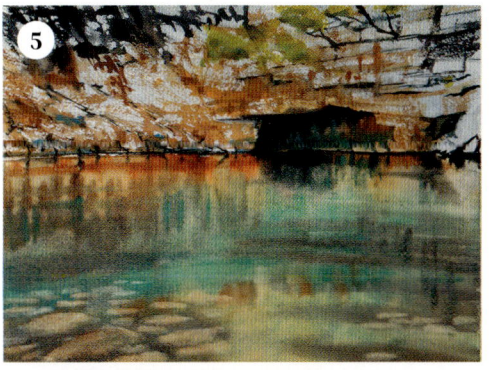

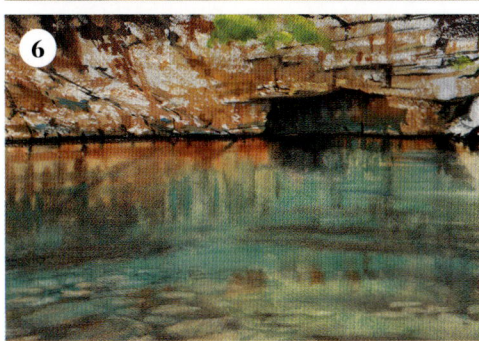

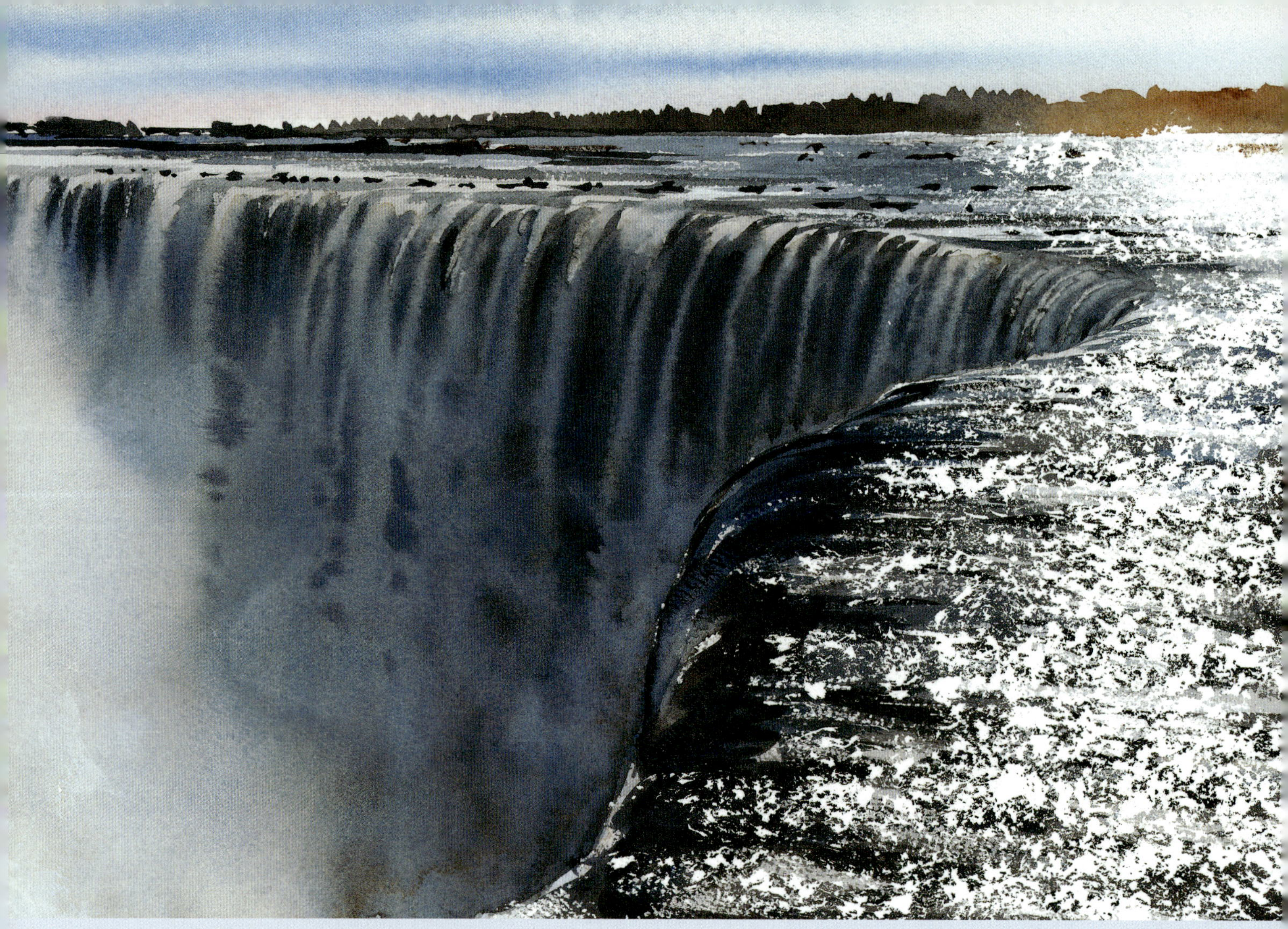

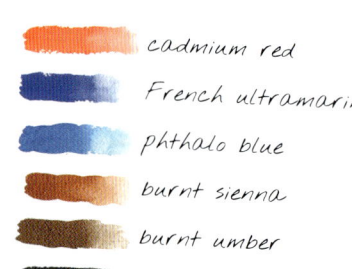

Falls

Paint strong contrasts – every part of this painting is light against dark, or dark against light. Wet-in-wet painting achieves the mist and masking with a rough hog-hair brush produces the glint on the water. The dark patches in the falls are wider spaced as they accelerate down into the mist and disappear.

Artist insight: The masking fluid is removed, and a few nicks with a knife blade are made on the plunging water. This painting of Horseshoe Falls, Niagara is entirely about tone. Even a slight amount of colour has a powerful effect; on the horizon it indicates heat from the sun and relieves the tonal monotony. Rough and jagged masking creates the rushing water as it churns up surface glints in the sunshine. Sky and falls light greys are cobalt blue and burnt sienna, with a little cadmium red and streaks of phthalo blue wet-in-wet in the sky. The darker greys are French ultramarine and burnt sienna, including the horizon skyline. The intense darks are Payne's gray.

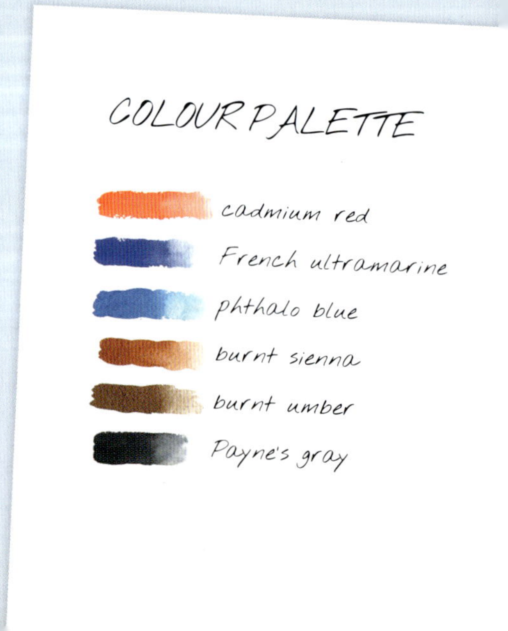

COLOUR PALETTE

cadmium red

French ultramarine

phthalo blue

burnt sienna

burnt umber

Payne's gray

Techniques: tonal values, page 15; washes, pages 18–21; mixing greys, page 23; skies, pages 54–55; masking sparkles (bristle brush/hog-hair brush), pages 42–43, 104–105, 108; masking sparkles (old brush), pages 92–93; waterfall, pages 78–79; mist/fog, pages 120–121.

PAINTING FALLING WATER

This technique produces glints on water bouncing off a sun that is directly ahead. Use a large bristle hog-hair brush, dabbed gently into the surface of masking fluid in the pot. Gently dab the brush vertically on the paper so the bristles each individually touch the surface and produce complex marks. Rotate the brush after each dab so each shape is different, and work along horizontal tracks. Delicate use will give smaller marks for distant glints. Add a few lines and spatters. Very few marks will go over the edge – they stop when the water drops because the angle changes and no longer reflects the sun.

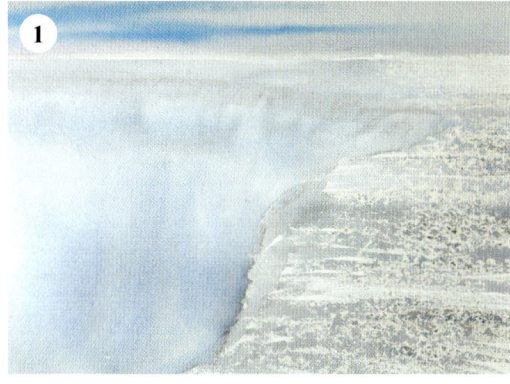

1 After the masking has dried, wet the sky. Apply a grey wash, adding streaks of blue while wet. Let it dry. Dry-brush pale blue-grey horizontal strokes onto the water, curving them over the falls edge. When dry, wet the cascade area and add a pale blue in a patchy mist up to the lip of the waterfall, leaving no white paper.

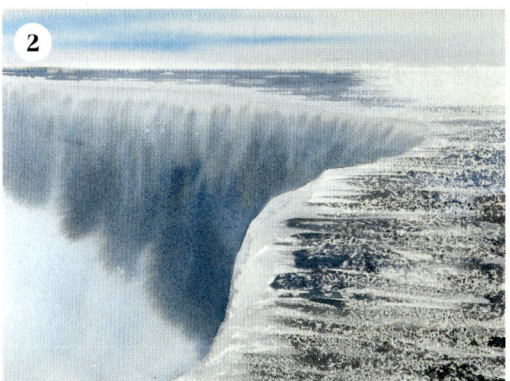

2 Rewet inside the cascade and add darker blue-grey in vertical swathes, with smaller ones and more light showing at the top. When dry, drag darker horizontal streaks across the upper water area. Save the distant sparkle zone above this area. Drag the darker colour in bands across the distant water to the left above the fall.

3 Rewet the lower cascade area. Apply strong darks, streaking them up with the point of a brush. The top is more sharp focus where the water plunges over, so drag the dark up into this area wet-on-dry, tapering the marks off to a curving point. The darks in the drop-off area become wider spaced and more diagonal the lower they go.

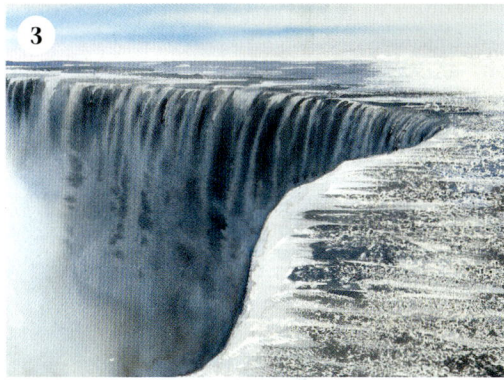

4 Drag intense dark along the foreground water on the top of the fall, keeping it straight. Leave a few lights. Where the water reaches the edge it plunges down directionally – leave some spaces and infill these with paler tone. Paint the rocks and long islets. Start to paint the distant horizon backdrop edge.

5 Complete the distant horizon backdrop and paint it with a lighter version of the colour mixed with burnt sienna where it crosses the track of the sun, adding a little water here to make sure it is paler. Add some additional marks of this colour for the rocks in the water on the right of the picture.

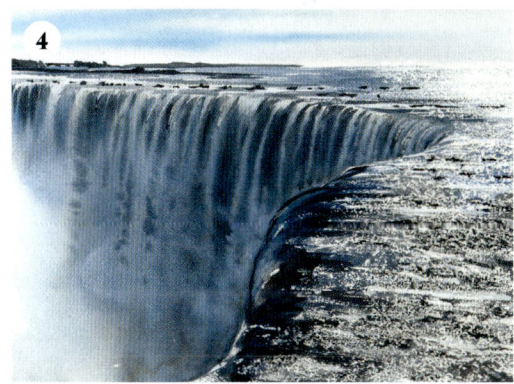

Direction of water

Directional brushwork charges the painting with energy. Keep the strokes of colour horizontal when overpainting the masking. The water plunges around a curve before dropping near vertically – built up with directional darks, saving lighter tone in the previous wash, wet-on-dry in the high contrast tones at the top and wet-in-wet in the shaded falls. Brush thin distant strokes of tone. The diagonal line of mist helps contain the image compositionally – and it was there! Before removing the masking, a few horizontal streaks were lifted.

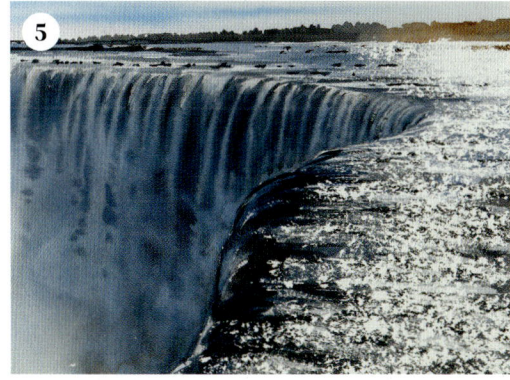

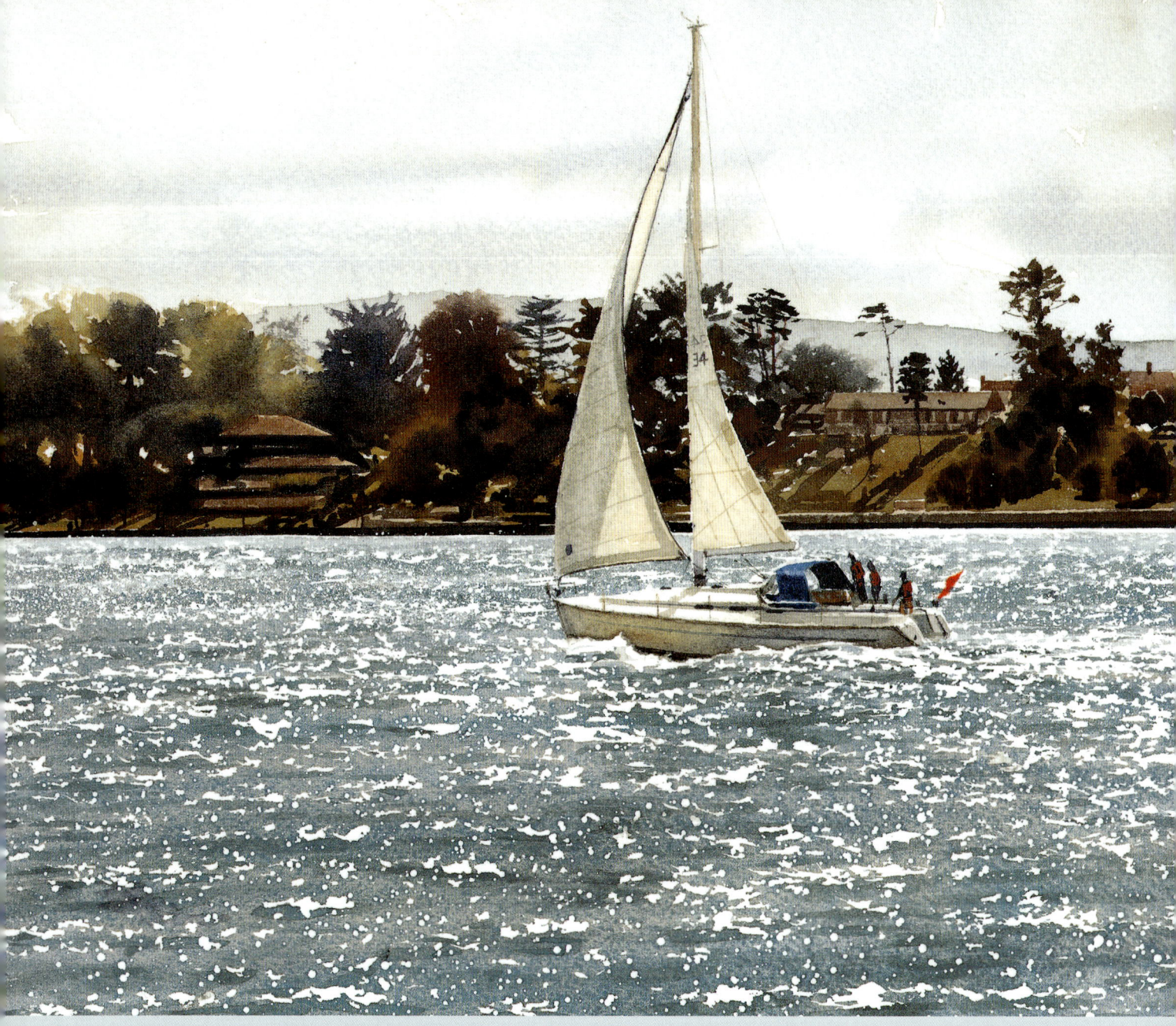

Boat sailing on the sea

The sparkles on the sea are created by a number of physical forces and laws that interact – light, wind, waves, tide and perspective. Together they create randomness within order; chaotic and yet within certain limits that define them and make them instantly recognizable. Here the question is – how to get these long stringy lights into a rough sea?

Artist insight: To achieve the effect shown, mask the sea with a small piece of ripped and tightly-coiled typing paper dabbed on the paper horizontally, then add toothbrush spattering and streaks. Brush the sky with cobalt blue and burnt sienna, and the sea with cerulean blue and cadmium red. Use a brush to apply more wave marks.

COLOUR PALETTE

- new gamboge
- cadmium red
- quinacridone magenta
- French ultramarine
- cobalt blue
- cerulean blue
- Hooker's green
- yellow ochre
- burnt sienna
- light red
- Indian red

CREATING SPARKLES

1 Dab masking fluid with an old brush caked with dried masking fluid. Here a grey wash contrasts with ragged highlights with the masking removed. Spatter distant sparkles with masking fluid from a toothbrush by dragging the thumb across the bristles. Protect the sky above the horizon with a cover. The masking fluid is applied in horizontal tracks with large gaps between the tracks nearer the foreground.

2 Brush a second wash on the sea, leaving long streaks of light as saved whites. The masking is complemented with a little dry brushwork to save further whites. The horizon is contrasted both dark and light against the grey sky. Keep the emphasis on the complex random sequences of nature rather than trying to be over tidy.

3 Masking fluid produces a range of textures, and some areas can be almost blocked out with random masked patterns. Paint pale colour into the masked area to accentuate glare. Paint rough, dark streaks across the masked areas, but keep most of them out of the central 'dazzle' area. Scrub vertical 'rays' across the large masked foreground highlights for additional glare and movement.

Techniques: washes, pages 18–21; mixing greys, page 23; sparkles, pages 42–43, 90–91; rough brush masking effects, pages 48–49; masking sea effects (surf), pages 102–105; boats, pages 94–95; figures (in boats), pages 82–83; figures (in action), pages 94–95, 106–107; sea and sky, pages 98–99.

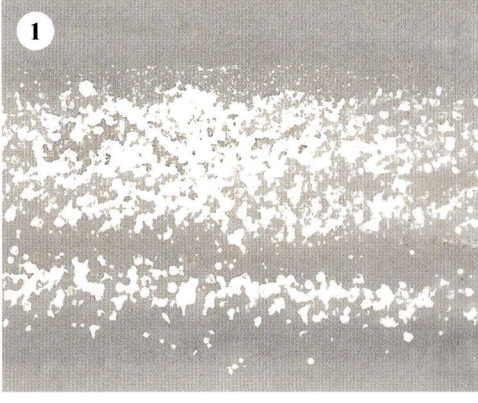

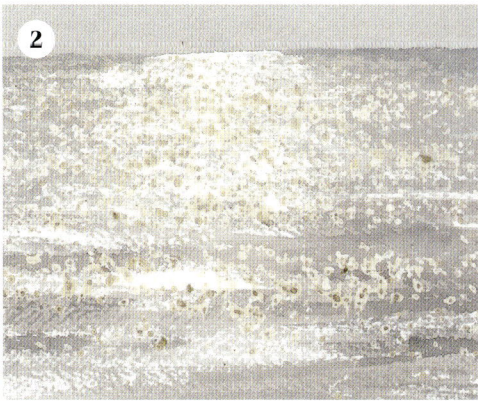

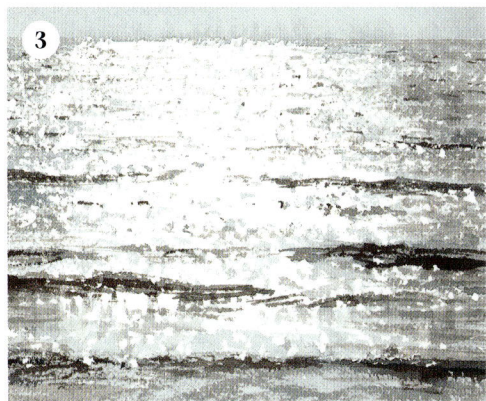

Lifting out sails

In the main painting, the sails are masked, but they can also be lifted, as here. The amount that lifts varies with paper type and the colour used. Scrub with a soft or a stiff damp brush depending how easily the paint lifts, then dab with kitchen towel. Be careful not to spoil the surface of the paper. Staining colours, such as phthalo green, do not lift easily.

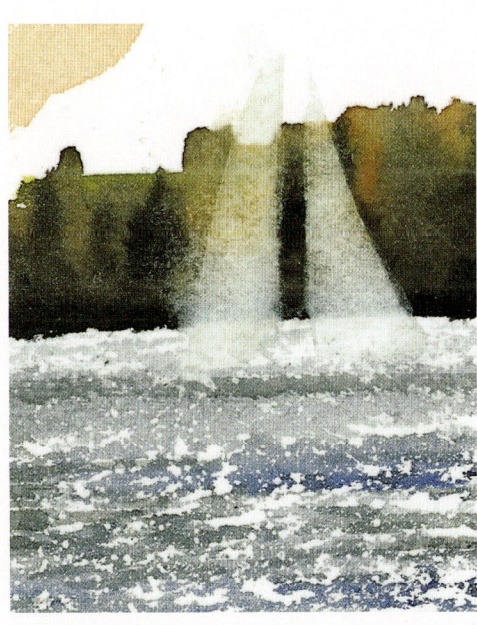

Reflecting light

A small coiled-up, ripped-up piece of typing paper dipped into masking fluid and used lengthways gets the texture of reflected light on the sea. Get rid of excess fluid before testing it to see if it is rough enough, then dab it on the paper horizontally, working along the paper in horizontal tracks, but varying it a bit to avoid regularity. Impose further randomness by spattering from a toothbrush.

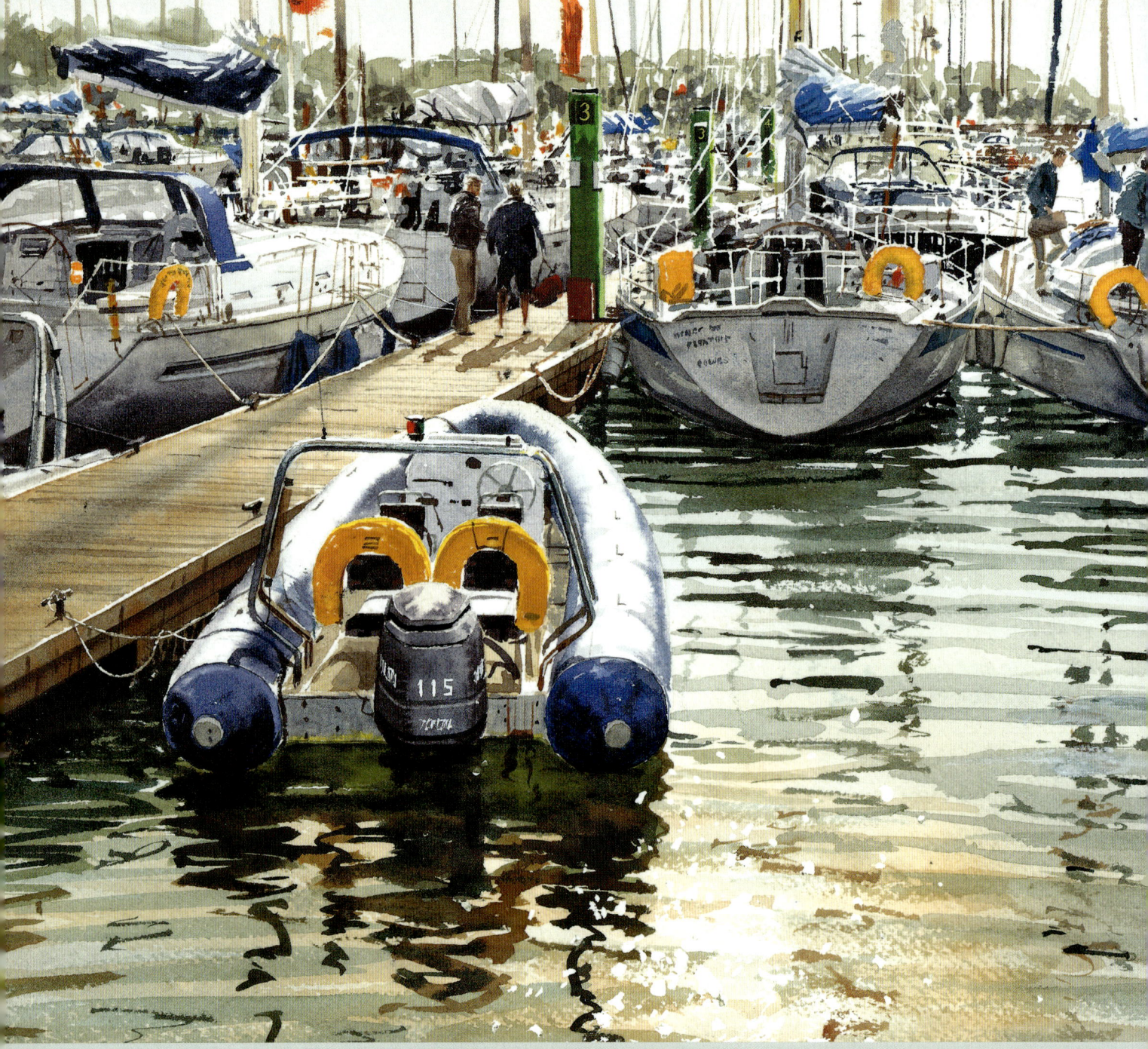

Yachts in a marina

A jumble of boats looks confusing, but you can keep the painting process simple. Start with the lightest tones, add darker ones and save the whites as you go. Do not paint exact detail in the distant clutter – just an abstract pattern – but paint the foreground detail as you see it. The use of masking builds the complex look.

Artist insight: Painting a busy harbour like this one involves organizing the saved whites. Mask the key edges of the foreground boat and pontoon, railings and ropes of the larger boats, the yellow life-saving gear, and railings and ropes on nearby and some distant yachts, and some canopies. Leave small shapes, patches of light, and rigging, as white or to paint later. Mask the sparkles in the sea using an old rough brush. The ripples were painted loosely from the point of a size 7 sable brush.

COLOUR PALETTE

- cadmium lemon
- cadmium yellow
- cadmium red
- quinacridone magenta
- French ultramarine
- phthalo blue
- cobalt blue
- phthalo green
- Naples yellow
- burnt sienna
- Indian red
- Payne's gray

Techniques: perspective, pages 16–17; wet-on-dry, page 19; mixing greys, page 23; sparkles, pages 42–43, 78–79, 90–91, 92–93, 108; ripples, pages 78–83, 86–87, 122–123; masking detail, pages 32–33, 46–47, 116–117, 120–121; boats, pages 85–87, 92–93; figures, pages 16, 82–83, 106–107.

Painting figures

Keep the heads and feet small, and aim for the correct angle of stance for the figure. Don't worry about painting figures. Paint the clothes they are wearing – the jackets, jeans and shorts – rather than the people themselves, then it will look convincing. If you are on the same level, people of your height will have their eye level on the horizon whatever their size. If you are above them, their eye level will be below the horizon.

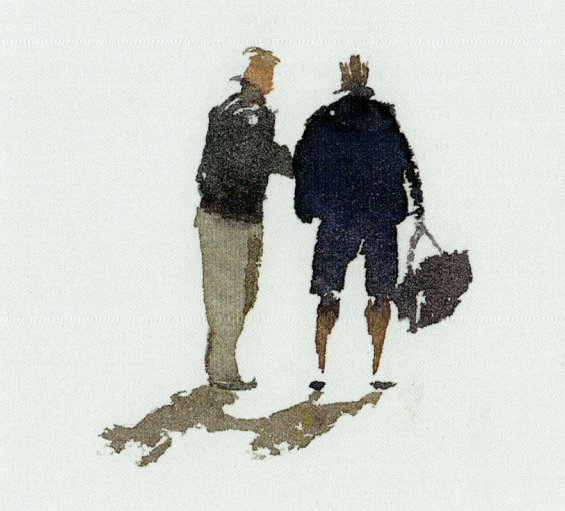

PAINTING A MASS OF BOATS

Keep background items as a series of small broken shapes, with just a few meaningful details here and there such as masts and canopies. Build up the boats in layers, saving plenty of whites, before putting in a few bright colours and intense dark accents.

1 Mask the lines and rails. Mask some of the masts, and simply leave many of them out. Paint the boats with a grey mix of cobalt blue, burnt sienna and quinacridone magenta. Use cadmium lemon, cobalt blue and burnt sienna for the distant trees.

2 Darken the hulls with a mix of cobalt blue, burnt sienna and quinacridone magenta. Use some of this colour for the distant boatyard 'jumble', which reads as an abstract texture. Add canopies to the boats using cobalt blue, with a rough indication of shape.

3 Wet the hulls and add a dark mix of Indian red and French ultramarine to define them. Use this colour for detail on the boats. Dash tiny areas of bright colour – red and yellow – in random places to add life to the scene.

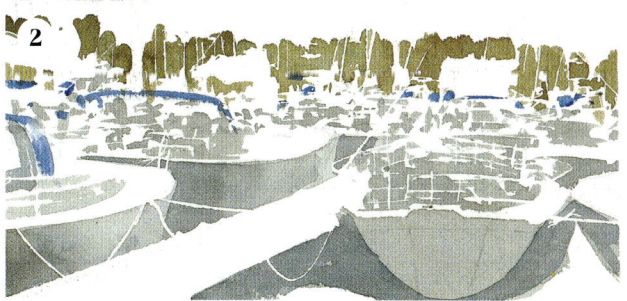

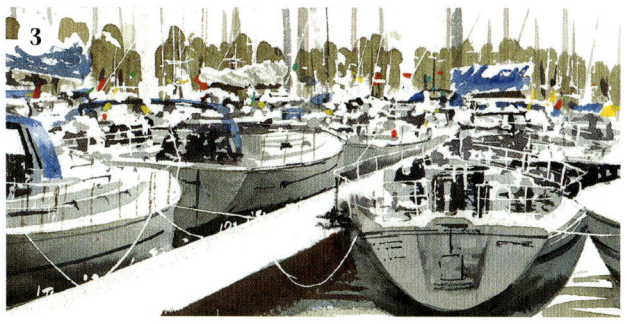

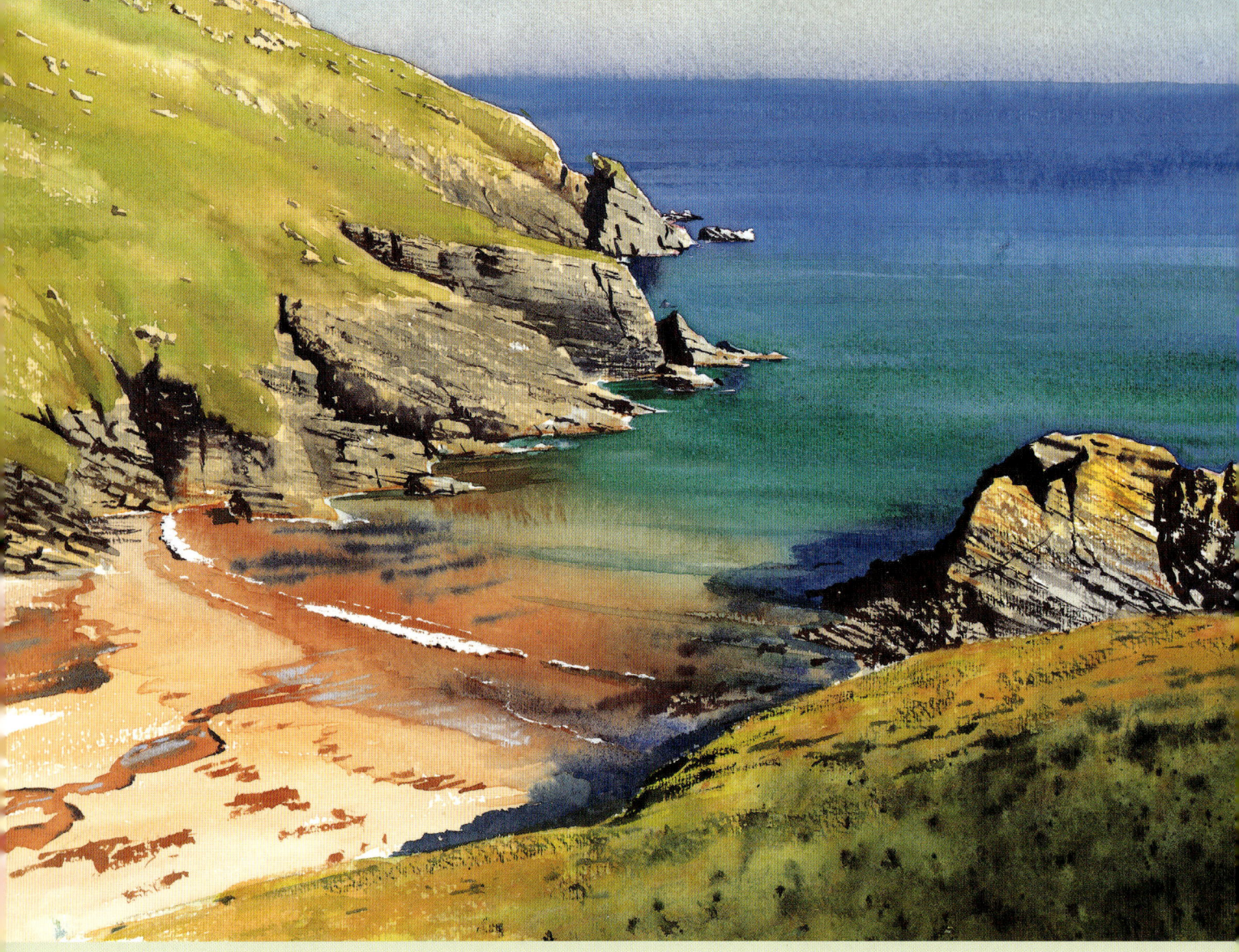

Sandy cove

Although this painting is of a cove, the sea and sky provide the main tone and form. The sky and sea can be painted in one go, with only the last sea wash distinguishing it from the sky. Building up the sea colour one wash at a time gives a more realistic, stronger result.

Artist insight: The sequence of colours painted down from the sky ends with streaks of Indian red on the beach and dark accents. The painting is built with the strong wet-in-wet sea wash, placing sun on the land by contrasting its lighter values – pale glazes of yellow and orange – with the darker tones. Over the glazes a pale grey of burnt sienna and cobalt blue was dry-brushed for the cliffs, and darks of French ultramarine and Indian red. A green mixed from cadmium yellow, burnt sienna and a little phthalo green gave the grassy hillside colour.

COLOUR PALETTE

- cadmium yellow
- translucent orange
- quinacridone red
- French ultramarine
- phthalo blue
- cobalt blue
- phthalo green
- Naples yellow
- burnt sienna
- light red
- Indian red
- white gouache

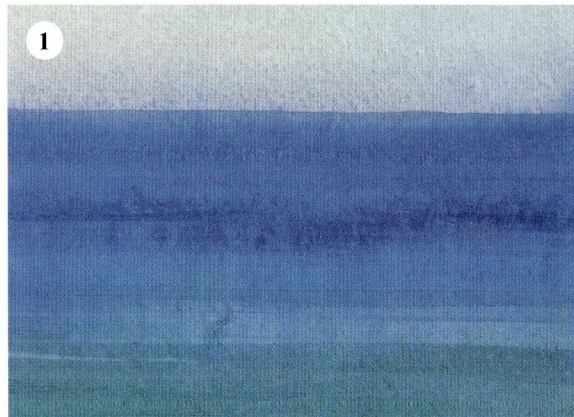

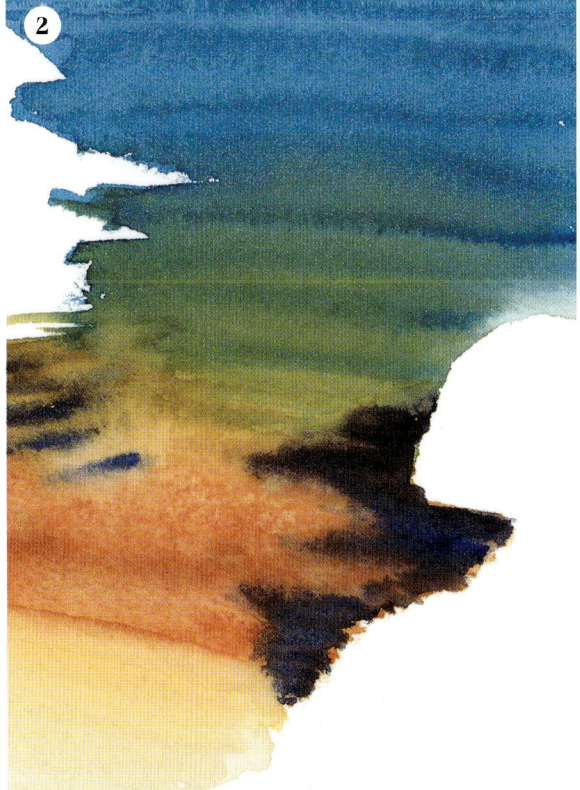

PAINTING SEA AND SHORE

The following steps explain how this landscape was painted, which unifies sea and sky by painting them together. Although you can use saved whites for the breakers, white gouache can work well, as shown here.

1 Paint the sky wet-in-wet with pale washes of quinacridone red, orange and phthalo blue. Brush the sea into the still-wet sky for the soft horizon, defining land with a hard edge as a contrast with the distance. More detailed instructions on painting the sea are given in step 2. See the main image for the slightly soft horizon.

2 Paint the sea using a sequence of colours from the top down. Underglaze the blue sea area with quinacridone red and paint over with phthalo blue. Then run cobalt blue along the horizon. Working downwards, apply phthalo green so the colour shifts first towards green, then yellow with Naples yellow and light red, wet-in-wet. Darks of French ultramarine and Indian red provide shadow in the sea. Stripe colours wet-in-wet for the deep swells.

3 Brush the breakers with thick white gouache, using opaque body colour in small areas. Define the shadow with intense dark. Paint the small waves blowing up on the wet sand, and streak in body colour of cobalt blue and white. The beach consists of mixes of Naples yellow and light red with indigo wet-in-wet in the sea.

Paint grass with mixed cadmium yellow, burnt sienna and phthalo green. On the point of drying I sprayed the foreground with water from a sprayer to give it texture, and spattered in a dark of phthalo green mixed with a blue-black of Indian red and French ultramarine. When dry, I dragged and streaked some of this colour across, and then dragged burnt sienna on top.

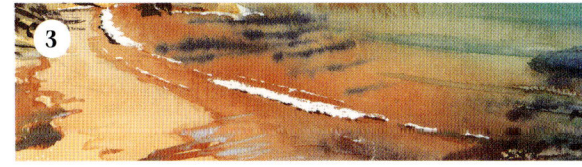

Techniques: mixing greys and greens, page 23; foreground spatter, pages 30–31; beach and sea, pages 72–73; rock formations, pages 36–37, 66–67, 72–73, 88–89; skies, pages 54–55; sea and sky, pages 98–101; surf, pages 102–105; cliff top grass, pages 100–101.

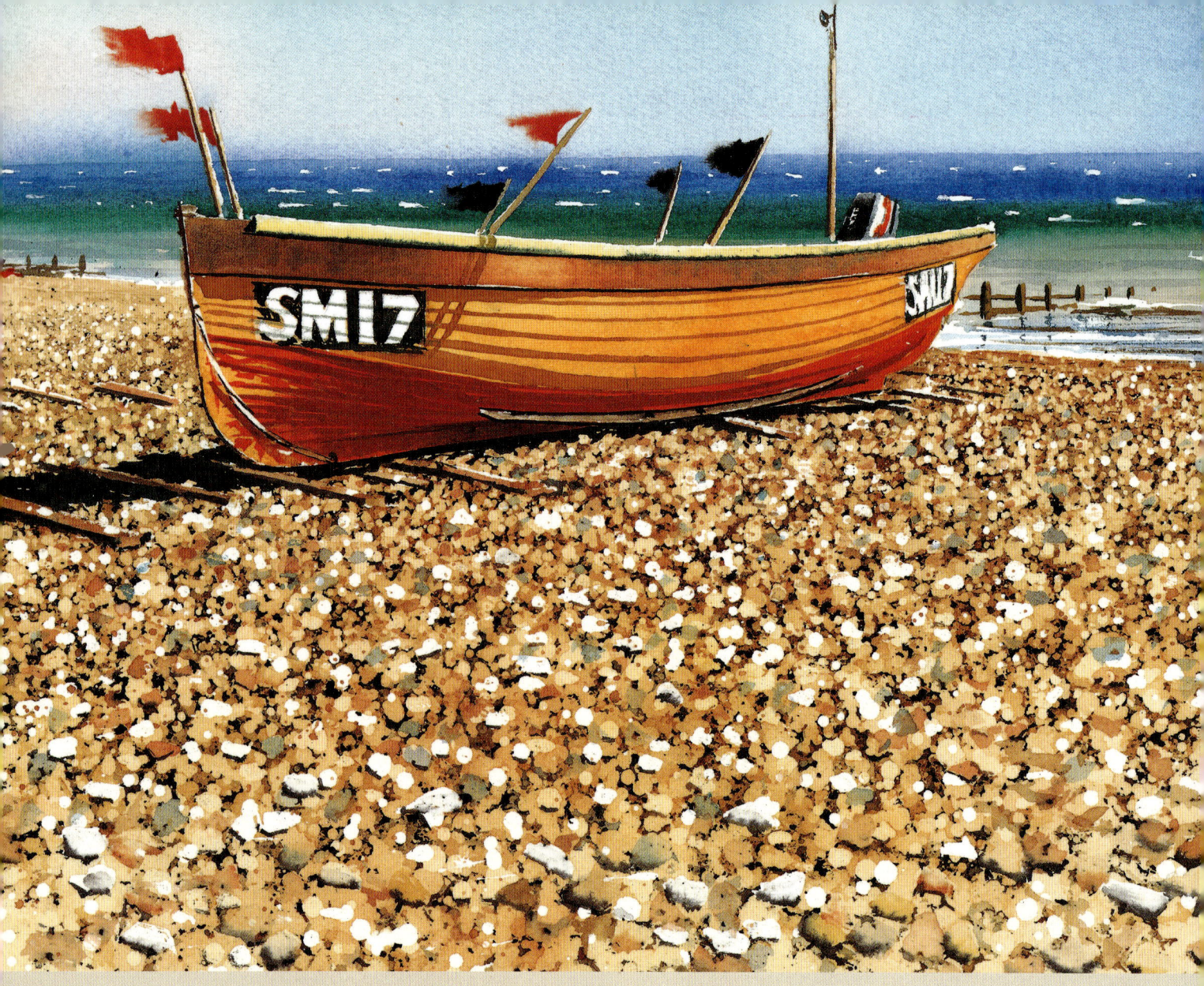

Shingle beach

A million pebbles on a beach, jumbled one on top of the other, all different colours, all in perspective! Thankfully, toothbrush spatter will enable you to achieve a realistic effect of shingle. Each droplet is a single pebble, so try not to allow the droplets to coalesce.

Artist insight: To paint three-dimensional stones, wet a few large stones, then apply grey to the shadow sides with the point of a brush. Colour spreads into a soft edge. These are lost and found (soft and hard) edges, graduating dark to light — this adds three-dimensional form. Add strong dark to shadow edges.

COLOUR PALETTE

- translucent orange
- cadmium red
- quinacridone magenta
- French ultramarine
- phthalo blue
- cobalt blue
- phthalo green
- Naples yellow
- yellow ochre
- burnt sienna
- light red
- Indian red
- Payne's gray

PAINTING THE SCENE

1 Mask the boat, outboard, planks, flagpoles, a few white horses on the sea, and some large jagged stone shapes in the foreground by hand. Spatter smaller stones with a toothbrush; work from bottom to top so that the droplet sizes get smaller.

2 Paint both the sky and the sea with the same overall wash wet-in-wet. Add a little colour to the sky, phthalo green to the lower middle of the sea, and some Naples yellow along the shore. Brush a mix of Naples yellow and burnt sienna onto the beach.

3 Wet the sea and brush a mix of French ultramarine and Indian red into the mid distance. Spatter masking fluid from the toothbrush over the beach again, covering the boat to protect it.

4 Make sure the beach is completely dry. Brush in a layer of burnt sienna and a little cobalt blue over the beach to add variety and colour. Each successive layer of colour alternates with a layer of masking.

5 Spatter masking fluid onto the beach again following the same procedure, working from bottom to top. Load the toothbrush with masking fluid. Bang the brush handle down on the palm of your hand, bristles facing down.

6 Brush another layer of deeper colour – light red and cobalt blue – onto the beach. When this is dry spatter some colour wet-on-dry for yet more texture.

7 When this is dry, wet the beach again and add dark of Payne's gray over the whole beach except the foreground area. Selectively place intense dark round some of the pebbles as shadow (**7a**). Let it dry. Peel off the masking fluid to reveal the shingle (**7b**).

8 Touch in some stones – the masking may lift some of the colour. Paint the boat. The flags are simply wet in their respective shapes, and have cadmium red, or a mix of Indian red and French ultramarine touched in at the flagpole ends, letting the colour spread towards the flag ends.

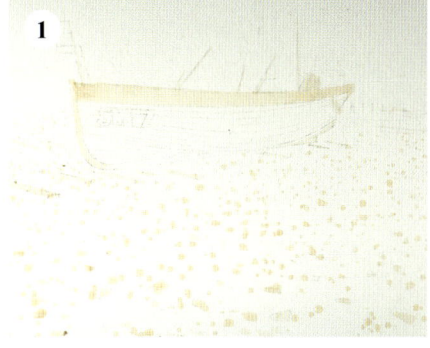
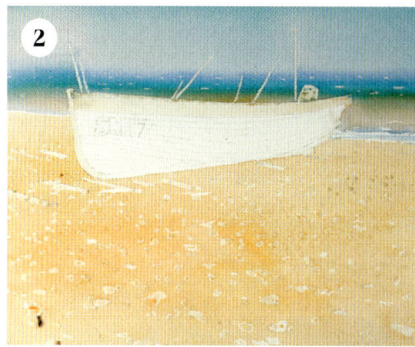
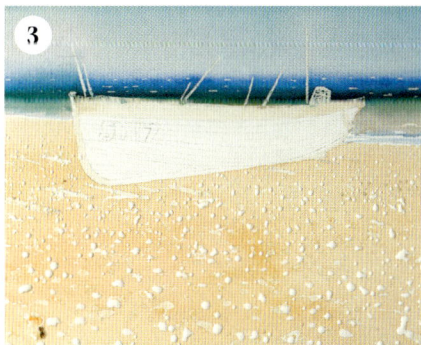
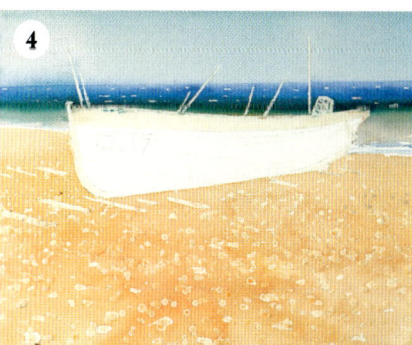
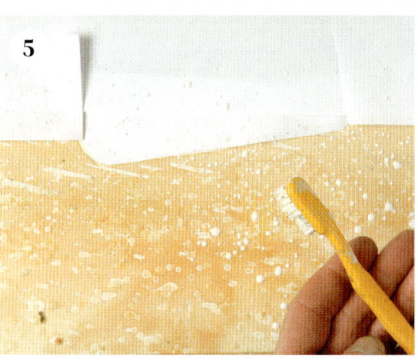
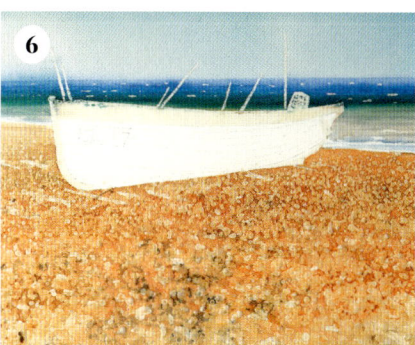
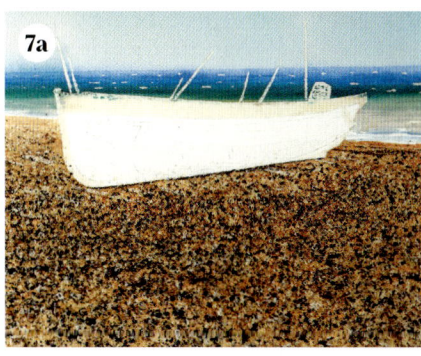
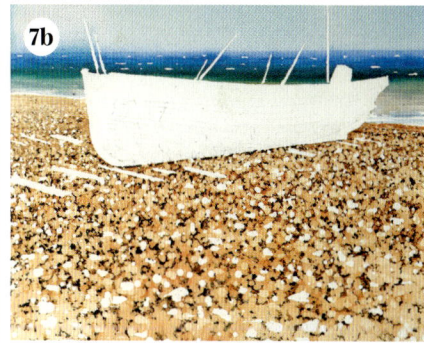
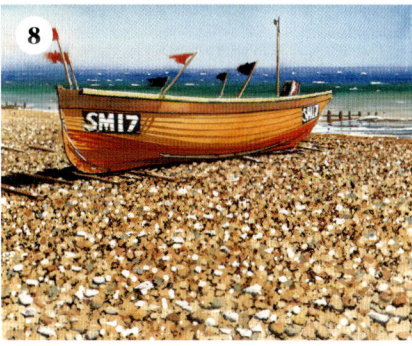

Techniques: *washes, pages 18–21; skies, pages 54–55; sea, pages 72–73, 96–97; spattering dark, pages 30–31; rowing boats, pages 82–83; masking detail, pages 32–33, 94–95; masking boats, pages 54–55; masking boat detail, pages 84–85, 94–95; masking sea lights, pages 92–93, 102–105.*

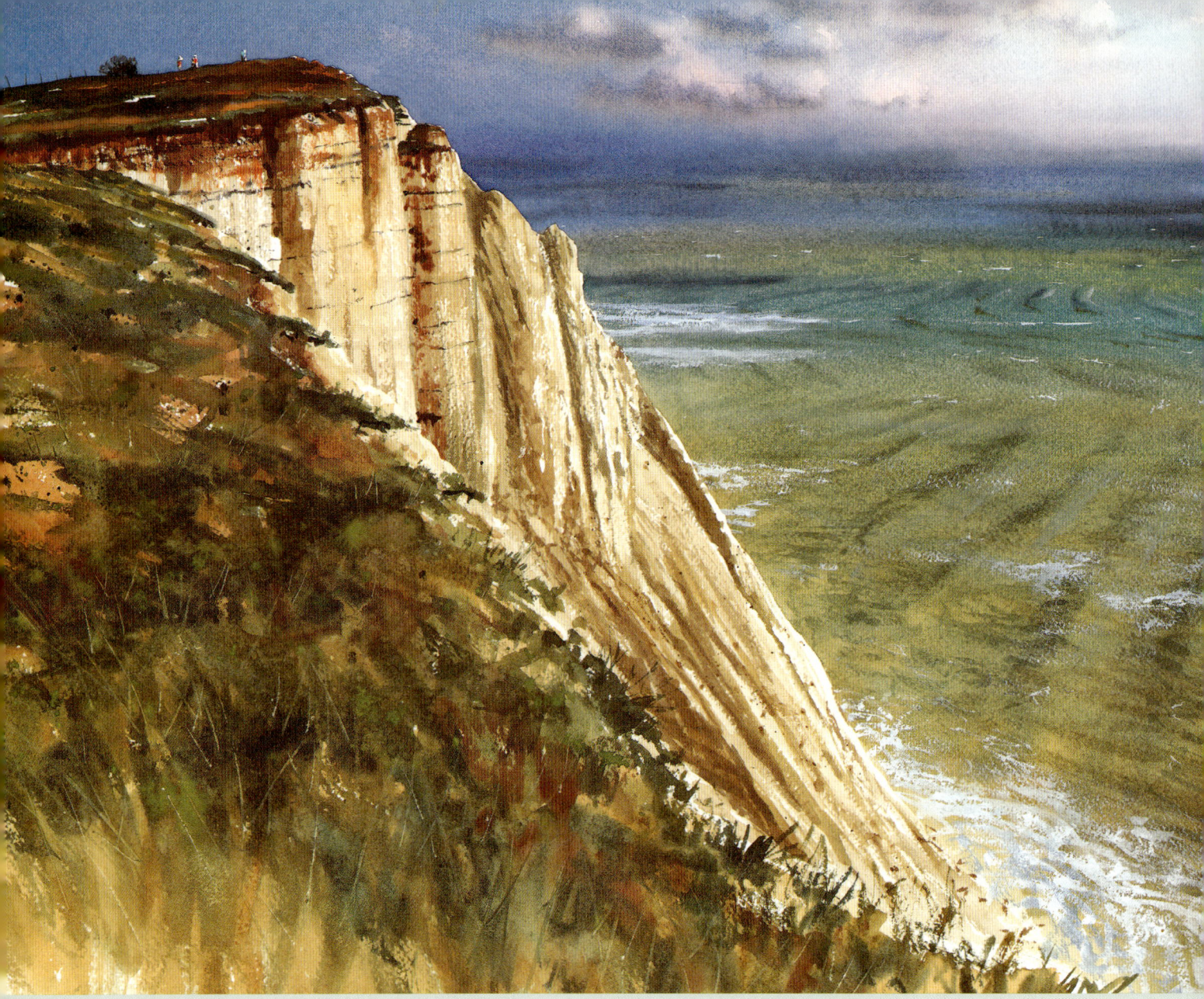

Cliff scene

Masking fluid retains the shape of the cliff while
you proceed with the sea and sky. Geometric swell
patterns, which are only visible from a height, are a
measure of wind or distant storms; notice, too, the
linear streaks indicating great distance. Near shore
the churning sea turns to mud or sand colour.

*Artist insight: The horizon is visible from vast distances at a height. It tends
to be lost in haze so a disappearing horizon gives an impression of altitude. The
darks in the sky put the sunshine onto the land and sea. Cloud shadows enhance
the sense of distance. Ranks of swell patterns could be plotted to vanishing points
on the horizon — even the sea obeys the laws of perspective. Distant linear swell
highlights and shoreline surf patterns are brushed with white gouache.*

COLOUR PALETTE

- cadmium lemon
- quinacridone red
- French ultramarine
- phthalo blue
- cobalt blue
- cerulean blue
- phthalo green
- raw sienna
- burnt sienna
- Indian red
- neutral tint
- white gouache

Techniques: perspective and distance, pages 16–17; brushmarks, pages 20–21; foreground grass (wet-in-wet), pages 38–39; skies, pages 54–57; sea and sky, pages 96–99; breaking seas and surf, pages 72–73, 92–93, 102–105; cliffs and crags, pages 36–37, 66–67, 72–73, 88–89.

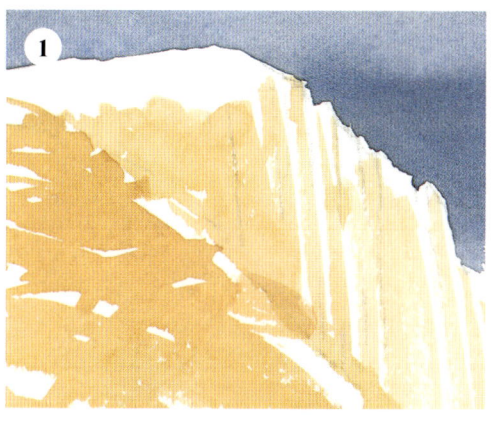

PAINTING THE CLIFF

1 In the main image the cliff edge was masked; here it was saved white. Wet the sea and sky. Apply colour to both, with a darker sea. Use a light wash of raw sienna for the fissures and textures of the cliff. Leave to dry, then brush over a mix of raw sienna for the grass underglaze.

2 Paint burnt sienna into the tops of the cliffs. Roughly paint foreground grass with a green mixed from cadmium lemon, phthalo green, burnt sienna and some Indian red touched in wet-in-wet. Brush raw sienna, cobalt blue and burnt sienna into the cliff face to shape the fissures. Brush colour into the distant sea.

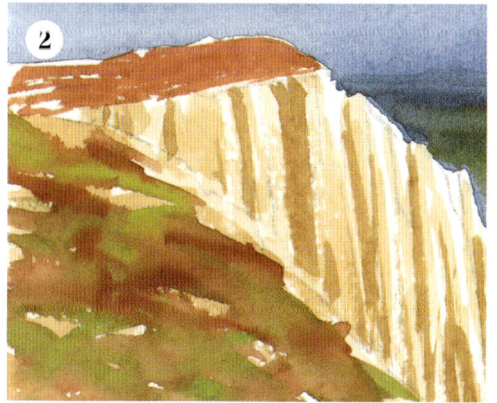

3 The foreground cliffs are a series of brushmarks, left to dry, then overpainted. Many colours are simply thrown in for the grass. Paint intense mixes of French ultramarine and Indian red for dark accents. These also serve as contrast against the light face of the cliff. Drop several colours wet-in-wet into the foreground.

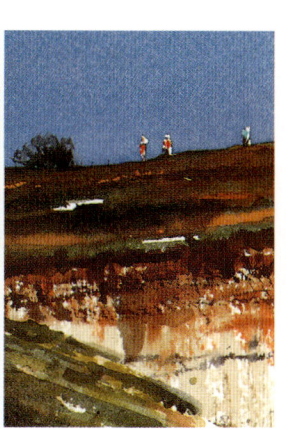

Adding scale

A few tiny people on the cliff top add scale to the scene. These were masked. The red colour gives a powerful message for people seen at a distance. Textured patterns reduce in scale with distance. Foreground texture opens out into broad and angled swathes. The high horizon accentuates the drama of height. The sharp tonal contrast of the cliffs pushes the sea back.

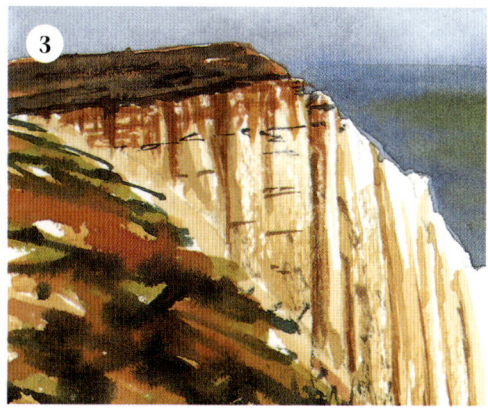

Building up the sea and sky

Many colours can be glazed in succession. Build up the sea and sky with quinacridone red and then phthalo blue, for example. Add French ultramarine to the soft horizon and then, working downwards, apply phthalo blue, cerulean blue, raw sienna and cadmium lemon. Add cerulean blue and a little burnt sienna for the groundswell. Paint distant cloud shadows on the sea with neutral tint, and waves with white gouache.

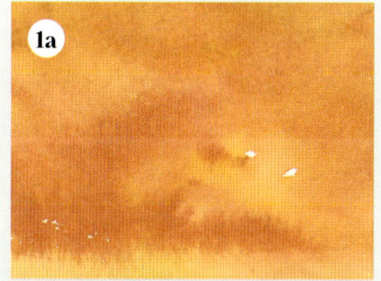

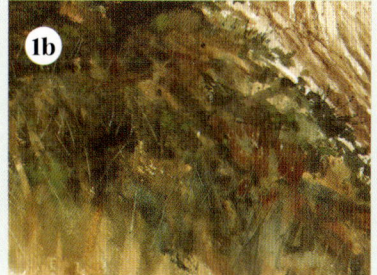

PAINTING CLIFF-TOP GRASSES

1a Apply raw sienna, leaving some lights. Look for textures and tones in grass, and paint these.

1b Brush and spatter darks of Indian red and French ultramarine mixed. Spatter the green mix. Opaque cadmium colours can cover underlying colour. Let it dry a little, but while still damp use a brush handle pressed firmly down to 'draw' the grass blades in the dark foreground. The handle pushes the colour to one side for the blade effects.

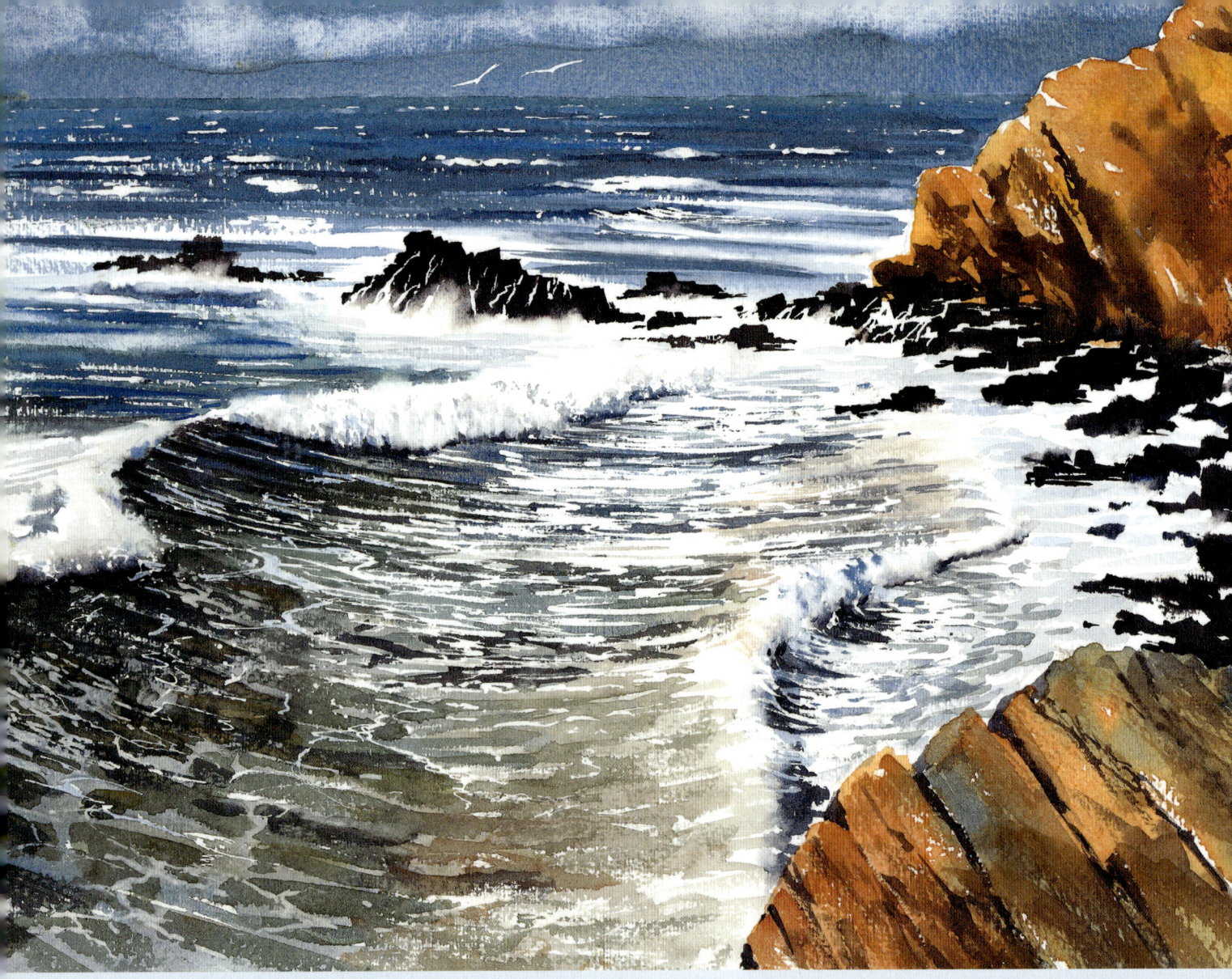

Surf breaking over rocks

For a wild sea, apply dabs of masking fluid and loose applications of colour, and overlay glazes using a sweep of the hand. Masking allows you to place two separate textures across the sea and let them indicate the rhythms of a sea in motion.

Artist insight: When painting the headland and far rocks, ensure that these are accurate geologically: you don't have to go into detail, but get the lines and fissures right. The seagulls were added at the end, using white gouache. Low cloud was lifted with a damp brush and dabbed with kitchen towel. Some lights were lifted on the sea.

Techniques: rough brush masking effects, pages 48–49; skies, pages 54–55, 98–99; rocks, rock formations, crags, and cliffs, pages 36–37, 66–67, 72–73, 88–89, 100–101; sea and sky, pages 96–101; sea foam and texture, pages 72–73, 92–93, 96–101, 104–105; lifting out, page 111.

COLOUR PALETTE

cadmium yellow

French ultramarine

cobalt blue

Hooker's green

light red

Indian red

Creating waves and foam

These sketches demonstrate a number of ways of portraying waves and surf. You can combine them for effect or use them singly.

A The distant highlights were masked, and the long white foreground streaks were left unpainted.

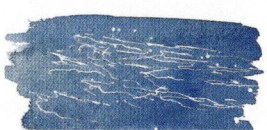

B A pen was used for masking, and fluid was spattered on from an old toothbrush.

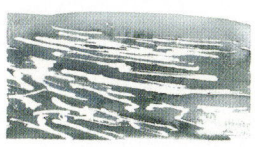

C The foam was masked using a colour shaper.

D The highlights were masked with a rough hog-hair brush, then lightly overpainted.

E No masking was used: the breaker was left as white paper, which was then wetted so the colour ran into it.

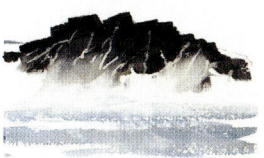

F The water coming off the rock was masked with a pen nib. The colour ran off the rock into the wet paper.

PAINTING THE SCENE

1 Use a pen nib to mask the highlights, and a brush for the breaking waves and foam in the sea. Add the rocks and headland, then the sky and distant sea. Lift out the clouds.

2 Build up the far sea with a variety of mixes and bring these colours down the page. Use a very pale wash for the near side of the breaking waves in the foreground, and when dry, soften the edges with a damp clean brush. Lift cloud with a damp brush and dab with a dry towel.

3 Brush in the foreground water in long streaks of paint; work up to the next crest on the right, leaving this as white paper. Wet the paper below the central rocks and bring the dark wash down into it from the top, to give the impression of spray crashing into the rocks.

4 Strengthen the underside of the crest of the foaming wave, using alternately strong and weak mixes. Add the rocks on the right and develop the headland. Remove the masking fluid and touch in some of the whites with cool greys.

5 The thin line of dark colour running along the bottom of the breaker, spreading up into a lighter wash with a very few pale marks on the foam itself, is what produces the three-dimensional appearance. The darks are mixed from Indian red and French ultramarine.

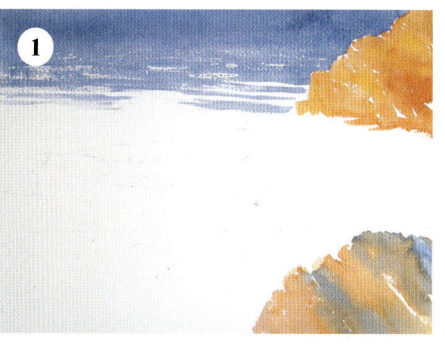

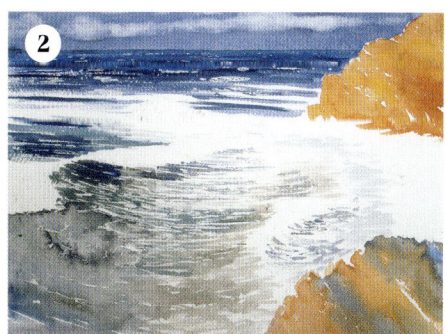

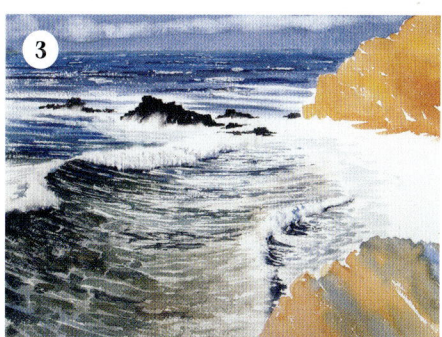

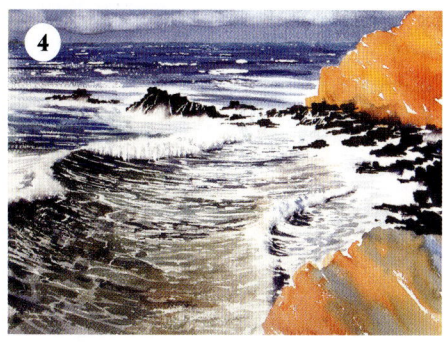

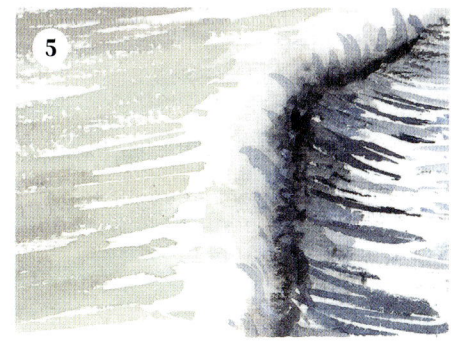

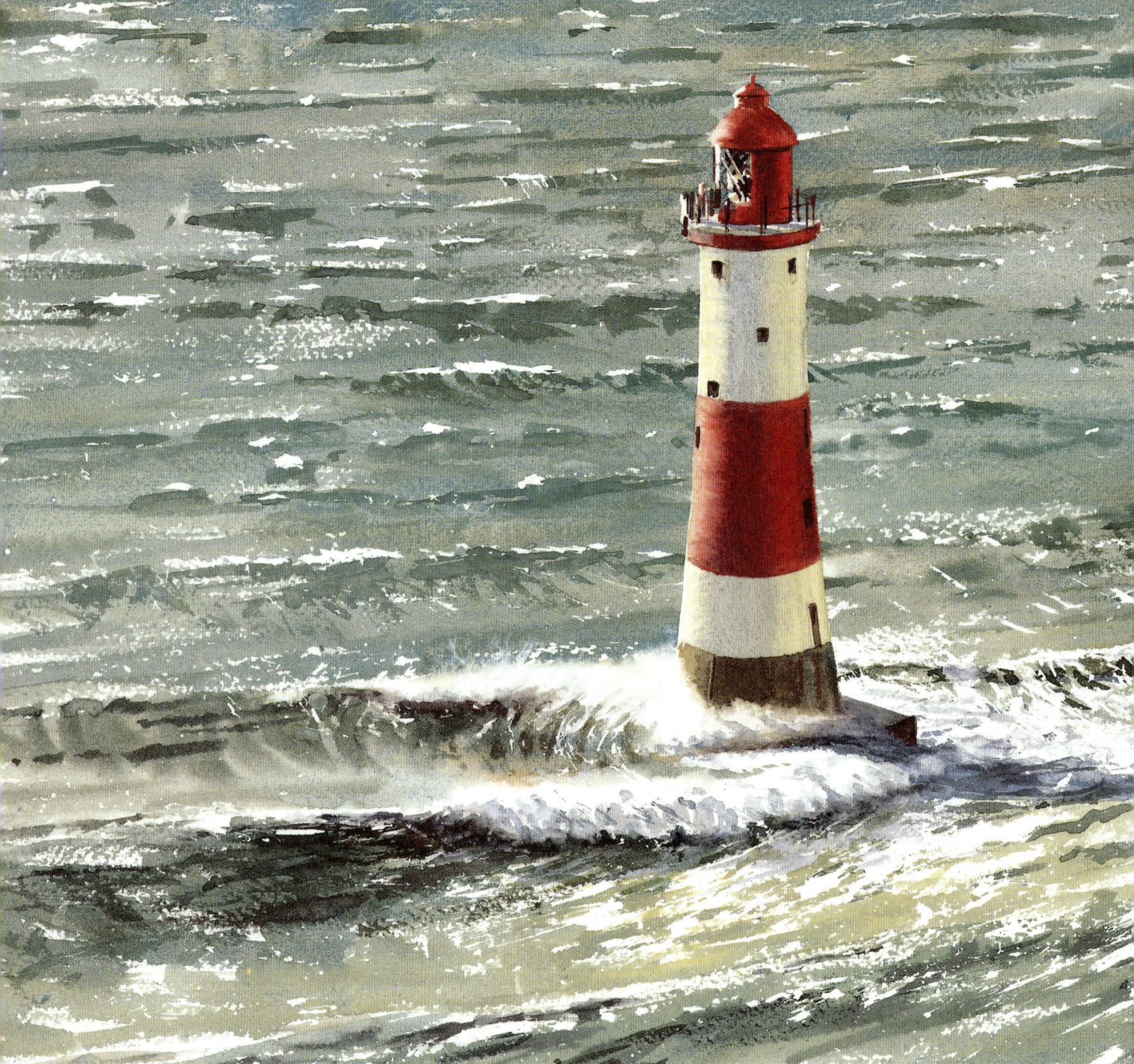

Lighthouse

The impact here is in the contrast between the smooth vertical lighthouse and the ragged sea that sweeps the image horizontally. Masking allows you to work the two separately, protecting the lighthouse while you work on the sea. Masking fluid is also used as an art material in its own right to get the sea effect.

Artist insight: Light on the right of the lighthouse is due to back light from nearby sunlit cliffs. The placement of the lighthouse to one side is crucial to this simple composition.

COLOUR PALETTE

- cadmium lemon
- quinacridone red
- French ultramarine
- cobalt blue
- cerulean blue
- phthalo green
- Naples yellow
- burnt sienna
- light red
- Indian red

Techniques: *composition, pages 10–11; composition format, pages 12–13; washes, pages 18–21; tower and masked detail, pages 32–33; rough brush masking, pages 48–49; sea, pages 72–73, 96–97, 102–103; sea sparkle, pages 92–93; surf, foam and breakers, 102–103; saved light objects (left white or masked), pages 72–73, 76–77, 83; dry-brush, pages 26, 109.*

PAINTING A LIGHTHOUSE

1 Mask the lighthouse with a colour shaper, but use a pen nib for the lookout. Use the side of a small, tightly coiled-up piece of paper to dab in the masked whites of the waves. When dry, brush in a sea wash of cerulean blue, Naples yellow and light red, with added cadmium lemon in the foreground, leaving soft-edged whites for waves breaking around the lighthouse. An alternative to cerulean blue could be phthalo blue.

2 Brush in a mix of cobalt blue, cerulean blue and light red roughly in lines for the waves, keeping many of them lining the underside of the masked white breakers. Roughly dry-brush cobalt blue mixed with a little light red into the breakers and around the lighthouse base. Paint the lighthouse shadow across the sea to the right.

3 Dry-brush darks across the foreground water. Wet the breaking waves and brush colour along their bases, letting it diffuse. With the sea completed, remove all masking. Brush water into the lighthouse, and brush pale Naples yellow into the wet wash. Add a blue-grey mix of cobalt blue and burnt sienna for soft shadow down the centre of the lighthouse.

4 Mix quinacridone red and Indian red. Wet the red areas. Add the mix to the centre and allow to spread. Add cobalt blue to the mix and repeat. Wet the bottom band and add Naples yellow with a soft lower edge. Add a dark of Indian red and French ultramarine to the middle, letting it spread. Darken the colour in the middle and right, leaving it lighter to the left.

5 Lift a highlight from the cap. Paint the turret platform and railings. Re-mask detail in the lookout. When dry, touch in dark details in the windows and on the lighthouse. Finish foam texture with blue grey. Remove the masking.

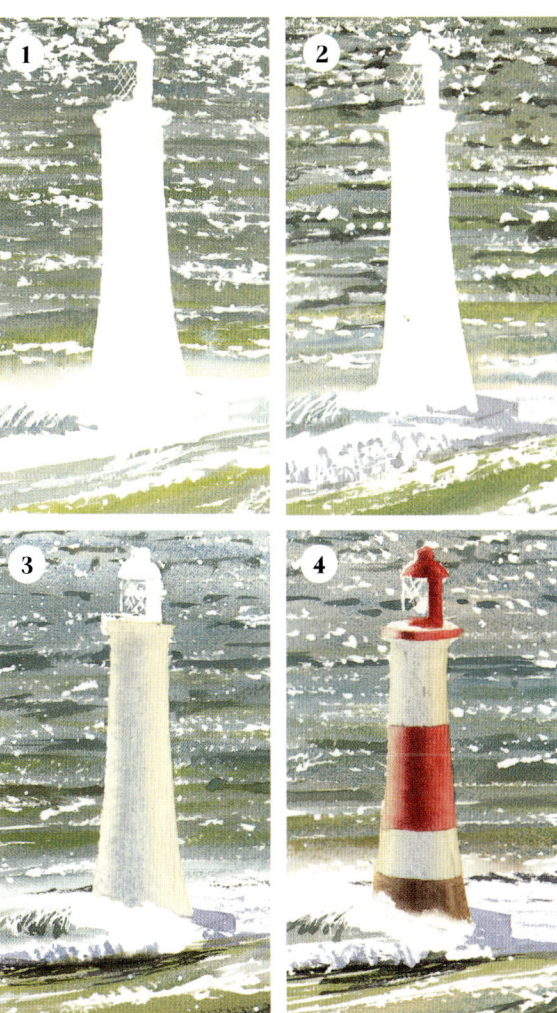

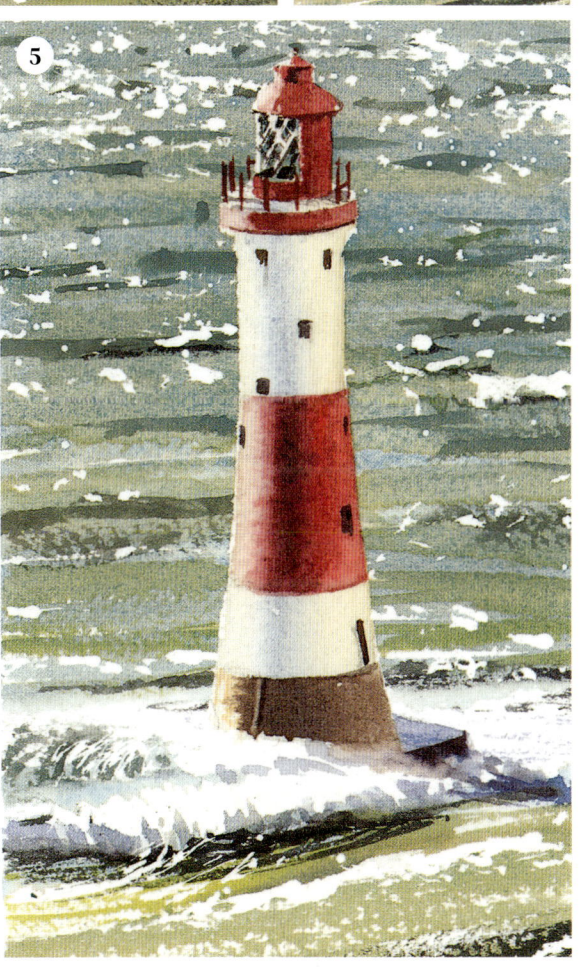

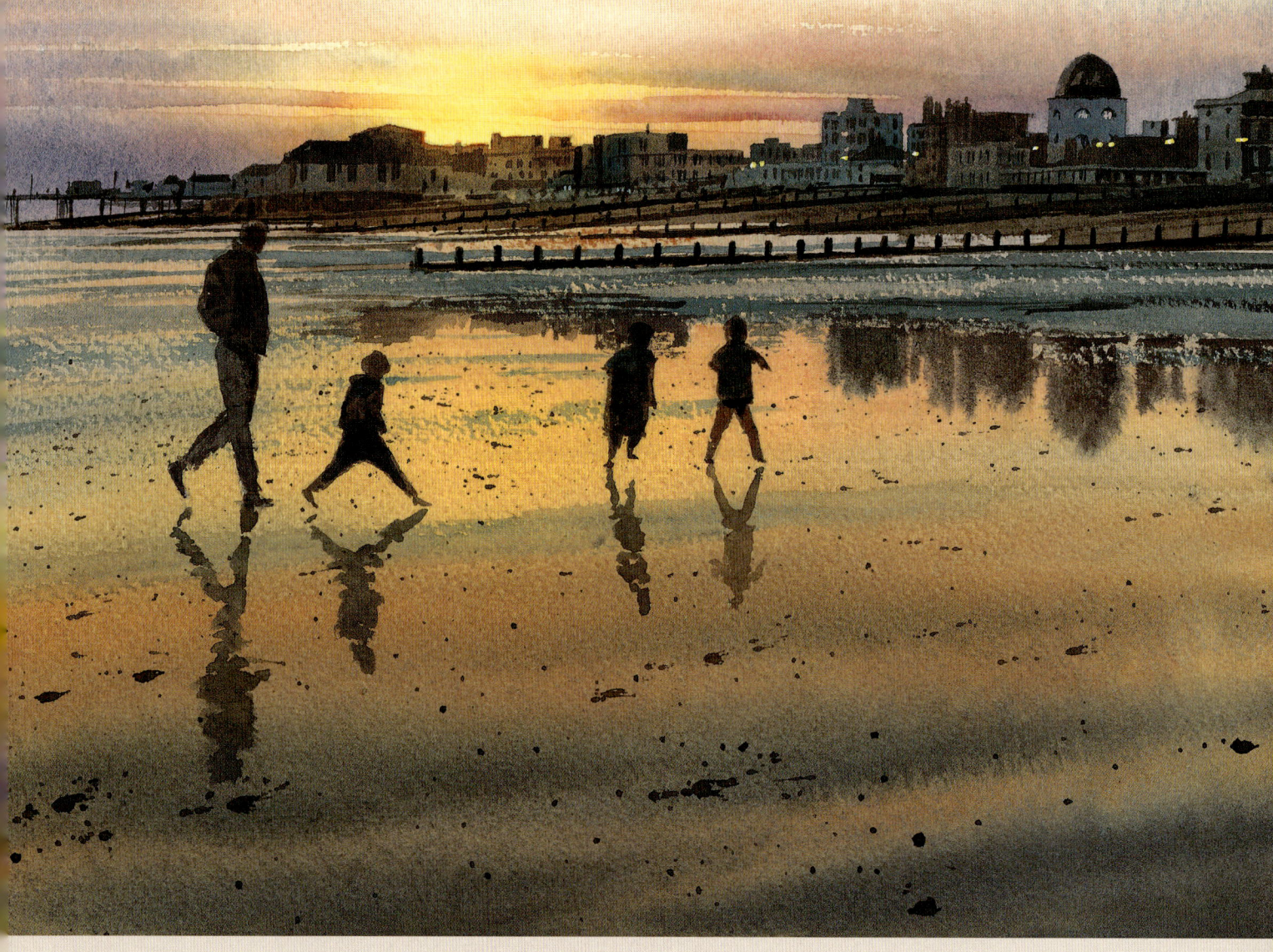

Evening beach

Wetting the paper and adding many subtle greys from two or more colours will give a silky smoothness to a picture. Leave it to dry before putting the darks on. The light is enhanced by the darks. The wetness is confirmed with the streaks across the wet sand and the soft reflections of the buildings.

Artist insight: Brush in the reflections of the figures and buildings with light washes of grey. Spatter the stones with horizontal brushstrokes, stencilling off the paper above the spatter zone and moving up for more distant spatters that become smaller as the brush uses up charge. Brush in the street lights with yellow and gouache white body colour, then touch in the light centres with a dab of white for dazzle. The space between the figures and their reflections enhances the feeling of movement.

Techniques: wet-in-wet and washes, pages 18–21: mixing greys, page 23; warm evening light, pages 38–39; figures, pages 94–95; evening sky and clouds, pages 56–57; sunset, pages 108–109; sunset effect, pages 62–63; reflections (soft focus), pages 70–71; harbour buildings, 86–87.

COLOUR PALETTE

- cadmium yellow
- cadmium orange
- alizarin crimson
- French ultramarine
- cobalt blue
- Naples yellow
- burnt sienna
- burnt umber
- white gouache

WET SAND REFLECTIONS

1 Paint the buildings and the base colour of the sand.

2 Wet the beach. Add a little gum arabic. Let the colour run down into this and leave to spread.

3 The gum arabic slows down the spread of paint, giving an interesting 'wet' texture.

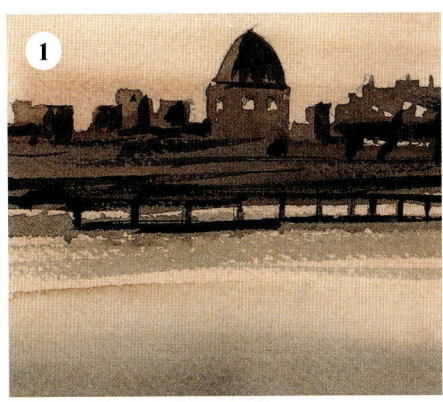

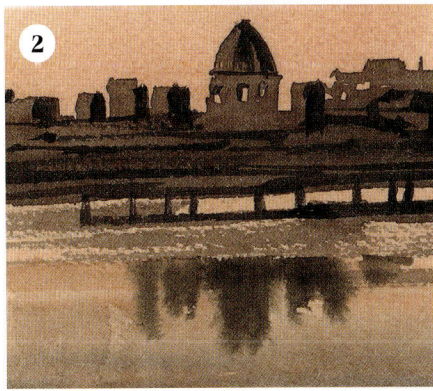

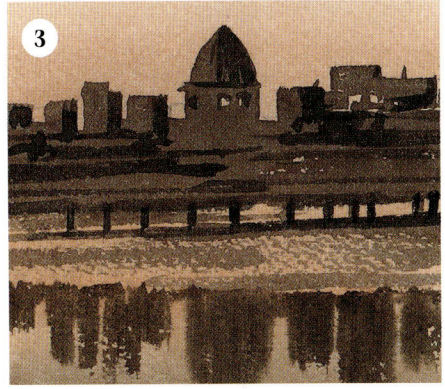

BACKGROUND WASH

To create the background wash of the main painting, begin by wetting the paper and covering it with Naples yellow, keeping it pale at the top. Mix Naples yellow with a grey of cobalt blue and burnt sienna. Apply cadmium yellow in the sun's vicinity and its beach reflection. Brush the grey mix, keeping it away from the sun. Add burnt sienna to the beach and lower sky. When dry, add sky washes of mixed crimsons, violets and greys, wet-in-wet, saving dry streaks of light. Brush burnt umber and French ultramarine on the lower beach area. Always preserve light areas around the sun and its reflection. Next paint the town and people. When the wash is dry, use French ultramarine and burnt umber for strong dark spatters and the figures.

Painting children

Paint the figures with a well-pointed sable brush. Do not aim for accuracy when painting children, just a sense of movement. Paint some of the feet so that they are 'floating' just above the ground to give this impression of movement. They are at impossible positions to be posed stationary; they are often leaning forwards, caught in action. Keep the heads large, the feet small, and the legs thin. An infant's head size in relation to its body is much greater than that of an adult, and a child of three can be around half the height of its parent.

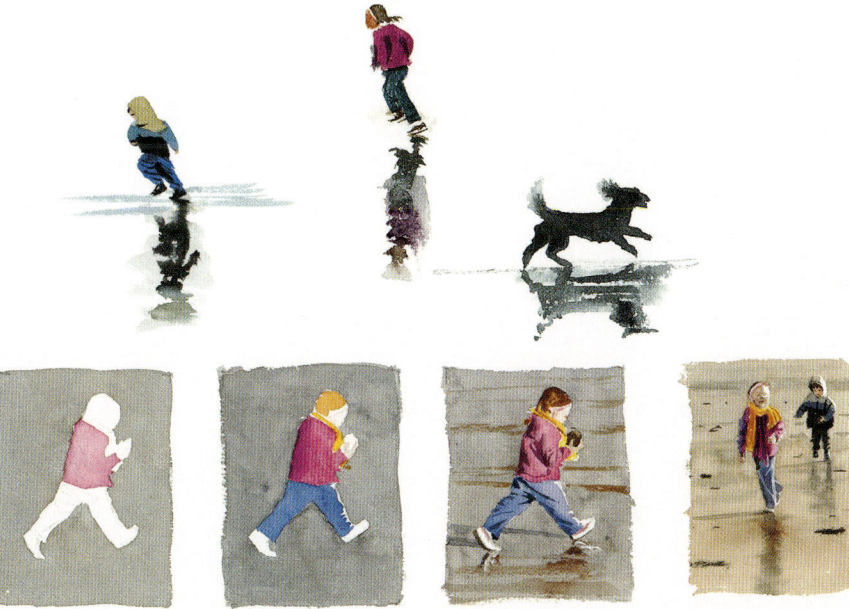

GUM ARABIC

Gum arabic is a glue-like binder in tube watercolours. Adding more increases control of diffuse effects. Colours can merge with a soft edge, rather than blending completely. It hinders the movement of colour, allowing wet-look soft-focus effects, especially in reflections. It gets hard to apply colour if you use too much, so use tiny quantities.

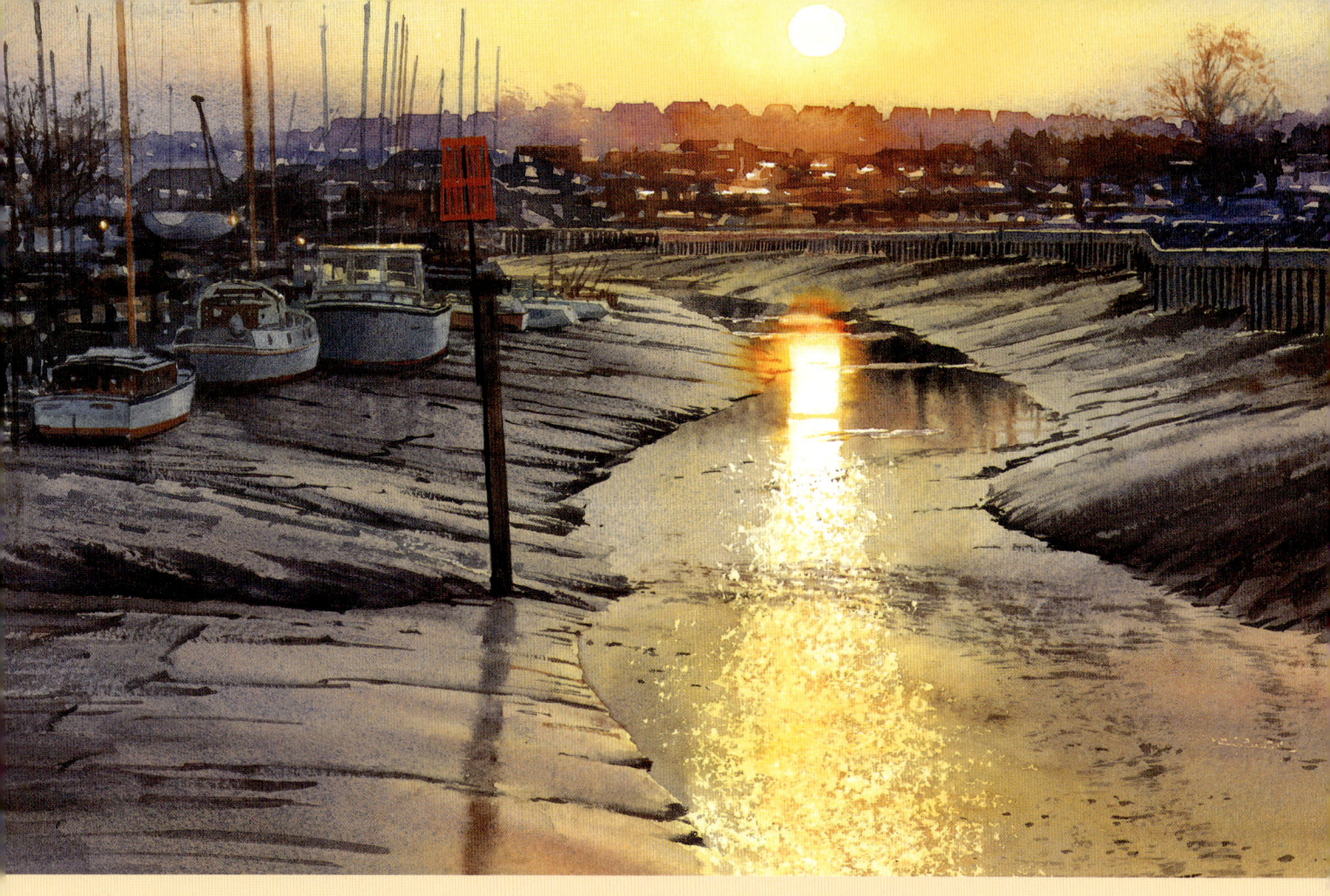

Sunset over low tide

You can paint the sun by masking it. Painting very pale sky colour around it will give an impression of glare; keep colours around the vicinity of the sun yellow, further away more orange and on the edges grey-blue. The sun's reflection is masked over yellow, using a rough hog-hair brush.

Artist insight: Here, a masked blob represents the sun's glare. Naples yellow and cadmium lemon covered everything, and darkened further from the sun with cobalt blue and burnt sienna. Sun reflection and sparkle were masked, the latter using a hog-hair brush over the yellow. The paper was alternately rewet, painted with mixes of cobalt blue, quinacridone magenta and burnt sienna, and dried. Different areas were selected for each application. This built up the light and dark patterns on the mud and water. More colour was allowed to flow wet-in-wet into the sky. A mix of light red and cadmium red was applied to the marker post. Payne's gray was used for a few intense dark accents, to make the light look brighter by contrast.

Techniques: X factor for light, page 14; warm evening sky, pages 38–39; sparkles, pages 42–43, 90–93, 94 (image only); sunset halation effect, pages 53–54; sunset with clouds, pages 56–57; masking shimmer and dazzle (glinting/glittering lights), pages 52 (under 'Artist insights'), 53 (step 5); painting the setting sun, pages 62–63; masking the sun (or moon), pages 110–111; boats in a harbour, page 95; painting wet mud or sand, pages 106–107; soft focus reflections, pages 106–107.

COLOUR PALETTE

- cadmium lemon
- cadmium yellow
- cadmium orange
- cadmium red
- quinacridone magenta
- French ultramarine
- cobalt blue
- cerulean blue
- phthalo green
- Naples yellow
- raw sienna
- burnt sienna
- light red
- Indian red
- Payne's gray

PAINTING A SUNSET

Keep the sun white, tones pale in the immediate vicinity, and use the full tonal range from the white of the paper to the deepest darks. Use glare on a principle of warmest and yellowest near the light source and coolest further away, following a sequence of yellow, orange and red. Use bright colours for the glare colours and balance them with intense darks elsewhere in the painting. You can use bright colour, straight from the tubes.

1 Brush a mix of Naples yellow and raw sienna over the whole sky, leaving a white patch for the sun. Brush cadmium yellow across the middle, cadmium orange wet-in-wet from the bottom up, adding cadmium red along the horizon. Brush cobalt blue wet-in-wet at the top.

2 Mix cerulean blue, cobalt blue and cadmium red for clouds. Rewet the whole sky and add these colours for clouds, keeping them redder near the sun.

3 When dry, add water to the clouds. Keep the sun area in the cloud dry and add a ring of yellow away from the edge of the sun, and outside this a ring of red. Let the cloud colour in from the point of a brush, keeping it redder near the sun and blending on the edge of the sun. Wet the land, and paint with some dark blue-green washes.

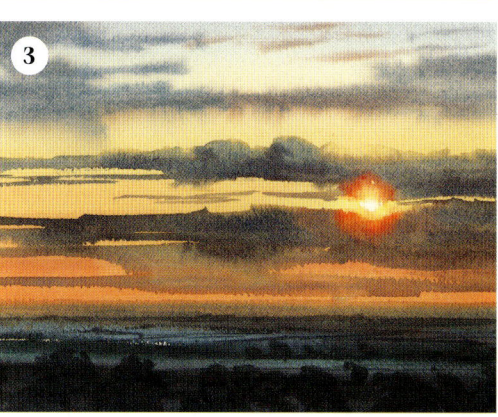

Sunset over buildings

Mask the sun and wet the sky, applying cadmium lemon and Naples yellow around the sun, burnt sienna further away, then quinacridone magenta and cobalt blue, letting colours blend and grey slightly. When dry, paint the buildings wet-in-wet, warm near the sun, cooler and darker further away. Use the same principle for the lower level of buildings, but darkening with Indian red and French ultramarine.

Dry-brush darks

Brush on an underglaze of burnt sienna, Indian red and phthalo green in a variegated wash, saving white for the sun area. Paint the distant trees in the sunset with cadmium lemon and burnt sienna, darkening to burnt sienna and dark greys. Dry-brush streaks of dark grey across the water. Place the buildings, boats and masts with darks.

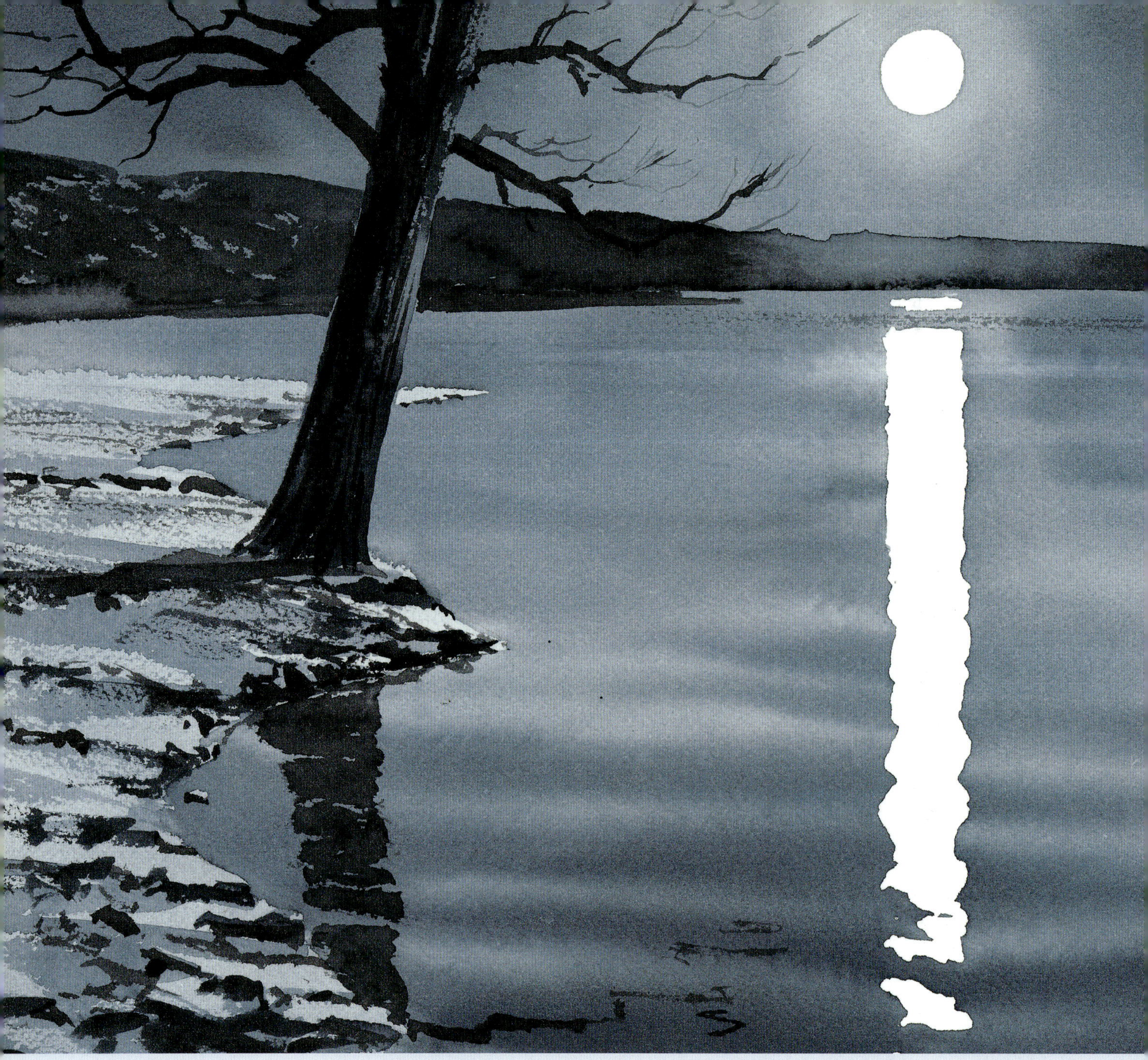

Moonlight on water

The moon is unique in the landscape, along with the sun, because it stays the same size from wherever you see it. Remarkably the moon occupies almost the same sized space in the sky as the sun – from our viewpoint it is identical in dimension. Always draw the moon larger in your paintings than you think it should be.

Artist insight: A transparent wash of colour brushed wet-in-wet produces a moonlit sky. Water was added around the moon to pale the sky and place the moon in a tranquil pool of light. Strong darks contrast the whites and lights. Only two colours plus the white of the paper were used here.

Techniques: washes, pages 18–21; skies, pages 54–55; dark skies, pages 58–59, 60–61; wet-in-wet sky (blue), pages 98–101; trees, pages 52–53, 62–63; trees and tree reflections, pages 78–79, 112–113; washes for deep water (harbour), pages 86–87; washes for soft focus wet effect, pages 106–107; sky reflection (puddles), pages 112–113.

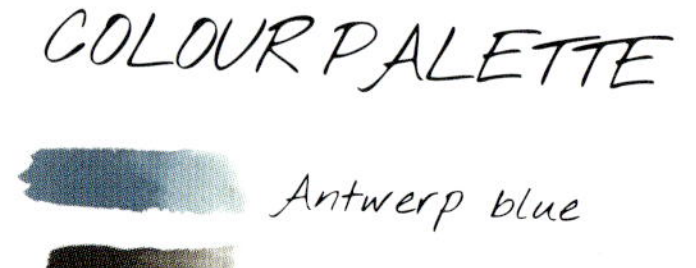

COLOUR PALETTE

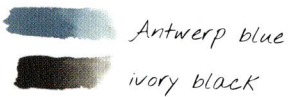

Antwerp blue

Ivory black

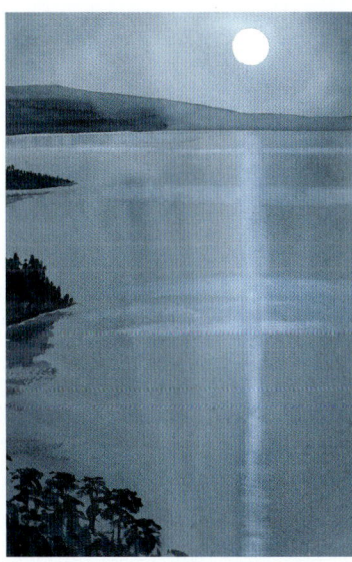

Painting the moon

- Make all tones silhouetted, with only a little discernible detail.

- Use one colour – very little colour is visible even in the brightest moonlight. A black with a little blue bias works well.

- Make the moon perfectly round and sharp. It is simply bright – not dazzling like the sun. It is also clearly edged and sits still in the eye, unlike the bright sun, which shimmers.

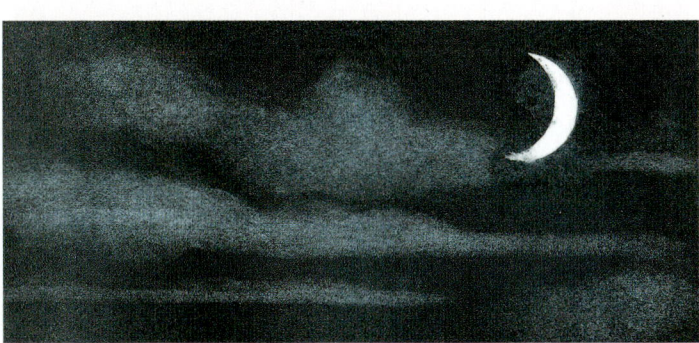

MASKING THE MOON

To mask the moon as a perfect circle, use a small coin as a template. With a sharp knife, cut out a neat round hole in masking tape, using the coin as a guide. Then place and stick the hole in the sky where you want the moon to be. Apply masking fluid across the hole. Quickly, but carefully, remove the tape before the masking becomes tacky or starts to dry. Mask the track of the moon's reflection using a colour shaper. Leave a break in the distance; make roughly straight edges further away and crooked ones nearer to allow for the rippling of nearby waves. Finish with a break-up zone where the moon reflection ripples off. Clouds in the image above were lifted.

CRESCENT MOON

The edges of a larger coin for the outer edge of the moon, and a smaller coin for the inner edge of the moon were used as guides for a knife to make shallow cuts into the paper (use a soft watercolour paper). The surface was carefully peeled away using the point of the knife.

Colours for lifting out

If you want a more distinct moon than you could achieve by lifting, but do not want the harshness of masking, use colours that lift more readily than others. Indigo is a staining colour and lifts to a limited extent. Antwerp blue and ivory black are colours that both lift well, so making a blue-black from these two gives an indigo-like colour that lifts much more easily.

Antwerp blue lifts well.

Ivory black lifts well.

Blue-black mixed from Antwerp blue and ivory black lifts well.

Lifting colour

Gently scrub with a damp brush and dab with kitchen towel to remove colour. Be careful not to scrub too hard or the colour will be absorbed into the fibres of the paper. The objective is not to remove all the colour back to the white surface, but to create a soft subtle effect.

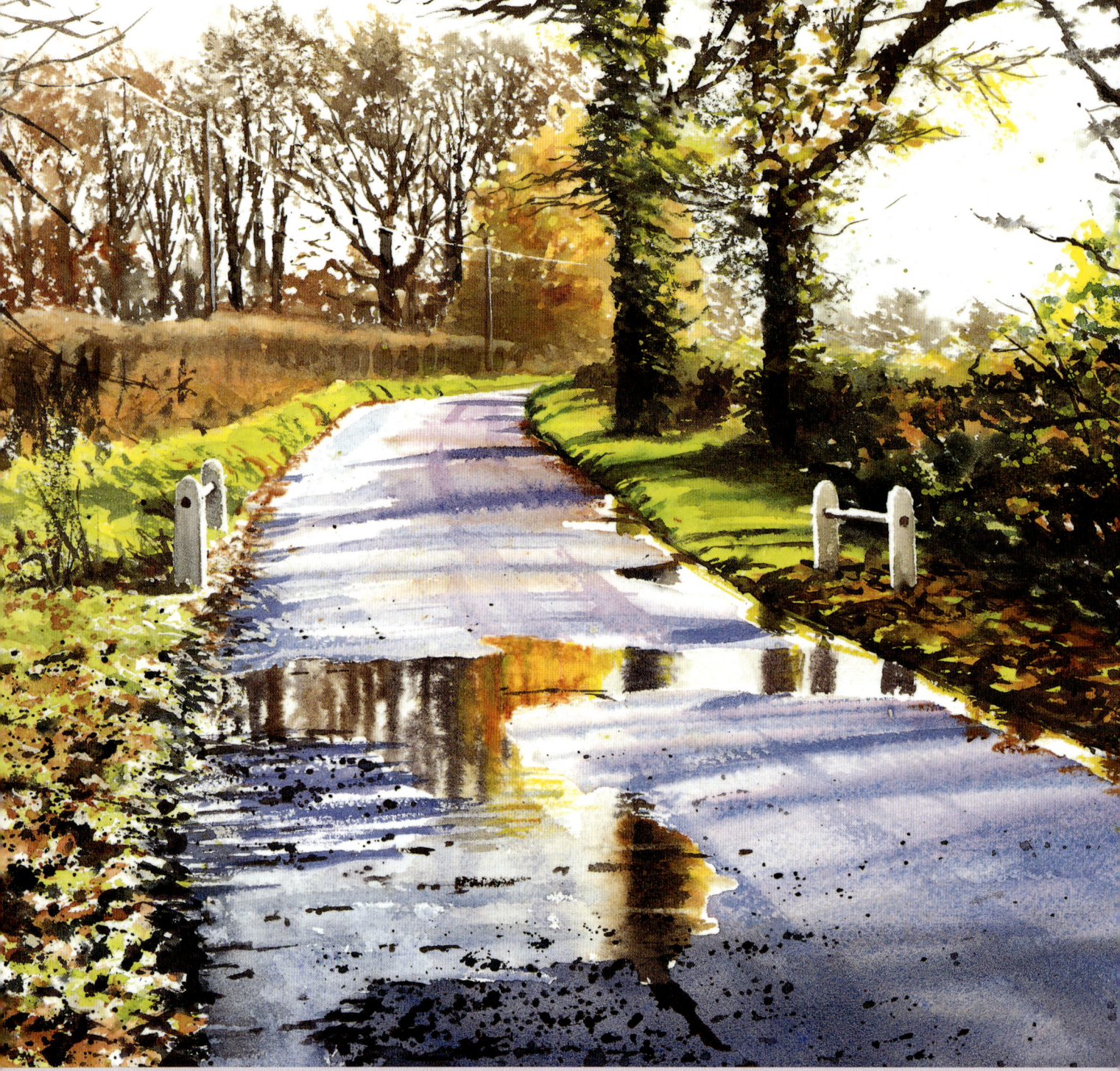

Lane with puddles

A portrait or square format allows you to compose a simple landscape.
It could just be a lane and a tree, with problems 'edited' out. Puddles add
interest. Here are useful techniques for rendering them. With variations
on this theme, you need never be stuck for something to paint.

Artist insight: *In this painting, the telegraph wire was masked with a dip pen. Small droplets of
masking fluid were spattered over the distant trees. The woodland was applied with the water
feathering technique. The puddle, railings and some leaves were masked. Autumn foliage colour was
applied with cadmium yellow and burnt sienna, with greys added later. Intense darks are Payne's gray.*

COLOUR PALETTE

- cadmium lemon
- alizarin crimson*
- quinacridone magenta*
- French ultramarine
- phthalo blue
- cobalt blue
- cerulean blue
- phthalo green
- Naples yellow
- burnt sienna
- light red
- Indian red
- Payne's gray

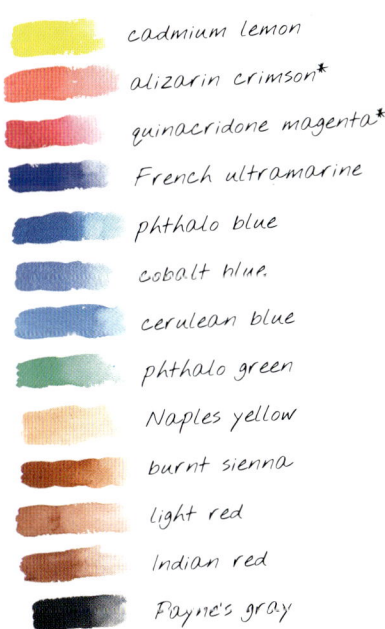

* *Alizarin crimson and quinacridone magenta are interchangeable.*

Techniques: simple landscape composition/portrait/various formats, pages 12—13; water feathering, page 19; granulation, pages 20—21, 124—125; wet-in-wet (use for puddle reflections), pages 18—19, 90—91, 106—107; sky hole spatter, page 28 (main image); puddles, pages 39, 54—55; masking details, pages 32—33; trees, pages 42—43, 78—79; dark spatter for texture on ground, pages 28—31; foreground foliage texture, pages 80—81.

Road surface texture

Mask the puddles. Mix violet with cerulean blue and quinacridone magenta, deep blue with French ultramarine and cerulean blue, and light red on its own. Wet the road. Brush in the pinkish violet. Brush the deep blue for shadows and streaks along the road. Add light red to the mid distance. Cerulean blue creates a granular tarmac effect. Apply nearby shadows wet-in-wet, distant ones wet-on-dry.

PAINTING PUDDLES

1 Saving white for the lane, brush greens of Naples yellow, cadmium lemon and phthalo green, and greys of burnt sienna, crimson, and cobalt blue or French ultramarine. When dry, wet the lane and apply a wash of phthalo blue, alizarin crimson and burnt sienna, working from the bottom up, dark to light. Leave the top as white paper.

2 Brush in the tree with burnt sienna and French ultramarine. Keep the foreground puddles longer and the curving lines more open, tightening them with distance. Brush the distant tree reflections down into the lane wet-in-wet or wet-on-dry, right across the drawn lines of the puddles.

3 Brush the tree with a dark of light red and French ultramarine. Brush the reflection with tree colour down over the reflection wash, wet-on-dry; mirror the exact height of the tree. Measure from the lane surface next to the tree. Brush the lane surface with a dark of Indian red and French ultramarine, leaving holes for the puddles.

4 In this finished version saved white for the distant house was touched in with light red for the roof and darks for the windows. The lane was dry-brushed with darker colour and the distant trees were water feathered. A pale sky helps place light on the land.

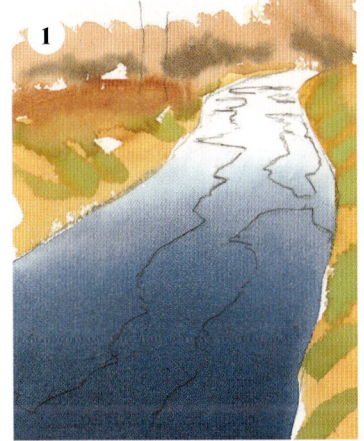
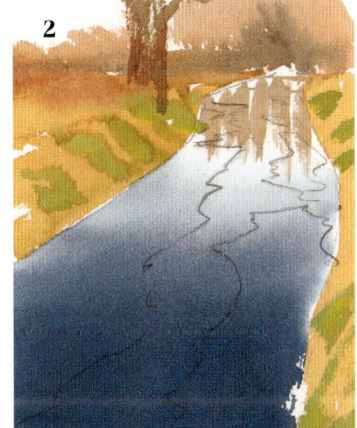
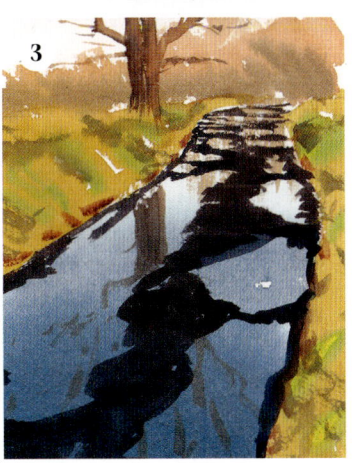
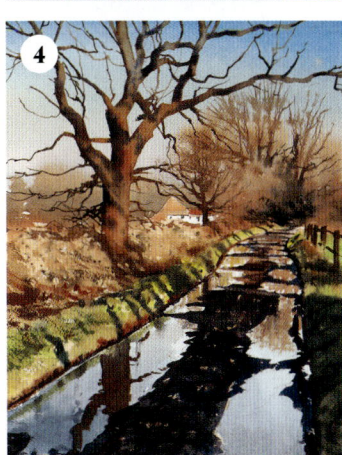

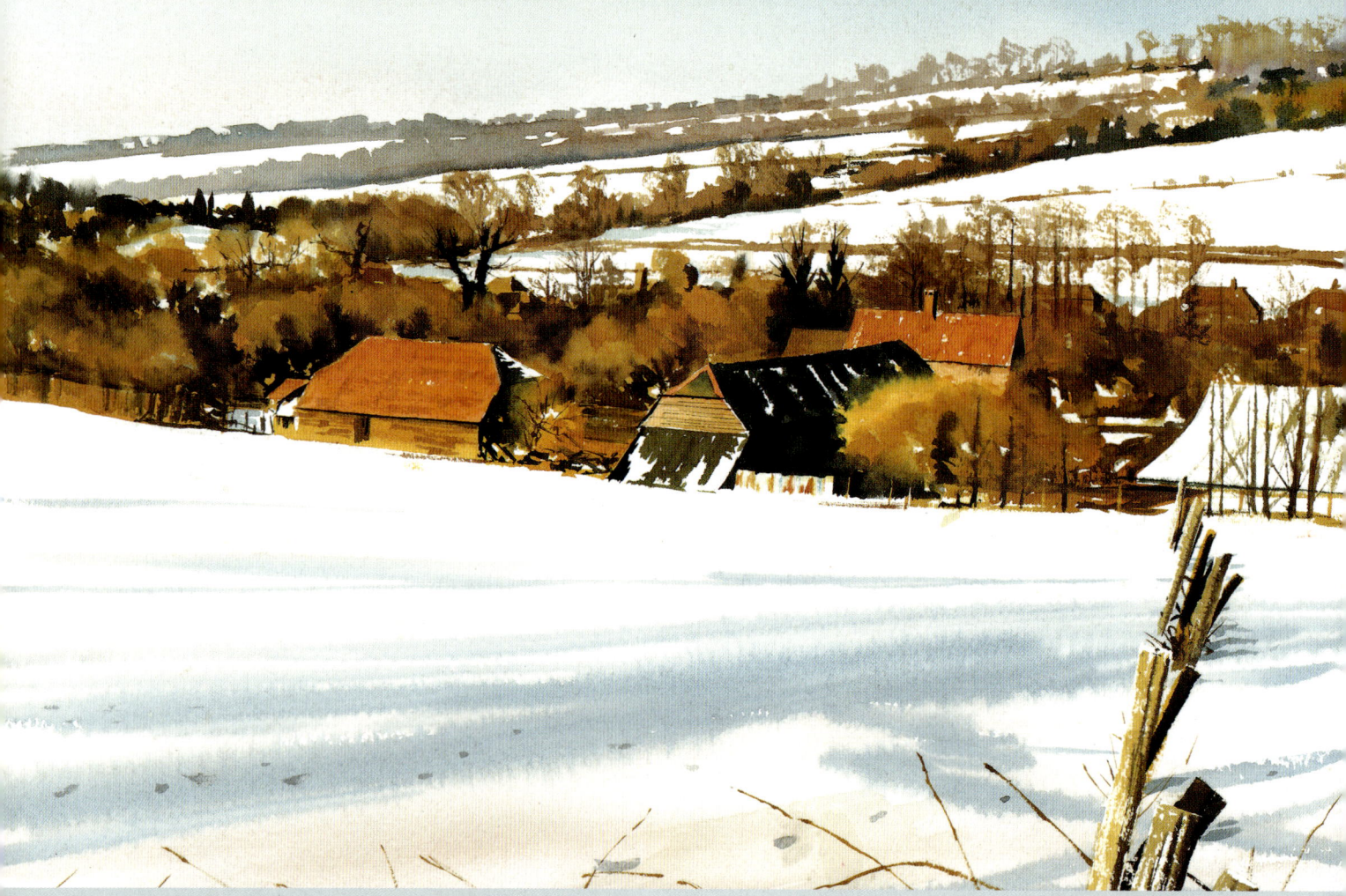

Buildings in the landscape

Great swathes of open countryside can be straightforward to paint. Here there is a simple contrast between the clear straight lines of the buildings against the free-form foliage and loose ragged lines of the field edges. Using a three-part brown as a base colour gives vibrancy and enables you to explore colour.

Artist insight: For buildings in the snow, viridian, red and transparent yellow make the greenish dark for the slate on the front of the right-hand barn. Sepia is used everywhere to define the edges of buildings, to paint tree trunks, to define the outside edge of the field edge fence and to put contrast into the painting. The dry plant stems in the foreground are brushed in with brown from the palette. Foreground posts were masked and snow shadows painted across them. With the masking removed, they were dry-brushed with water. A yellow version of the three-part grey was added, (see 'Exploring colour'), leaving lights from dry-brushing as speckled snow on white paper. For a hard and soft shadow edge, dark was added to the right-hand sides while they were wet. Vertical fissures were added when dry.

Techniques: receding bands (landscape in perspective), page 17; wet-in-wet, pages 18–19; mixing greys, page 23; buildings (rural), pages 26–27; buildings (in landscape), pages 40–41, 74–75; buildings (city roofscape), pages 118–119; distant landscapes, pages 34–35; skies, pages 54–55; leaving out white or light (without masking), pages 83–85; dry-brush, pages 27, 109; snow, pages 46–47, 64–67, 116–117.

COLOUR PALETTE

- transparent yellow
- cadmium red
- cerulean blue
- viridian
- sepia

PAINTING BUILDINGS

Paint the shapes of buildings first, or paint round them. Light shapes are revealed by darker surrounding tones. When painting darks round the buildings, paint straight washes along the outsides of the edges, overshooting the corners until the straight washes link up leaving a straight faceted hole – your building. Constantly turn the painting to suit your hand. Work from the outside; for example, upside down when defining roofs.

1 Mask the light fence posts. Wash in the sky and foreground wet-in-wet using watery mixes of greyed cerulean blue. Add the red on the barn roofs with a mix of transparent yellow, cadmium red, and a little viridian to calm the red down. Add a patch of transparent yellow for the trees in the sun, like those on the right.

2 Paint the distant hilltop trees with a blue-biased mix of cadmium red and cerulean blue. The nearer ones are made with browns of cadmium red and viridian. Allow pigment to blend on the paper with colour variations, defining the barn edges. Paint the walls with the roof mix, watered down and with more viridian.

3 Build up the rich browns with cadmium red, viridian and plenty of transparent yellow in a warm brown mix. Add darks wet-in-wet with sepia, used also for deep darks on the shaded barn sides. Dry-brush some of the trees. Work others wet-in-wet. Provide tonal contrasts, such as the dark barn wall against yellow foliage.

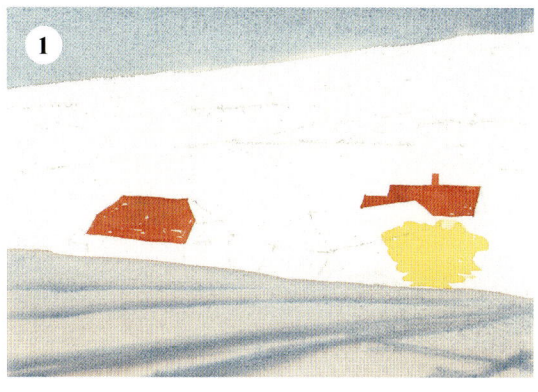

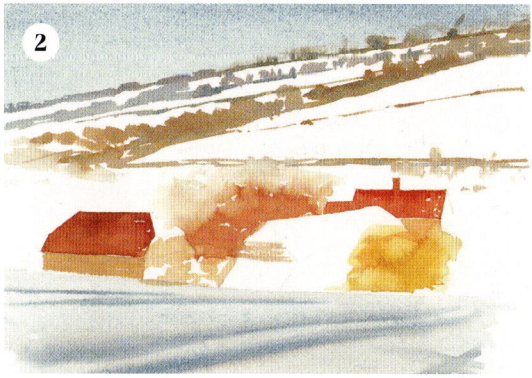

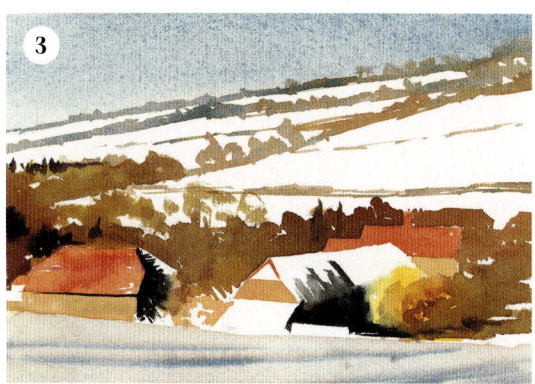

Setting the tone

A pale wash of tone has great power. Though not dominant in the finished painting it unites and projects lights and whites. Here the image is unified at the start by painting land and sky with the same mix, and leaving the vast space of snow-covered hill white. Shadows are a darker mix of cerulean blue and cadmium red.

Exploring colour

Often a watercolour painter uses burnt sienna as the base colour, or another warm earthy colour such as burnt umber, light red or yellow ochre. Changing your normal palette is a great way of experimenting with colour for a lively result. A three-part brown from cadmium red, viridian and transparent yellow, contains the three primary colours – red, yellow and blue – the latter two make up the green. This means the mix has the potential for mixing any red, brown, yellow, green or black, so it fulfils all the needs of the painting. Inject heat into the colour by using a lot of transparent yellow. If you add new gamboge or transparent yellow to burnt sienna, it can become really vibrant, even when dry.

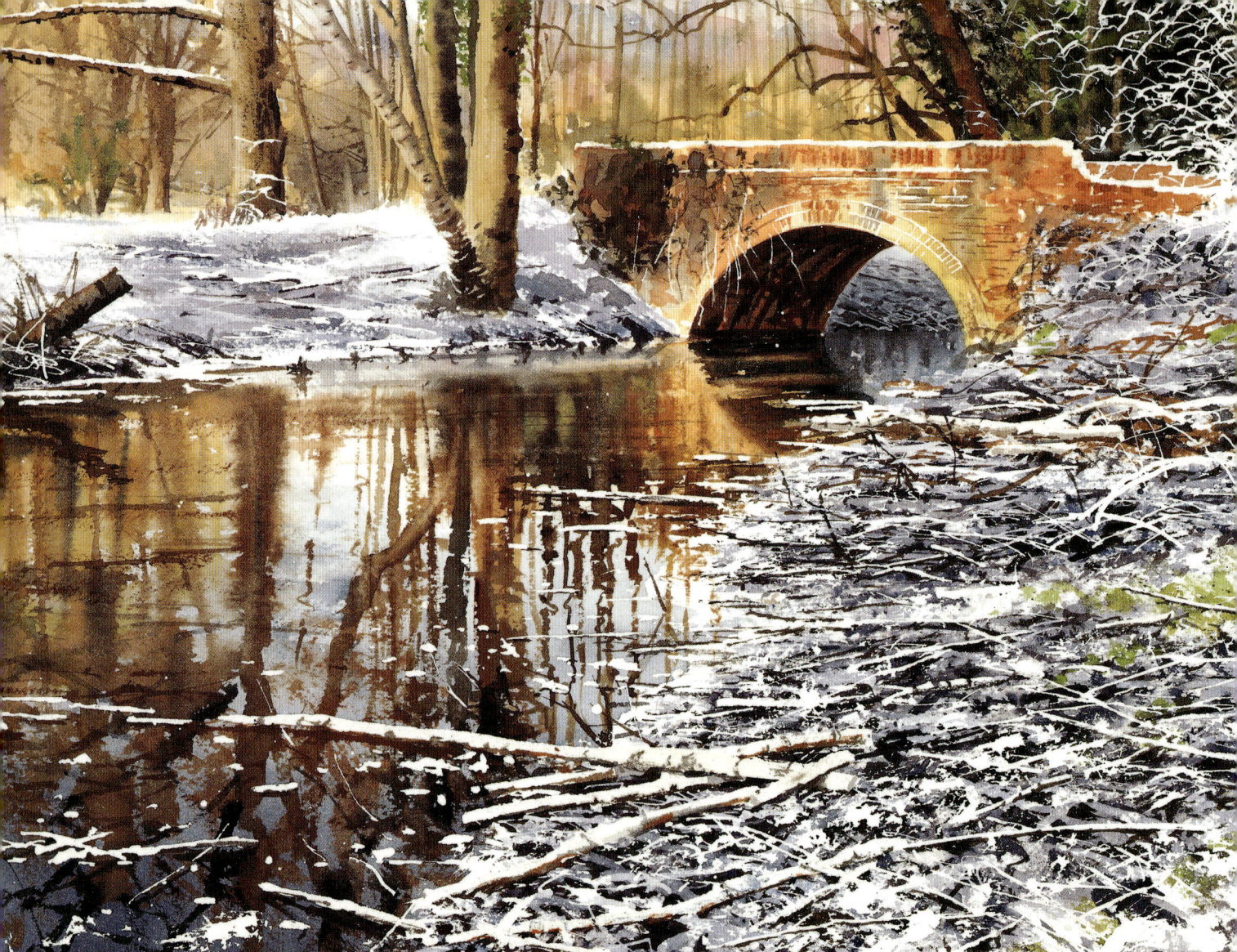

Little bridge

Working one layer and one area at a time makes a complex-looking painting simpler to paint, part of the illusion you can create. Snow on the parapet is masked for convenience, but masking is also used creatively to make fallen branches rather than just solving painting problems. Water is painted both dry and wet-in-wet.

Artist insight: To complete the painting, the water was worked wet, with vertical soft-focus marks dragged down, as well as hard-edge vertical marks on dry, all painted loosely. Dark lines were brushed in above the horizontal brick courses and to the left of the upright ones on the bridge. Darks were brushed into the fallen mass of branches. All the masking was removed and the whites retouched a little. All the masking was removed and the whites retouched a little with a blue-grey mix of cobalt blue and burnt sienna. Some intense dark was lined in from the point of a brush, wet-in-wet.

COLOUR PALETTE

- cadmium lemon
- alizarin crimson
- French ultramarine
- phthalo blue
- cobalt blue
- phthalo green
- Naples yellow
- yellow ochre
- raw sienna
- burnt sienna
- light red
- Indian red
- neutral tint

Techniques: washes, pages 18–21; tree canopies, page 19; reflections, pages 42–43; masking fallen branches and textures, pages 50–51; winter trees, pages 46–47; water and reflections, pages 66–67, 76–85; snow (on landscape), pages 114–115; snow (on mountains), pages 66–67.

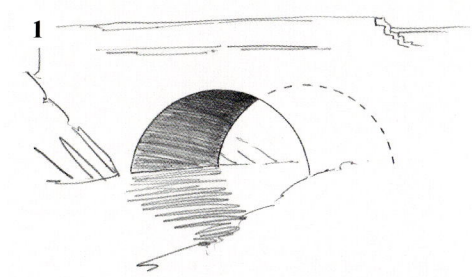

PAINTING THE BRIDGE

1 Construct the bridge carefully in pencil, by drawing two arches, one behind the other, to get the shape of the opening – these are virtually semi-circles seen dead on. Place the second circle to the right of the first to map out the back of the bridge opening, but draw only the visible part of the curve.

2 Mask snow on the bridge and masonry courses, twig mass and branches. Lay the first washes. Paint the snow with a mix of cobalt blue, alizarin crimson and burnt sienna. Wash the bridge with Naples yellow and a little light red. Brush a mixed wash of phthalo blue, neutral tint and alizarin crimson into the wetted water area. Allow to dry. Brush under the arch with light red.

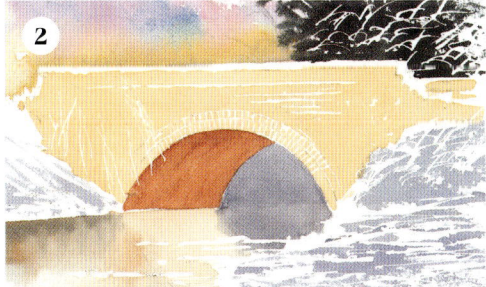

3 Brush the bridge with light red. When dry, touch in the bricks again with light red and a little cobalt blue. Add the shadows to the bridge with cooler versions of this. Drag some dry-brush accents across. Wet under the arch. Brush in Indian red and French ultramarine mixed as a dark, leaving a few lights. Put plenty more colour in and paint the bridge reflection soft focus in the wet area.

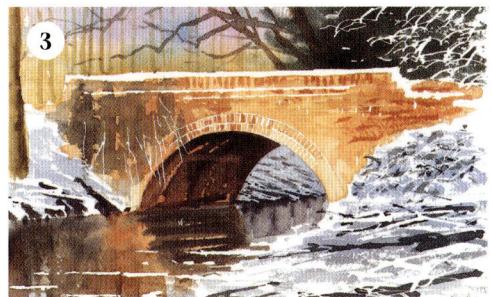

DIAGONAL COMPOSITION

By keeping the horizon high, and the focal point of the painting well off centre, you will create a good composition at the start. The diagonal theme is important, with counter-balancing diagonal lines creating a rhythm in the foreground landscape. This is drawn at crouching height – as though you are sitting on the bank, giving an exaggerated foreground perspective. The first few metres make up the bottom half of the painting; the rest of the scene is compressed into a relatively thin strip. When planning the foreground river bank texture, think in terms of broad diagonal lines that define underlying form – deeply slanting and long in the foreground, shorter and flattened off in the distance. Practise a series of lines on scrap paper to get the feel of the required perspective.

Painting brickwork

You can mask brickwork courses over white and paint over, or paint them and mask over, as shown in these three examples.

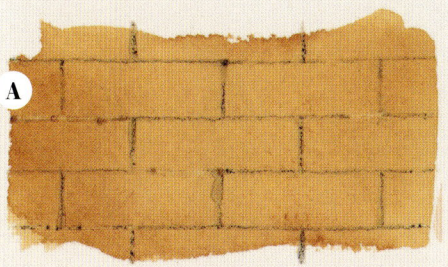

• Raw sienna with courses masked over (**A**).

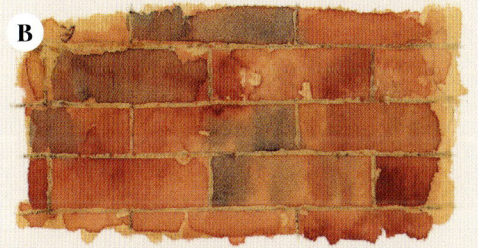

• Light red with added French ultramarine and yellow ochre brushed over the courses (many other browns and blues can be used) (**B**).

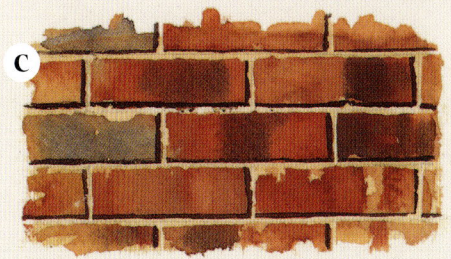

• Shadow lines painted above the masked courses and alongside the perpendicular ones (**C**).

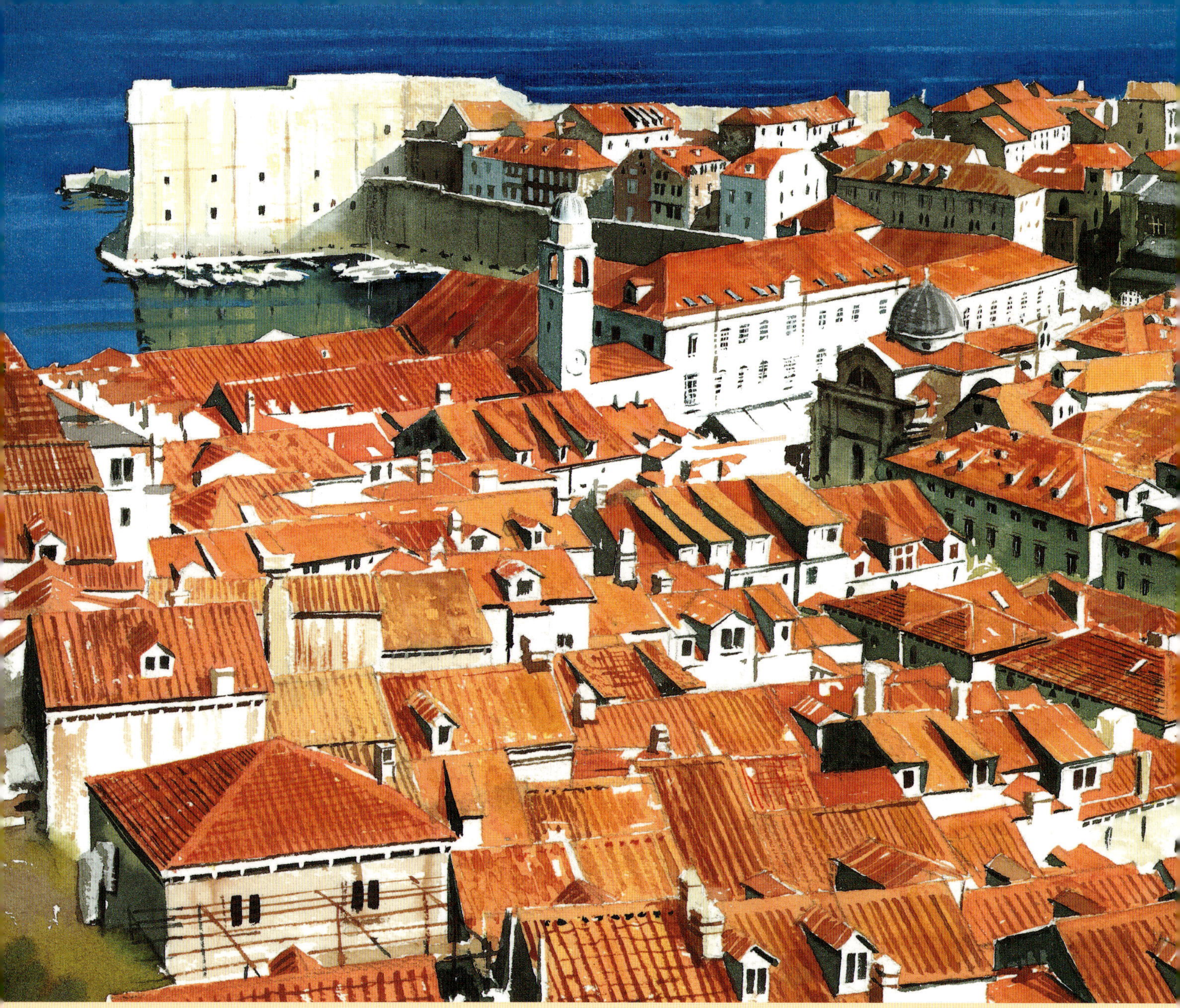

Medieval city and harbour

Build up a maze of roofs and a cityscape by defining basic shapes, then working the tones from light to dark. The principle is the same for any apparently complex painting – break it down into manageable areas and handle one at a time. Save and maintain the whites; the painting jumps into life when the darks are added.

Artist insight: The darks in the completed painting pull the image together. Dark indigo detail is painted onto the building faces for shadow under the eaves, in window apertures and for deep shadow on the sides of dormer windows. The light harbour wall is reflected on the water with a wash of Naples yellow and white gouache applied wet-on-dry. A few textures are dragged with a dry brush onto the white building faces.

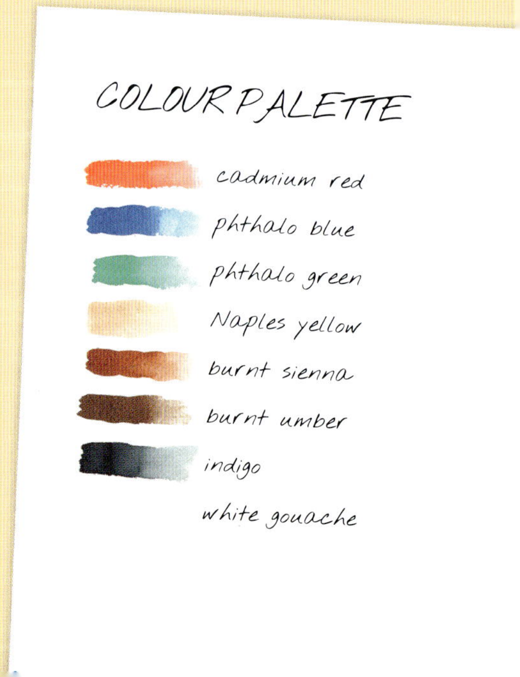

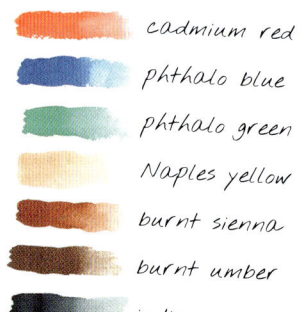

COLOUR PALETTE

cadmium red

phthalo blue

phthalo green

Naples yellow

burnt sienna

burnt umber

indigo

white gouache

BLOCKING IN A COMPLICATED HARBOUR SCENE

'Block in' the basic shapes by working the tones and colours one layer at a time, letting each dry and saving the whites as you go. Painting small areas and working these one at a time prevents confusion. Do not think about it all at once – get one stage complete, then move to the next and darker layer of tone.

1 By not painting the object in view, but painting around it to define its shape, you are working tonally. Wet the sea area and brush a blue wash mixed from phthalo blue and phthalo green, and paint the sea around the harbour wall and city.

2 Add a stronger sea wash to prevent the wash drying too pale. Prepare a mix of Naples yellow, cadmium red and burnt sienna in a hot red orange mix ready to paint the roofs.

3 Rather than painting individual roofs, paint them all together, ready for the next layer of tone, when the first is dry. Leave lights for dormer faces and sides. The domes are grey; build these up with a mix of cobalt blue and burnt sienna.

4 Paint shadow tones for the walls in a grey of burnt umber and phthalo blue. When dry, apply the dark detail, with added indigo for intense darks.

Techniques: perspective, page 17; buildings, pages 40–41, 86–87, 122–123; buildings in landscape, pages 74–75, 114–115; saving whites in blue sea, pages 72–73; leaving out shapes, pages 83–85; painting sea, pages 96–97; deep blue sea, pages 72–73, 96–99.

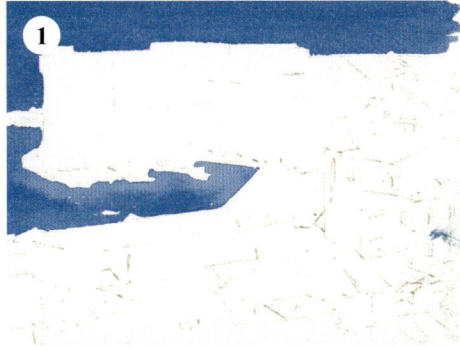

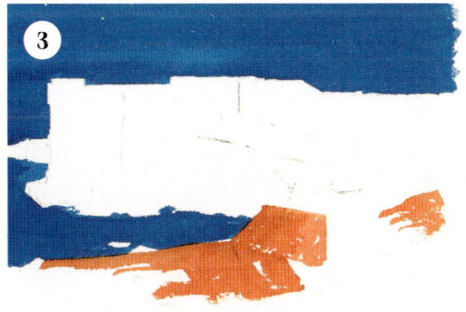
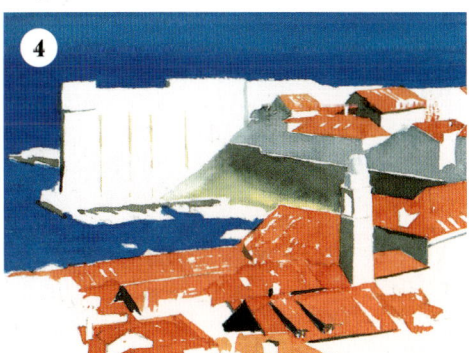

Painting ridges and tiles

To paint the shadows in the dips of the Roman-style roof tiles up to where they meet the roof ridges, protect the ridges with masking tape, or position a piece of card to protect them. Paint the lines up to the protected area, painting the little shadows under the ridge tiles where they cross the dips in the tiles.

Painting windows

Mask window bars right across longer building frontages with a pen nib so that they all align when painted over. Paint other lines over windows in shaded areas with 'body colour' or white gouache added to the building colour. Window slats can be masked, left out or painted with body colour. All these methods were used here. Another method would have been to lift some of them.

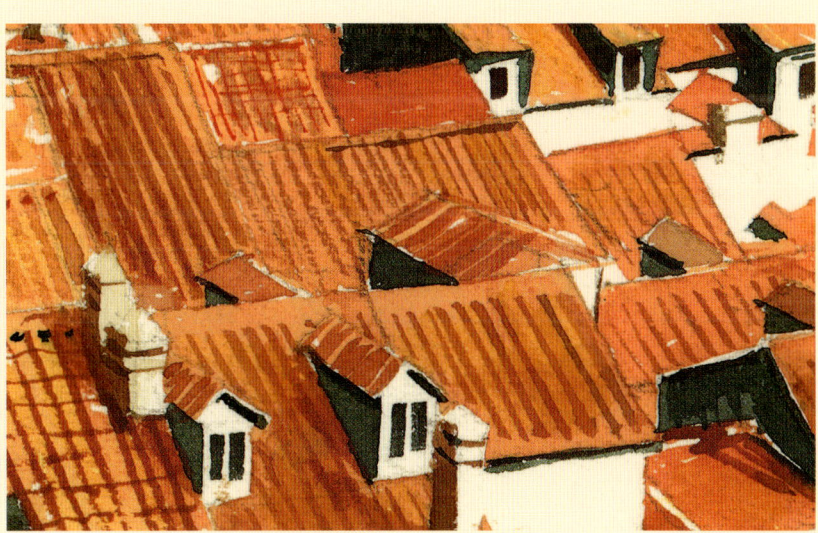

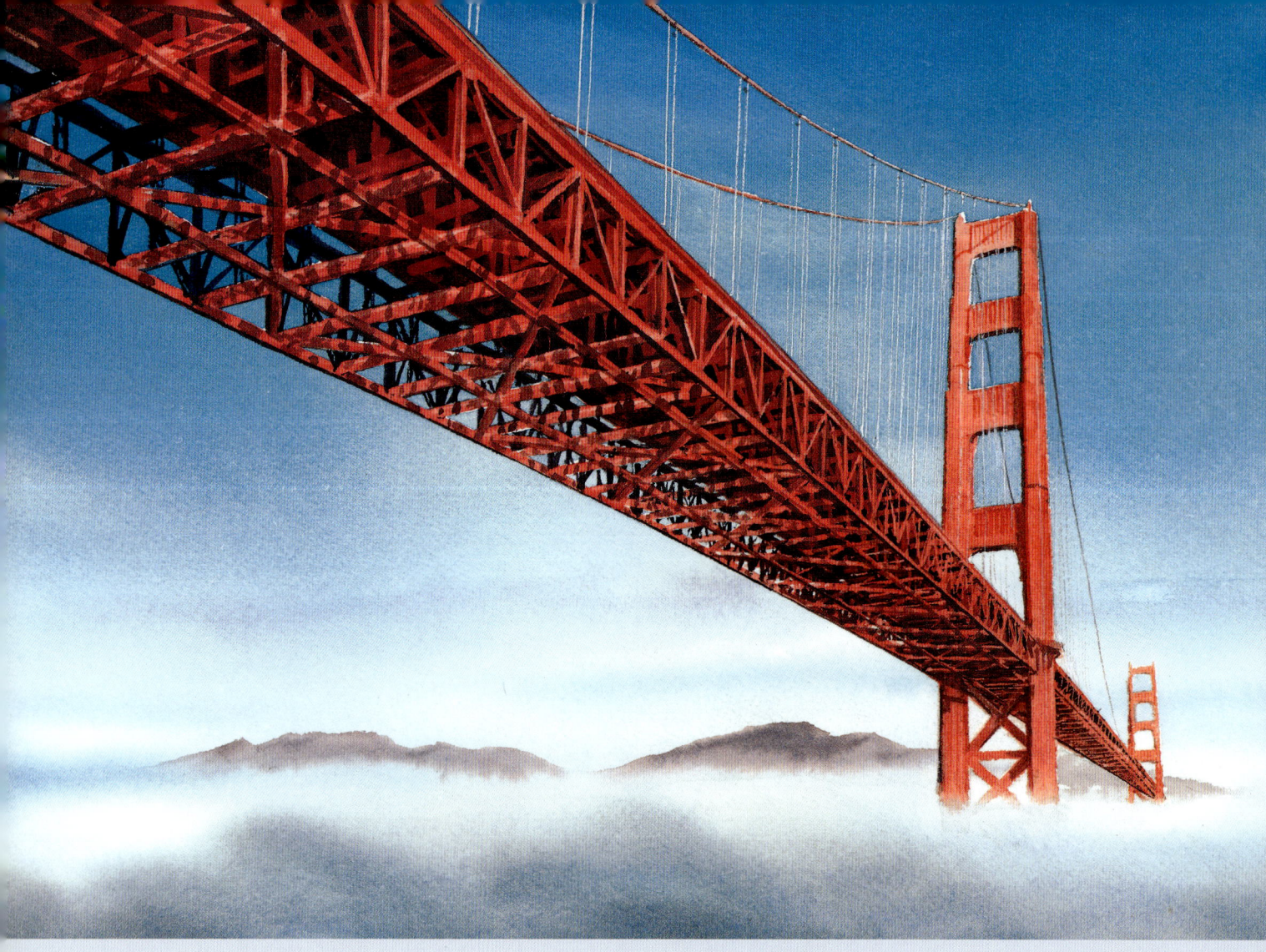

Golden Gate Bridge

Local fog conditions are ideal to present the vast height and span of the Golden Gate Bridge. Its shade of vermilion, based on nearby landscape colour, is lit by low sun, lighter against a dark sky. A perspective drawing enables the repetitive steelwork to be drawn easily, and masking simplifies the painting.

Artist insight: Referring to the finished painting, touch in the main cables with the bridge colour and fine line some dark under them. Place detail and shadow on the piers with a little French ultramarine and Indian red added to the basic bridge colour. Place finer dark shadow with French ultramarine and Indian red on its own. Use white for highlights down the piers, and a mix of white and the bridge colour for the vertical suspender cables in pairs. Notice these attach to the bridge above the apexes of steel. Mix the bridge colour with light red, permanent rose and new gamboge, and greys of French ultramarine added to this mix or use with light red for a dark.

COLOUR PALETTE

- new gamboge
- permanent rose
- French ultramarine
- phthalo blue
- cobalt blue
- yellow ochre
- burnt sienna
- light red
- white gouache

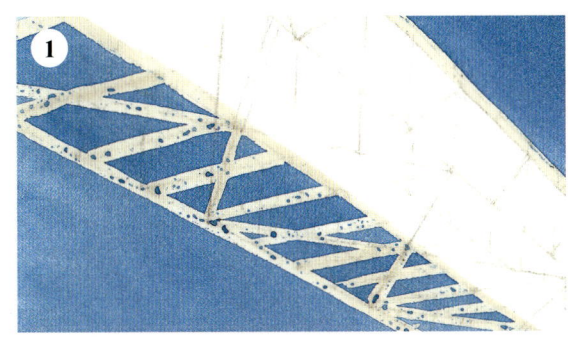

Techniques: composition X factor, pages 14—15; perspective, page 16; perspective vanishing points, page 17; wet-in-wet, pages 18—19; mixing greys, pages 23, 114—115; lost edges (hard and soft edges), pages 57, 124—125; mist, pages 68—69, 90—91; masking, pages 32—33; skies, pages 54—55; masking (layered), pages 48—49; masking (detailed), pages 94—95, 98—99, 104—105.

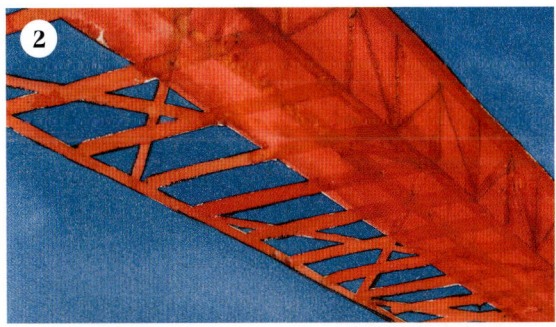

PAINTING THE BRIDGE

1 This layered masking technique can be applied to many subjects including steel structures, cranes and complex installations. Draw the framework, mask it and paint the sky, avoiding the white area. Only the areas and edges requiring protection from the sky wash need masking.

2 Remove the masking fluid. Paint the deck with a mix of light red, new gamboge and permanent rose. When it is dry, re-mask the structure of steel girders within the deck. Next paint with the bridge mix and a little French ultramarine added.

3 Paint the darks with a mix of French ultramarine and light red. Leave lights of the previous wash to reveal the tracery of girders within the structure, defined by dark shadow. Now paint the dark girders on the far side of the deck and remove the masking.

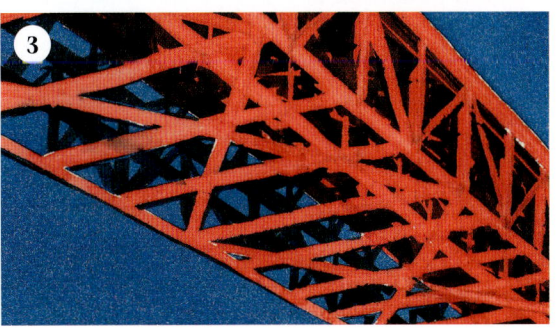

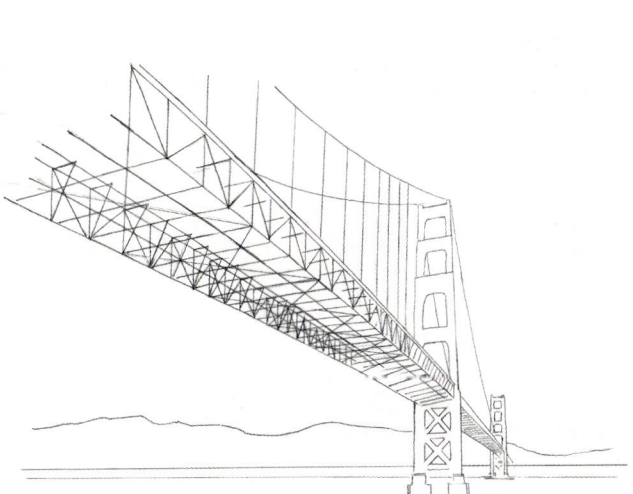

Drawing steelwork

All lines are plotted from three vanishing points. Vertical lines converge to a high vanishing point above the image. If the vanishing point were central, the piers would lean in and look wrong. I placed the vertical vanishing point directly above the near right-hand pier with a long steel ruler. All other vertical lines are projected from this vanishing point. I ignored the technicality of a small deviation from vertical on the curving deck as it is barely noticeable. There are two other vanishing points, to the left and out of the image, and at the far end of the bridge.

PAINTING FOG AND MIST WITH LOST EDGES

Wet the paper. Apply watery permanent rose from the mountains up, and a little yellow ochre up from the mid sky. Brush phthalo blue from the top down. Apply a grey of cobalt blue and burnt sienna from the bottom up. Dry it. Rewet the paper along the base of the mountains. Run a mix of cobalt blue, burnt sienna and bridge colour along the mountain ridge. It should spread down in a lost edge. The piers are wet and touched in with colour well above the fog. Again it spreads down in a lost edge.

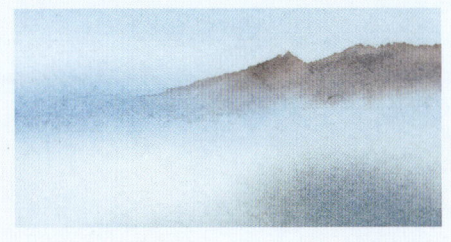

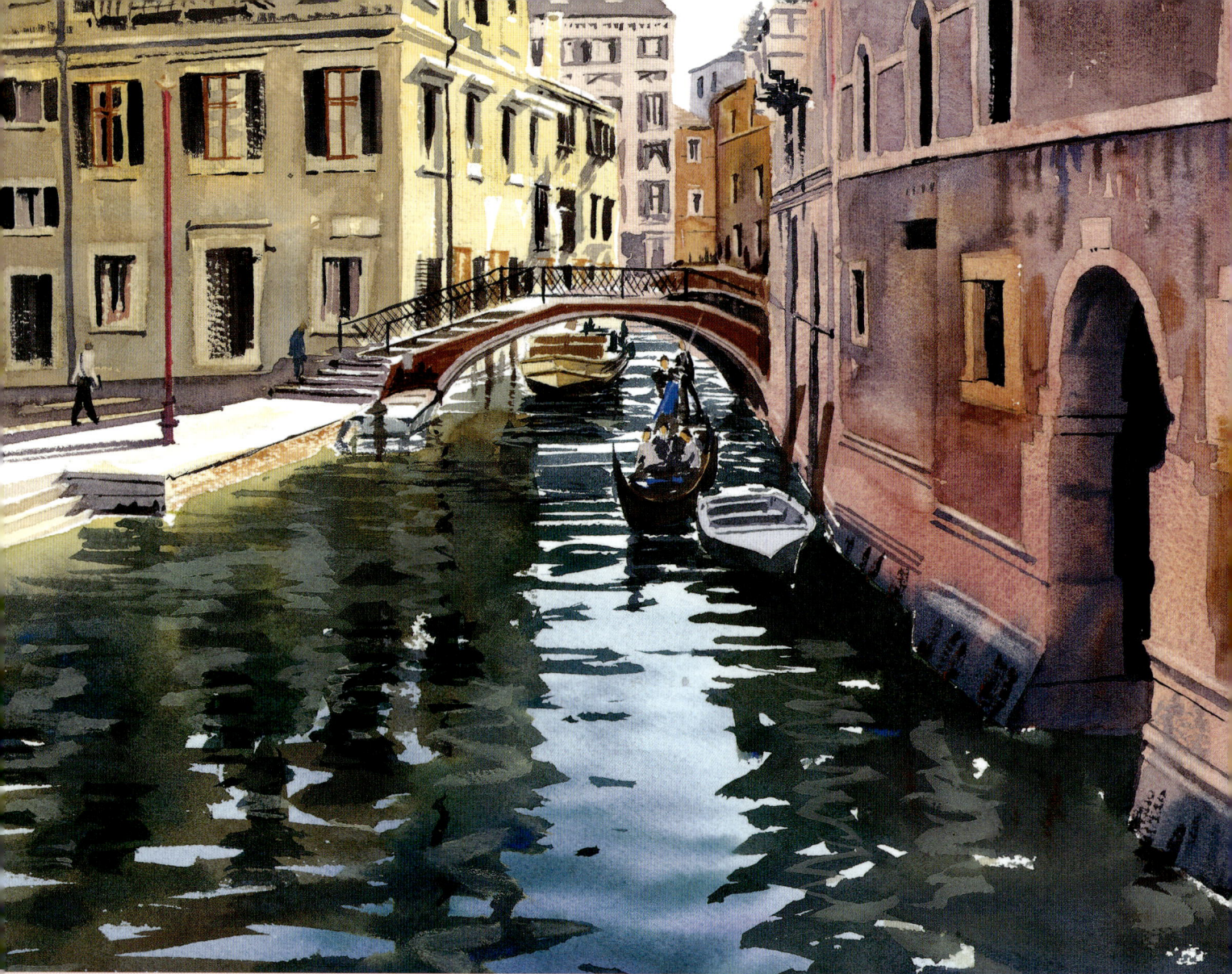

Venetian bridge

The bridge seems incidental here, but it is vital in linking the composition and giving it depth because although you can see past the bridge, it obscures enough of what is happening behind to maintain a kind of mystique. The buildings are constructed from interesting greys in a panelled and layered approach, one layer at a time.

Artist insight: To complete this painting, mix large amounts of colour for the water reflection. Phthalo blue, phthalo green, cadmium lemon, Indian red and French ultramarine were prepared, ready for some dark blue green mixes. Yellow down one side of the canal captures the light. Plenty of lights are left in the water. Some Naples yellow is brushed over the canal both for soft wet-in-wet highlights, and as light semi-opaque ripples.

Techniques: washes, pages 18–21; brushmarks, pages 20–21; boats, pages 82–83, 86–87, 92–95; rippling water, pages 78–81, 86–87; bridge arch, pages 116–117; buildings, pages 40–41, 86–87; windows, pages 118–119.

COLOUR PALETTE

- cadmium lemon
- permanent rose
- manganese violet
- French ultramarine
- phthalo blue
- phthalo green
- Naples yellow
- yellow ochre
- burnt sienna
- Indian red
- Payne's gray

BUILDING UP WASHES

Painting a darker wash over a lighter one is a simple, but important, technique. Instead of painting everything at once, paint layers, saving whites each time. When you paint a second wash, save the whites and some lights in the first wash. When you come to paint darks you will have created four layers of tone with two washes and a few marks!

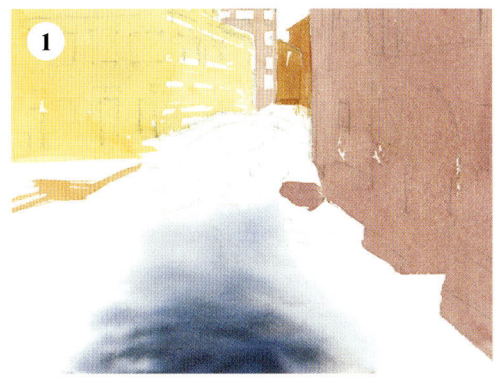

1 Paint shadowed buildings with mixes of yellow ochre, manganese violet and some permanent rose, and those in the sunshine with Naples yellow. Distant buildings are manganese violet, yellow ochre, permanent rose and burnt sienna mixes. Leave the bridge and window details white. Paint the water wet-in-wet with phthalo blue, phthalo green and Indian red mixed, stronger colour wet in wet for ripples.

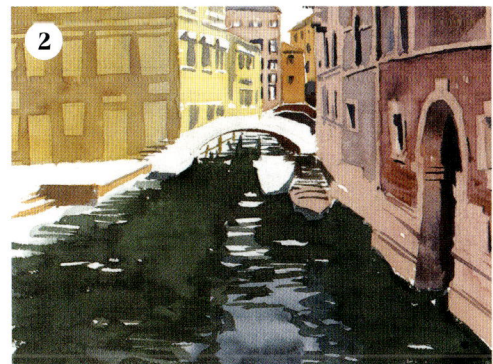

2 Brush in darker tone and lines to the building on the right with manganese violet and French ultramarine, leaving lighter undertone, and on the sunny side use yellow ochre and manganese violet mixed. Add French ultramarine for window detail. Dry between each stage. For intense dark detail, use French ultramarine and Indian red mixed.

PAINTING WINDOWS

Windows can be left as rectangular spaces in previous washes, or painted as dark shadow marks, often tapering downwards. Darker shadow can be applied to the window detail, and finished with detail of intense dark. Work one stage at a time.

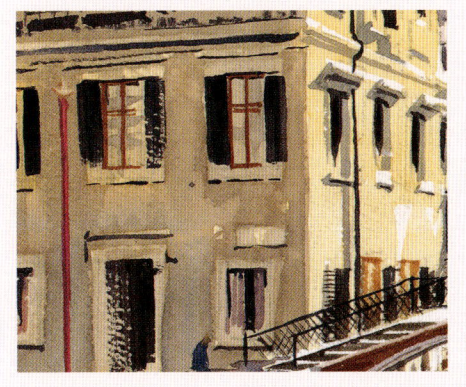

Working loosely

Blocking in colour loosely is a key to glazing in watercolour, and it allows your style to develop. Loose, rapid washes look lucid and free, so leave them alone – be a little untidy. Results can be natural and lively.

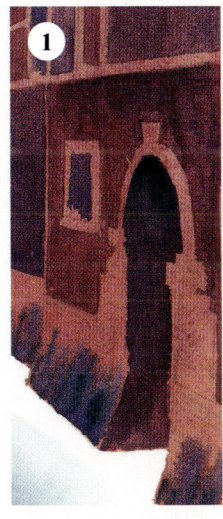

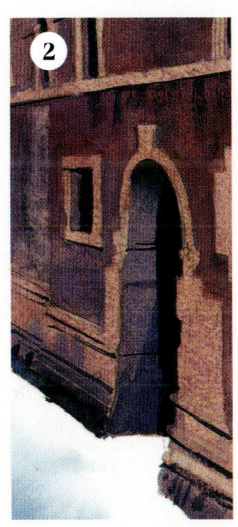

PAINTING ARCHES

Practise drawing arches first. Draw a box around the arch and then link corners with an 'x' through the middle. A vertical line through the 'x' finds the top of the arch. Practise a smooth transition curve through this point.

1 Apply darker tone outside the arch, saving lights. Wet the interior arch dimension. Apply colour from the top down. The entire arch shape is defined with tone. Add intense tone to the dark underside top of the arch. Add any additional stonework colour to this wash. Allow to dry.

2 Wet the narrow interior space of the archway, within the thickness of the walls, without going over the interior edge of the arch itself. Apply a dark of Indian red and French ultramarine in a cool mix to define the inside edge of the arch, and draw detail lines across it.

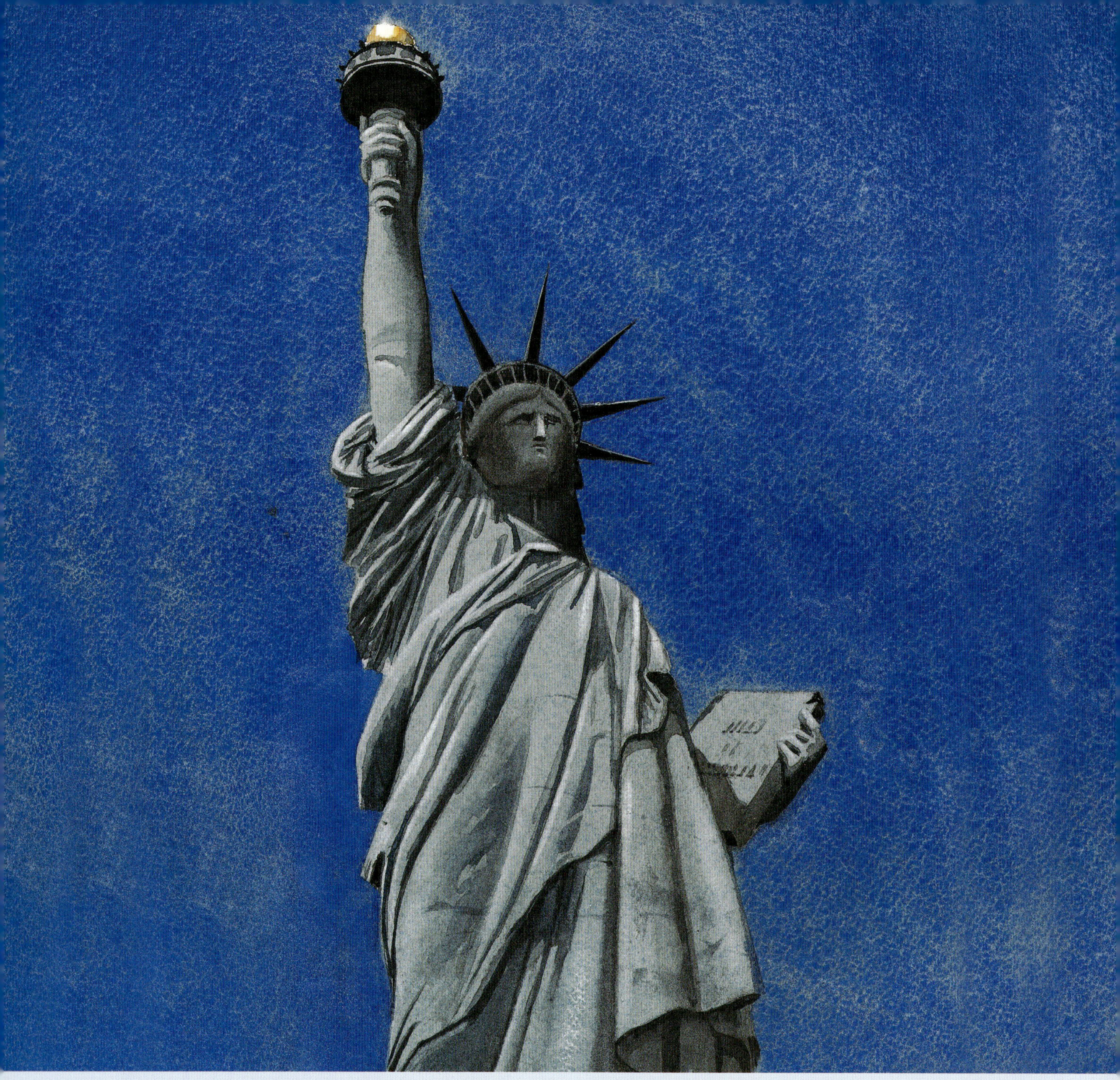

Statue of Liberty

There is a simple choice here – is the statue going to be darker, or lighter, than the sky? This image portrays the latter, which is the more difficult approach, but you could equally paint the statue dark against light sky.

Artist insight: *A 'lost' edge of colour fades to nothing, a diffuse foggy edge. Paint on wet paper so the colour flows without a distinct edge. A 'lost and found' edge is a soft edge/hard edge wash. One side of the wash is painted on dry paper and has a hard edge; the other diffuses into a wet surface.*

COLOUR PALETTE

 cadmium lemon

 quinacridone magenta

 French ultramarine

 cobalt blue

 viridian

 burnt sienna

 Payne's gray

white gouache

Techniques: tonal composition, pages 14–15; wet-in-wet, pages 18–19; granulation (as seen in sky), pages 20–21; dry-brush, pages 26–27, 66–67, 109; sky (contrasting a structure), pages 32–33; skies, pages 54–55; hard and soft edges (lost and found edges), pages 56–57, 120–121; scratching out, pages 36–37; masking fine lights and glints, pages 62–63; leaving out shapes in an underlying wash, page 83; knife peeling/knife lifting, page 111.

PAINTING THE SCENE

1 After drawing the statue, one tiny piece needs to be masked – the top of the torch. Wet the whole paper and apply a wash of greenish grey – the statue colour. Burnt sienna, cobalt blue, viridian and quinacridone magenta make a good grey. Mix enough to complete the statue.

2 Allow the grey undercoat to dry. Then rewet the paper around the statue, but not right up to the edge. Apply a wash of French ultramarine all over the background, defining the edge of the statue with the paint. Rapidly apply French ultramarine wet, and leave it alone so it 'granulates'. French ultramarine does so with a linear effect of attracted granules in stringy formations, known as 'flocculation'.

3 Rewet the statue, one area at a time. Add darker shadow of Payne's gray to the edge of the rewetted area. Build up sharp-focus darks wet-on-dry around the fingers and torch, defining the lights.

4 Work up the face with pale washes of the original statue mix. Use Payne's gray for darker detail and the rays on the crown.

5 Each of the folds has a sharp edge and a soft edge. Carefully wet and paint one at a time; apply the statue colour along the sharp edge and allow it to flow into the water, producing a soft lost edge. Gently scrub the masked torch to produce some glare for reflected sunshine.

6 Remove the masking and paint the tip with a tiny amount of yellow, leaving a white hole in the middle. Add a little grey to the outside of this, then lift lighter highlights all over the statue with a damp brush and dab with kitchen towel. The statue colour used in faint passages hints at very slight panels – changes in the underlying surface from its means of construction. Finally, dry-brush a few very pale streaks of grey across the statue for a weathered effect.

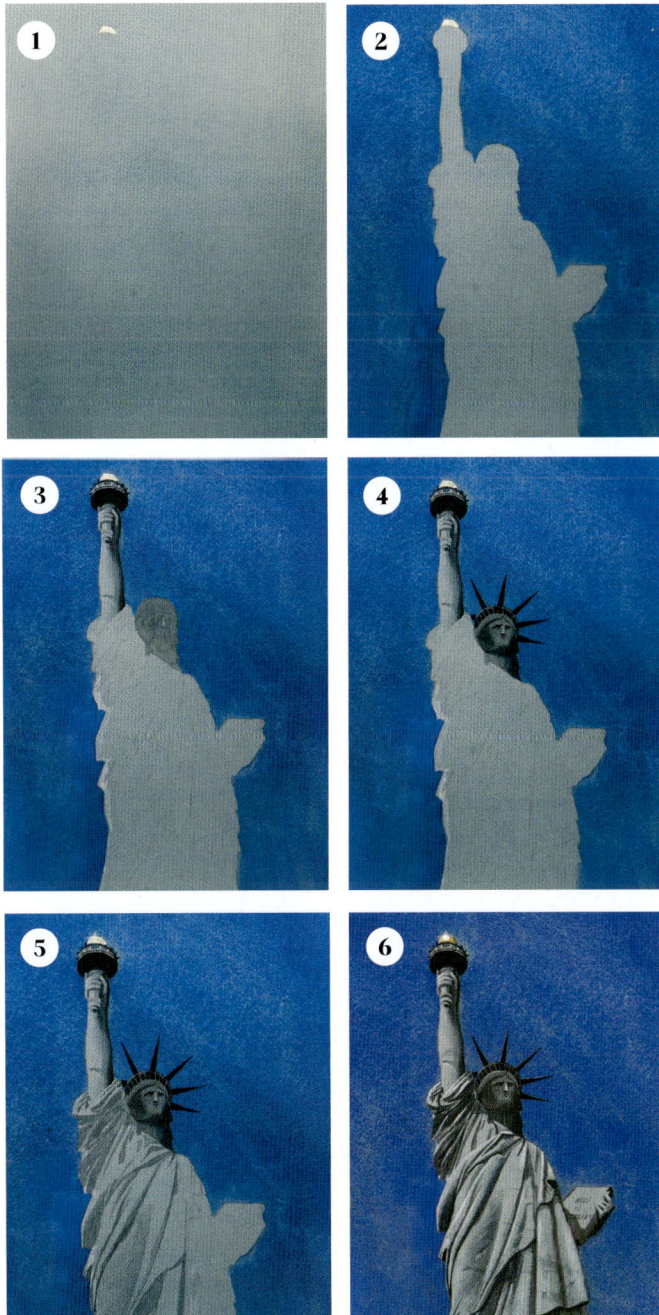

One piece at a time

Simple initial washes are worked one at a time over large areas, but what about the mass of tones that define the statue? You can only work small areas, so tackle it 'one piece at a time'. Many soft lost edges were produced here by carefully wetting only the outer diffuse edges of shadow areas before applying colour. Check each area is dry before working on the neighbouring one. Mistakes often do not show, and if they are bad they can be corrected – for example, by simply lifting with a damp brush, dabbing with kitchen towel and starting again when dry. White gouache was applied to highlight the rays and the brightest edge was cut off in a thin strip with a craft knife.

Closing thoughts

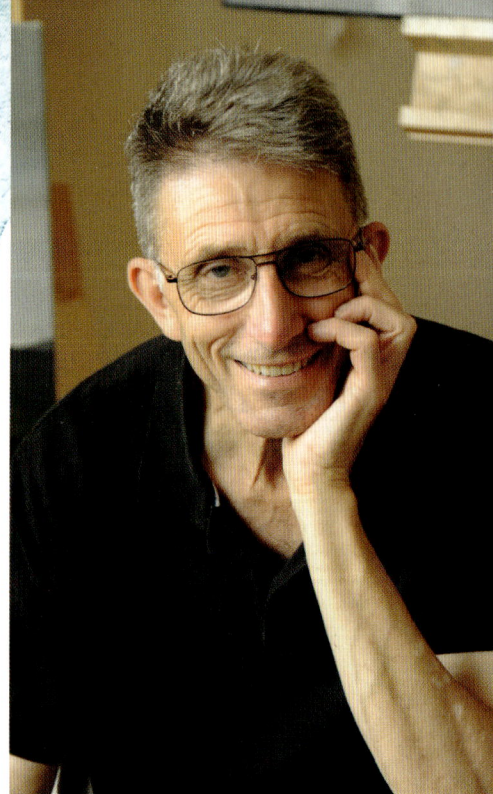

ABOUT THE AUTHOR

Joe Francis Dowden was raised in a musical and creative family in the Surrey Hills of Southern England. In these surroundings his father taught him watercolour. He painted, sketched and drew out of doors from the age of six. His books and articles have been published in many languages. In the UK, he has exhibited at the Royal Institute of Painters in Watercolour, the Royal Society of Marine Artists, the Royal Watercolour Society, the Dorchester and Park Lane hotels, the UK Masters exhibition, and the International Watercolour Masters. He has also featured in many one-man shows. Joe has been an invited artist at international exhibitions globally. He has painted for government and private collectors and his paintings are in permanent collections around the world. He demonstrates painting and these paintings have been among those exhibited internationally. Wherever he goes he seeks new material, and his work is constantly changing. He has appeared on DVD and television. Joe's paintings can be seen at **www.joedowden.com**.

ACKNOWLEDGMENTS

Thanks to David and Charles for the opportunity to put down what I know in such a direct way, and for their immensely creative approach.

To my wife, Ruth, children Elise, Bernice, Felicity, Rory. To Graeme, Asher and Mya. To Cornel, Stanley, Peter and Lily. To Rory and Chloe. To my brothers and sisters, Juliette, Simon, Louisa, Dominic, Anna, Lucy, Johnnie, Matthew, and to Mick. To Mavis. To my friends Barry and Hillary, Milan, Dave and Mel, Graham and Rose, Barry and Sandra, Steve and Anne. To Max. To Colin Harding. To Stuart Greville-Brown. To Jed Armstrong for inspiration.

To Gwynn Sparrowhawk, and in memory of Janice Sparrowhawk.

In memory of my mother Ginny, father Prosper and father-in-law Charlie.

Remembering a school teacher, Dennis McCarthy, for encouragement in 1968.

Some of my favourite painters past and present are W L Wylie, 1851–1931, Edward Wesson 1910–1983, Rowland Hilder 1905–1993, Nita Engle, 1925–2019, Richard Thorn, Joseph Zbukvic, Sergey Temerev, Patrica Guzman, Sergiy Lysyy, Konstantin Sterkhov, Keith Hornblower, Rick Huang, Ken Knight, Richard Bolton, John Haskins, Alvaro Castagnet, Boonkwang Nonchareon, Ilya Ibryaev, Yuko Nagayama, LaFe, Anna Ivanova, Ong Kim Seng, Elena Basanova, Professor Ming Zhou, Lok Kerk Hwang, Vivienne Pooley, Thierry Duval, Amit Kapoor, Peter Brown, Olga Retunskaya, Julio Jorge, Eudes Correia, Kate Sava, Igor Sava, Richard Bolton, Geoff Butterworth, Michal Jasiewicz, Stanislaw Zoladz and David Poxon.

PICTURE CREDITS

Chris Bonington, Chris Bonington Picture Library – Cho Oyu, page 66, 'Mountain lake'.

Robert Grange – Melbreak from Crummock Water, page 61, 'Mountain lake'.

Pamela Cuthbert – Lokrum, Dubrovnik, page 88, 'Shallow water over rocks'.

Sarah Underhill – The Twelve Apostles, page 72, 'Rocky outcrops'.

Sarah Underhill – Horseshoe Falls, Niagara, page 90, 'Falls'.

Whitehallrow.com – Boats built and images from Whitehall Row, page 82. 'Rowing boat on a lake'.

For other picture locations and assistance, I acknowledge Jane and Andrew Winch, Alice Purvis for Dilton Farm, Rye Kingdom Hall of Jehovah's Witnesses, Michael Baxter of The Albury Estate, Handa Bray of The Shere Estate, Tony Reed of High House Farm, Milan Pleic, and Janet, Miro and Mark Kasumovic for the City of Dubrovnik and surrounding region, and Ruth and Jeremy Greenfield. For inspiration I acknowledge the mountain photography of Chris Bonington, Robert Grange and others.

Index

A DAVID AND CHARLES BOOK
© David and Charles, Ltd 2007, 2023

David and Charles is an imprint of David and
Charles Ltd, Suite A, Tourism House, Pynes Hill,
Exeter, EX2 5WS

Text and Artwork © Joe Francis Dowden, 2007, 2023
Layout and Photography © David and Charles, Ltd
2007, 2023

First published in the UK and USA in 2007 as *The
Landscape Painter's Essential Handbook*.

Joe Francis Dowden has asserted his right to be
identified as author of this work in accordance
with the Copyright, Designs and Patents Act, 1988.

The author and publisher have made every effort
to ensure that all the instructions in the book are
accurate and safe, and therefore cannot accept
liability for any resulting injury, damage or loss to
persons or property, however it may arise.

Names of manufacturers and product ranges are
provided for the information of readers, with no
intention to infringe copyright or trademarks.

A catalogue record for this book is available from
the British Library.

ISBN-13: 9781446309834 paperback
ISBN-13: 9781446309841 EPUB
ISBN-13: 9781446310373 PDF

This book has been printed on paper from
approved suppliers and made from pulp from
sustainable sources.

FSC
www.fsc.org
MIX
Paper from
responsible sources
FSC® C012521

Printed in China by Asia Pacific for:
David and Charles, Ltd
Suite A, Tourism House, Pynes Hill, Exeter, EX2 5WS

10 9 8 7 6 5 4 3 2 1

David and Charles publishes high-quality books
on a wide range of subjects. For more information
visit **www.davidandcharles.com**.

Share your paintings with us on social media using
#dandcbooks and follow us on Facebook and
Instagram by searching for **@dandcbooks**.

Layout of the digital edition of this book may
vary depending on reader hardware and display
settings.